HOTSPUR

HOTSPUR

Eighty Years of Antiques Dealing

Compiled by Nicholas Goodison and Robin Kern

Published by Two Associates

Contents

Introduction   ROBIN KERN   8

Reminiscences   ROBIN KERN   10

Hotspur: 1924–2004   NICHOLAS GOODISON   16

Hotspur and Temple Newsam House:
two eightieth anniversaries   JAMES LOMAX   26

An historic British collector: Sam Messer   CHARLES CATOR   48

A contemporary American collector   JOHN BRYAN   68

Matthew Boulton: ormolu   NICHOLAS GOODISON   94

Seat furniture   SIMON REDBURN   122

Glass objects and chandeliers   MARTIN MORTIMER   158

Case furniture and carvers' work   ANTHONY COLERIDGE   184

Clocks, barometers and other objects   ROBIN KERN   240

Bibliography   282

Index   284

Photographic acknowledgements   288

First published by Hotspur Limited © 2004
This is number 936 of a limited edition of 2000 copies.

The right of John Bryan, Charles Cator, Anthony Coleridge, Nicholas Goodison, Robin Kern, James Lomax, Martin Mortimer and Simon Redburn to be identified as authors of this work has been asserted by them in accordance with the Copyright, Designs and Patents Act 1988.

All rights reserved. No part of this publication may be reproduced, stored in a retrieval system or transmitted, in any form or by any means, electronic, mechanical or otherwise, without the prior written permission of the publisher.

ISBN: 0–9546825–0–5
This book is sold subject to the condition that it may not be resold or otherwise issued except in its original binding.

A CIP catalogue record for this book is available from the British Library.

This book was produced by
Two Associates
14 Collinson Court, Great Suffolk Street,
London SE1 1NZ

Design and project management:
Ray Carpenter for Two Associates
Editorial and project management:
Mandi Gomez for Two Associates
Typesetting: Tom Knott
Proofreading: Judith Gray
Index: Hilary Bird
Repro, printing and binding: Singapore, under the supervision of MRM Graphics

COVER: (Detail from p. 225, cat. no. 18)
A yew-wood and marquetry commode, *c.*1765.

This book is composed of various sizes of Baskerville: roman and italic. The main text size is 12½ on 15½ pt. It was originally designed by John Baskerville in the 1750s and cut for him by John Handy. It is the epitome of neoclassicism and eighteenth-century rationalism in type, and considered to be very appropriate for the subject matter of this book. The face was far more popular in Republican France and the American Colonies than in eighteenth-century England, where it was made.

Baskerville was a Birmingham japanner, a letter-cutter and writing master, and in his type these disciplines produced magnificently controlled, generously proportioned letterforms. He also made a number of important innovations in ink, papermaking and printing. Passing wove paper through hot copper cylinders produced a smooth white surface that showed off the black type to perfection. He also developed a new open typographical style with wide margins and leading between lines. This gave the page an austere brilliance.

To our parents, ROB and BETTY KERN

Introduction

THIS BOOK CELEBRATES the eightieth anniversary of our family company, Hotspur Limited. I would like to record my very appreciative thanks to all those friends who have contributed to the firm's success and to this celebration.

First, I must thank my brother Brian, who has helped me and worked by my side for so many years. We have enjoyed our time together enormously; he has been a splendid partner, but he deserves his retirement … from me! Second, I thank all those to whom my family and I owe much of the success of our business – clients, fellow dealers and others in the trade, admirers, restorers and many others.

I salute with gratitude all those who have contributed to this beautiful book, and without whom it would not have materialised. Nicholas Goodison's academic yet highly readable books on Matthew Boulton and English barometers have been inspirational. He has from the start of this project been a most perceptive guide and adviser. He has also written two sections of this book. James Lomax, the great silver specialist, has kindly chronicled Hotspur's relationship with Temple Newsam House in Leeds, tabulating some of the many pieces they have acquired from us over the last thirty years. Charles Cator's experience of the fine art world and love of English furniture makes his contribution invaluable. He is an old friend for whom nothing is too much trouble and whose insight into Sam Messer's collection is so very enjoyable to read. John Bryan II is a collector whose knowledge and placement of objects within their natural settings is worthy of any museum. His depth of knowledge in the many fields he collects never ceases to amaze me. Simon Redburn is one of the most respected experts on English furniture on either side of the Atlantic. His vast knowledge in this area has been tapped by many an aspiring collector. Anthony Coleridge's fascination for English furniture and its historical significance has added much to the enjoyment of all those with a passion for eighteenth-century English furniture. We go back a long way together and I remember him at Knight Frank and Rutley in the 1960s as a young auctioneer. Martin Mortimer of Delomosne is a fellow dealer with whom Hotspur has had numerous transactions over the last forty years or more. He has a unique knowledge of English glass and an individual sense of fun. Mandi Gomez's professionalism in managing this publication has been exemplary; her warmth and humour have made the whole project such a pleasure to work on. Ray Carpenter's unerring eye for design and meticulous planning of illustrations and text have been a major contribution.

Most of the photographs are from our own archives. Raymond Fortt's photography is a benchmark for many other photographers. Thanks are due also to Peter John Gates and Philip Paddock (P. J. Gates Photography Ltd) for their colour photography – a 'secret weapon' in so many dealers' armoury – for the camera never lies!

Finally, I would like to say thank you to my wife Odile, who conceived the idea for this book to celebrate eighty years of Hotspur – thank you most sincerely and warmly.

I should say a little about the organisation of the book. The emphasis is on some of the objects that have passed through the firm over the last eighty years. The first three essays discuss three great collections that Hotspur had a hand in forming. The book then becomes largely picture led, looking at specific categories and opening with a short introduction to each, with extended written entries to selected pieces. Where possible, the authors have provided details of attribution, provenance, size, relevant literature and exhibitions, but sometimes the information is no longer available. The tone aims to be not too academic. The book is written by friends and colleagues who share my love – Hotspur's love – for these things. The bibliography, which you will find at the back of this book, is compiled for the avid reader rather than for the scholar. It supports abbreviated mentions of the sources' titles in the text and footnotes.

I would like to close with something said to us many, many years ago by Sir Richard Powell of the Institute of Directors, then in Belgrave Square: 'I have never regretted my extravagances, always my meannesses. Always, buy the best.'

ROBIN KERN London, 2003

Reminiscences

ROBIN KERN

I SET OUT to write a short introduction, but I soon found myself recording memories that have come to mind while looking back on eighty years of Hotspur's history – memories of my grandfather, father, brother, vicissitudes, some of the lovely objects that we have had the good fortune to work with, and the firm's many friends and clients.

My introduction to Hotspur in 1956 permitted a short period of study with my very elderly grandfather, F. E. L. Kern. I was guided too by my father, Rob Kern, who was immensely generous with his knowledge and who showed such patience with this new student. These early years guaranteed my devotion to being an antiques dealer. It is both my business and my hobby.

In 1963 my brother, Brian, joined us and we worked together for some thirty-five years before Brian retired to enjoy his numerous interests. But he keeps in touch, almost weekly, and comes to help for a few days each year at the Grosvenor House Fair.

My father encouraged us both in many ways, but for me one particular memory comes to mind. Amyas Phillips (Phillips of Hitchin) and my father were great friends and they decided that both their sons would benefit from a trip to America. Jerome Phillips, recently down from Oxford, and I were to travel around the country for a month, meeting the New York dealers, visiting our two firms' customers, and taking in Washington, Boston, Colonial Williamsburg, Chicago and Detroit. My enthusiasm knew no bounds and, as I had not yet started buying, I searched New York eagerly for something exceptional to report back home. At French & Co. they had a mid-eighteenth-century carved mahogany Gainsborough chair that I liked. At Stair & Co. I found a garniture of ormolu-mounted blue john, which I compared as best I could with examples at the Metropolitan Museum: I thought it might be by Matthew Boulton.

I raved about both items and, whilst we travelled around America, my father – to encourage me – purchased both the chair and the garniture and flew them home to await my return from my travels. Such was the quality of this fine man: what a wonderful thing to do to encourage your son in his new career!

Jerome Phillips and I travelled everywhere. On one occasion, on a wet evening in New York, we were trying to find a taxi on Park Avenue. Jerome insisted on stopping a taxi whose flag was down, as the driver was probably going home, and said 'we want to go to …' in his English accent, whereupon the taxi driver said 'I liked the way you said that, get in and I'll take you'. We visited the Ford family in Detroit and enjoyed being driven in a 1912 electric car from their motor museum, pushing a rod to go forwards and pulling it back to reverse. We were introduced to Judge Irwin Untermyer, surely the finest collector of decorative arts in America at that time, and enjoyed a wonderful visit to Colonial Williamsburg and the Governor's Palace, to which both Jerome and I had made many sales, and where, I recall, all the employees wore period costume.

On my arrival home, you can imagine my surprise at seeing both the Gainsborough chair and the garniture at Hotspur. The garniture turned out to be mid-nineteenth century, not eighteenth century, and not by Matthew Boulton either. It was sold on a qualified invoice for a small profit on the £700 it had cost. It was to be the catalyst that started my interest in Matthew Boulton's ormolu work. The Gainsborough chair was sold to an international museum and paid for my month's expenses in America.

The period of my indoctrination introduced me to some of the great collectors who were buying at this time, collectors like Sam Messer, the Moller brothers, Noel Terry and Judge Irwin Untermyer, with whom I spent countless hours contentedly looking at his collection, which was housed then in a duplex apartment at 960 Fifth Avenue, New York, and is now in the Metropolitan Museum.

I enjoyed many evenings with my father and Mr and Mrs Noel Terry, who lived in York. Every article in the Terry collection had a Dymo label, in code (i.e. one, two, three, four and so on), explaining where it was purchased, from whom, when, and for how much. Mr Terry quizzed me time and time again on the details of each piece. Just as well, for when Mr Terry died he left his collection to the City of York, and the new curator of this fine and handsome collection, Peter Brown, asked me if I knew what these labels meant. I was, of course, able to break the code and in no time a catalogue was produced with each piece duly recorded. This was an invaluable, perhaps unique, addition to the archive of this remarkable collection.

Sam Messer was equally generous with his time; he thoroughly enjoyed showing his collection to those of like mind with loving devotion, to the point of wiping off my fingerprints with his handkerchief.

Budgy Moller was keen on horses and kept a fine stable near Newmarket, where my father, my brother Brian and I spent many happy times together going through the collection and enjoying lunch afterwards in the dining room, where there were outstanding clocks.

At the same time, I was able to get to know Ralph Edwards, the peppery curator of furniture at the Victoria and Albert Museum, at a time when dealers and curators hardly ever met. Ralph Edwards's main contribution to my career was the publication of his *Dictionary of English Furniture*, which is still to this day a bible for dealers and collectors.

R. W. Symonds was no less demanding. I have the greatest admiration for his three most important books: *Masterpieces of Eighteenth-Century English Furniture*; *English Furniture from Charles II to George II* and *Furniture-Making in Seventeenth- and Eighteenth-Century England*, as they have contributed enormously to the depth of knowledge in eighteenth-century English furniture. Symonds's numerous articles on specialised subjects in this field that first appeared in the *Connoisseur* and *Antique Collector* are still highly regarded by the specialist. Hopefully, one day these will be republished together in one volume to make a valuable addition to the bookshelves of the enthusiastic collector and dealer.

Hotspur has dealt with many collectors over the years. The first of our collectors I met was Claude Rotch, an elderly gentleman who lived at 215 Cromwell Road, in an aged apartment at the top of the house. He collected Chippendale-period-furniture avidly and was a lover of fine music. Each time we alerted Claude Rotch to come and see something, he would arrive dressed in a black coat and hat and was invariably thrilled with what he had come to see. He always brought a loose cheque with him and usually ended up purchasing what we had found for him; one day, as he walked out of the front door at Hotspur, he handed my father his cheque and said 'you fill it out for whatever I owe you'.

We invited Claude Rotch to lunch on one occasion, to Wheelers, the famous fish restaurant very close by. He was appalled at the high cost of lunch (£15) and said that next time we should go with him to Soho, to his favourite Chinese restaurant, which we did. The hatcheck boy was given sixpence but had to give back threepence. Lunch cost £3, which Rotch felt was much better value for money. On his death, Claude Rotch left his substantial collection to the Victoria and Albert Museum.

Judge Untermyer was also frugal. Our last transaction with him was his purchase of a pedestal desk. We had to take another desk in part exchange. I refused his suggestion that we pay for the transportation of both pieces and his answer to this was to suggest that we send our desk first. He would then use our packaging to send his desk to us.

The relationship between dealer and client is sacrosanct, built up over years of advising and collecting; the inevitable friendship that results is a warm and rewarding partnership. I can remember on two occasions how a client of my father's bought from us without asking the price, knowing full well that this prized relationship meant his interest would be protected.

Similarly, an extraordinary occurrence happened to me after I recommended to a client a chair for sale at Christie's in New York. After much discussion, a decision was made to try to acquire this piece and I was asked (by our client) to bid for it. When discussing possible bids, I was staggered to be told 'you pay what you think is a correct price'. As this was a most costly article, it put enormous pressure on me to be accurate, fair and, most of all, to protect our client's interest. It was a most clever example of delegation and a fine example of the mutual trust that exists between Hotspur and its clients.

My father was a generous man; I remember on one occasion a very old friend and client, Lionel Golodetz, paid a visit to Lowndes Street and asked if he might purchase the brass ship's bell with the name 'Hotspur' on it that has been sitting in Hotspur's window for over forty years. The company's mascot

was not for sale, but I remember my father saying: 'Lionel, if I ever find a bell with the name 'Golodetz' on it I will buy it for you!'

Do objects do the rounds? According to one client they may well do. One of the most popular and regular visitors at Lowndes Street in the 1960s was the then Patrick Gibson, now Lord Gibson, who lived in London. He was invited to speak at a British Antique Dealers' Association City dinner and had the house laughing heartily when he recalled how he would do the rounds of Jeremy, then Hotspur and then Mallett in Bond Street, and see the same piece of furniture, rising steadily in price, which had passed from one shop to the other.

Many firms of antiques dealers are family based and their friendships continue from generation to generation. In the 1960s I was invited to the wedding of a fellow dealer who has become one of my oldest friends. I remember so well his wedding speech – he had his guests rolling about with the story:

I was always told:

- Never to buy anything without having it home on approval – I wasn't allowed to do this with my wife.
- Before purchasing anything always examine it closely for damage – I wasn't allowed to do this with my wife.
- Examine for woodworm; remove the drawers and pat them for any signs of dust – I wasn't allowed to do this with my wife.

… and so on. Suffice to say this marriage has endured and born fruit.

I have also benefited from knowing many dealers from the old school, most of whom are no longer with us. They were an invaluable part of my upbringing. Names that come to mind are: Leonard Knight, Joel Wolff, S. W. Wolsey, Amyas Phillips, Cecil Turner and Alec Lewis, Frances Egerton, Henry Rubin and Reg and Frank Lumb, – all wonderful characters, each with their own personal area of expertise.

With regard to the Lumbs, I remember one

occasion when, on a visit to Harrogate with my father in the early 1960s, we called as usual at the Lumbs who took us to their workshops round the corner from their shop. Reg Lumb said he had a fine walnut shepherd's crook armchair somewhere and began to search for it. An arm was found here, a leg there; the beechwood frame was in pieces hanging on the wall, and so on. Eventually, we found everything and slowly we assembled the chair as best we could, rather like Lego. Since we were satisfied that we had found all the pieces, we walked out to the car carrying what looked like a bunch of firewood in a box. Reg Lumb cried with laughter as he saw us carrying away this 'bundle of wood' for which we had paid several hundred pounds.

Furniture certainly can hold some 'hidden stories'. One particular memory begins with a car that my brother and I decided to purchase for our father in the 1960s to thank him for all the help he had given us. We purchased a new Jaguar for £2,495 and presented it to him. The maiden voyage was to Wales to see a client who wanted to sell an important cabinet. I drove my father there. We purchased the splendid cabinet for £10,000 (a huge sum of money then for a piece of mid-eighteenth-century furniture) and from that moment things went from bad to worse. As I carried the cabinet to the car, the top part of pierced Chinese fretwork fell into the car's boot in literally hundreds of pieces. On the way home, I drove too close to the car in front and a stone broke the windscreen, which eventually collapsed into our laps as we reached London. The cabinet had been bought to be exhibited at the forthcoming Grosvenor House Fair, but there was no way it could be repaired in time. Finally, when the repairs were completed, our photographer, Raymond Fortt, came to photograph it in close detail on the same morning that a possible purchaser was due to come to see it. Fortt's photography was exceptional and he used enormous spotlights. Whilst he was taking the detailed shots his spotlights were too close to the cabinet and caused the polished surface to fizzle. It looked awful. At that moment the client arrived and we quickly put the cabinet against the wall to hide the offending burns. To everyone's delight he purchased it.

Sometimes the allure of a fine piece of furniture can land the unsuspecting dealer right in it, as they say; this particular memory has me cringing with embarrassment even today. It is rare for Hotspur to purchase French furniture, but we succumbed to an early eighteenth-century gilt wood console table with its original top. We were asked to send it 'on approval' to a house in Eaton Square and I travelled with the van to make sure all went well. The table was of the type that had two reverse 'C'-scroll front legs, while at the back there were no legs, because it would be screwed to the wall. The walls in Eaton Square were covered in silk, so our worthy carriers rested the table against the wall, but the client (and his wife standing beside me) wanted to see the marble top in place. It was duly put on top of the table and we all stood back to admire it. Suddenly there was a resounding crack, and the table literally broke into dozens of pieces in front of our eyes as the weight of the marble top took its toll.

I looked at my clients whose mouths, like mine, just opened wide in astonishment. The full weight of the original marble top compounded the fractures in the gilt wood frame, but it was cushioned from breaking by the debris. My client's wife said ruefully 'I think I will get a dustpan and brush'. I don't think I have ever been so embarrassed and, to cap everything, the client said that the table would have been perfect, although now, naturally enough, his interest had declined.

Of course the dealer is as susceptible to giving in to his own whims as anyone, and sometimes his enthusiasm can get the better of him. Francis Egerton of the fine art and antiques dealers Mallett used to call every Tuesday and usually purchased something. One such Tuesday I was thrilled with a new purchase of a fine mid-eighteenth-century breakfront bookcase. In my enthusiasm, I said to Francis: 'I am so pleased with this bookcase, that I could live with it', to receive the retort 'Robin, you may have to'.

I attended my first big furniture sale at the Sotheby's Cobham Hall sale, in Kent, where Hotspur was representing the Victoria and Albert Museum. We purchased several pieces under the watchful eye of Ralph Edwards and I shall never forget the excitement of the moment of bidding and the exhilaration when we were successful.

A great deal of the time my job does not feel like work, it is sheer pleasure. One of the great pleasures I have had over many years has been working with Dick Kingzett of Agnew's for English Heritage. They employ us to independently value the contents of some of the country's great stately homes that are being taken over in lieu of inheritance tax. Agnew's value the paintings and we value the furniture. This means that we have the privilege of examining wonderful pieces of furniture, seen previously only in textbooks or from behind ropes, at our leisure, in houses like Osterley, Kedleston, Ham House, Belton and Hopetoun. What a wonderful privilege. It is a busman's holiday and we get paid for it.

I began my career in 1956 and I have absolutely no idea when I shall stop; none of Brian's or my own children are interested in taking the business on. I have every confidence for the future, however, ably supported now by Christopher Payne and Simone Barnard whose patience and tolerance of my whims know no boundaries. Suffice to say that I take, and continue to take, great pleasure in buying things I like and selling them to people I like – a privileged way to indulge one's passion.

RABK

Hotspur: 1924–2004

NICHOLAS GOODISON

PREVIOUS PAGE
1. Robin and Brian Kern in front of the
Harewood lacquer Lady's secretary by Thomas
Chippendale, taken on the first floor gallery at
14 Lowndes Street, London, 1999, at the time
of B.K.'s retirement.

2. Frederick Kern (centre) with Her Majesty
the Queen at Streatham Lodge in Richmond
on Saturday 17 February 1940.

I FIRST VENTURED through the door – that curious glazed side-door to the right of the entrance – in the early 1960s. I was barometer hunting. I was compiling the material for my book on English barometers, and Ronald Lee, the leading dealer in his day in English clocks, had told me that Robert Kern (known to everyone as Rob) was an essential contact. He knew the leading collectors, he handled the best English furniture, and he had instructive files of photographs. The showroom, then as now, was impeccable and stylish. The furniture shone with beeswax polish, the gilt mounts gleamed. It was a little daunting. I felt underdressed in an open-necked shirt and casual trousers.

Rob Kern appeared down the stairs. He wore a dark suit. His welcome was disarming. Within minutes we had forgotten my errand – that could wait until we reached the top floor – and we were immersed in a tour of the furniture. He had detected an enthusiasm for English design; and the youth of his visitor, along with the suspected lack of a cheque-book, didn't matter. He wanted to share his own enthusiasm for each individual piece in the show-room, as if they were his favourite grandchildren or his collection of orchids. The tour was a wonderful lesson in design, construction and the art of the best cabinet-makers. As a fledgling businessman, I wondered how he made any money if he was willing to pass so much time with a tyro.

There are, as they say, dealers and dealers. There are those who treat their stock like sardines, for buying and selling. There are those who cultivate their clientele and know their tastes, but make little effort to research their stock beyond looking for photographic comparisons in the standard reference books, which they sometimes leave on show nearby. There are those who love to know as much as they can find out about what they own. Of course it pays them – every piece of furniture has a history, and the more intriguing the history the higher the value. But to some, and Rob Kern was emphatically one of them, the history is an excitement in itself.

I am not alone among authors in saying 'thank goodness for Hotspur'. For me, the Kern family has been an invaluable source of information, and im-peccable tutors in taste and the art of curiosity.

3. F.E.L.K., as he was known, in c.1955.

4. Rob Kern, 1974.

They have been fun to work with. I cannot pretend that Rob was pleased when I arrived with a screwdriver and other tools and took his Matthew Boulton vases to pieces, but I admired and was thankful for his tolerance. Rob and his two sons, Robin and Brian, have all been stimulating companions in the appreciation of quality. Their enthusiasm has always been infectious and a great thing to enjoy on a Saturday morning. It must be in their genes.

The family came originally from Heidelberg. Rob's father was Frederick Kern (known as F.E.L.K.), who was born in 1868. He was said in 1955 to have just completed seventy years in the antiques trade, having started in soft furnishings, decorations and panelled rooms. He became a director of the Paris firm Carlhian and Beaumartz, which had a branch in Soho Square. He was with the firm for twenty years until it closed in 1914, and was then briefly in business at 27 Soho Square as a director of Monday, Kern and Herbert, where he was in charge of the 'Antique Department and Reproductions'. The firm advertised 'unique examples of the historic furniture to be found in the best old English mansions', specialised in 'reproducing the best specimens of period furniture in English, French, and Italian Renaissance', and offered to submit designs for interior decoration and to treat woodwork specially 'for extreme climates'. Frederick lived at Loughton in Essex (where Rob was born in 1907). He died in 1958.

Rob too had started young. After working for a firm of restorers, he and his father founded Hotspur when he was only seventeen years old, at 16 Buckingham Palace Road. An early advertisement in the *Connoisseur* listed 'a rare collection of English glass, early oak Gothic and Tudor hutches and coffers', which may come as a surprise to those who associate Hotspur with the finest figured eighteenth-century mahogany furniture. There is a tale that Rob employed sandwich-board men to draw people's attention to the business. The tale doesn't record whether this led to a successful passing trade in Gothic or Tudor hutches and coffers.

A few years later Hotspur moved to Hazlitt's House at 6 Frith Street, a seventeenth-century house near Soho Square. Here Rob instituted the Hotspur

Copy.

TELEPHONE: GERRARD 6301.

HAZLITT'S HOUSE,
6, FRITH STREET,
SOHO SQUARE,
LONDON, W.1.

Dear Sirs, A reminder of our removal from 16 Buckingham Palace Rd and acquisition of the fine 17th century "Hazlitts House" Soho. Having been consistently buying during the recent depression we are able to offer a large selection of Genuine Antiques at exceptionally low prices which coupled with the £ at its present level is an opportunity for our American clients that will never occur again.

Hotspur Ld.

Photo Print by Lilywhite Ltd.,

One of the many original Pine Rooms built 1690. in
HAZLITT'S HOUSE. 6. FRITH ST., SOHO SQUARE. LONDON. W.1.

5. Gallery interior at Frith Street in Soho, London, c.1936.

A mid 18th Century elaborately inlaid serpentine Cabinet, with finely chased ormolu mounts, in the manner of John Cobb, circa 1765.

HOTSPUR
LTD.
14 LOWNDES STREET, BELGRAVE SQUARE,
LONDON, SW1X 9EX
Telephone: 01-235 1918

6. Trade card c.1968.

tradition of an advertising card with a photograph of a piece of current stock printed on it (Fig. 6). Announcing the move on the first of these cards, he told clients that 'having been consistently buying during the recent depression we are able to offer a large selection of Genuine Antiques, at exceptionally low prices which coupled with the £1 at its present level is an opportunity for our American clients that will never occur again'. He was of course right, except for the years of the Second World War, but it was a bold forecast at the time.

The photograph of the pine-panelled room at Frith Street (Fig. 5) shows, among other things: a fine glass chandelier (later a particular line of the firm, discussed in Martin Mortimer's article, pp. 158–83); two early eighteenth-century mirrors; a coat of arms, probably embroidered, in a carved wooden frame; a late seventeenth-century upholstered chair with turned legs; an upholstered armchair with cabriole legs of about 1740; a pair of gilt gesso tables of about the same date; a bureau desk and a big bureau bookcase of about 1720; a neoclassical two-branched silver or plate candlestick; two other candlesticks; and a cross stool with lions' heads and claws. There is no sign of Gothic or Tudor hutches, but this was only one room of several.

The photograph suggests a continuing interest in furnishing, and not just in fine pieces of furniture, and Rob's note to his clients makes it clear that clients in America figured large in his thinking. The firm's files show how important this transatlantic tradition has been to its success. The newspaper magnate William Randolph Hearst was an important client in the 1930s, introduced by the dealer Lord Duveen, who did so much to export works of art to the United States in the interwar years. Hearst bought individual pieces and a complete panelled room. Rob Kern was one of the founding members of the Grosvenor House Antiques Fair in 1934, another benchmark in the trade's development of the transatlantic market.

In 1939, at the outbreak of the Second World War, Kern decided to move the business out of London. He took it to Streatham Lodge (Fig. 7), a seventeenth-century house in Richmond. There, ten years later when celebrating the firm's twenty-fifth

7. Streatham Lodge, Richmond, c1949.

1924 Twenty-fifth Anniversary 1949

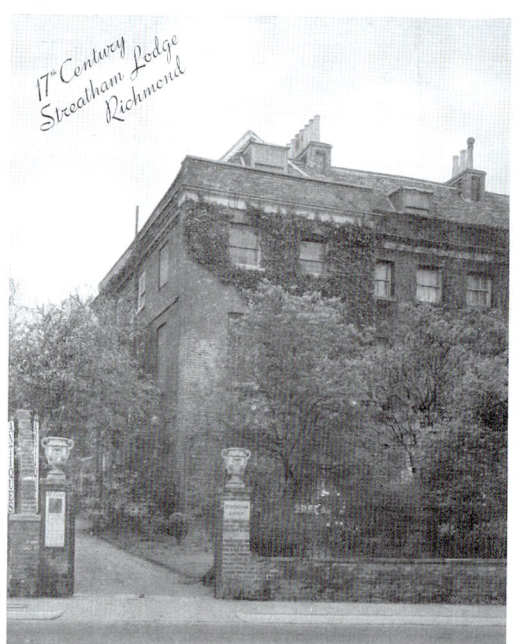

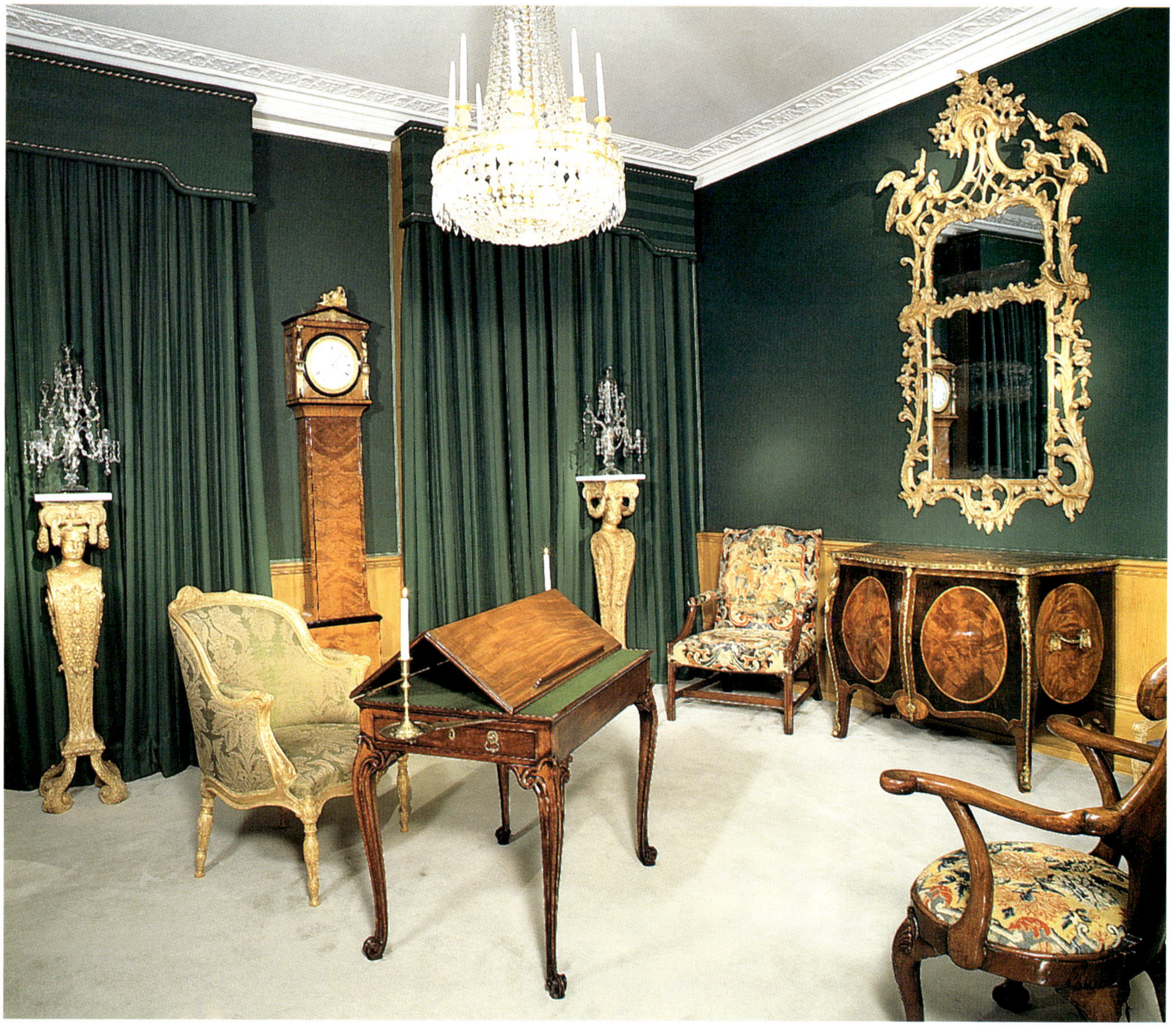

anniversary, he advertised Hotspur's 'important stock of 17th and 18th century English oak, walnut and mahogany furniture'. Interestingly, a photograph of the showrooms at Streatham Lodge shows that at least three of the objects in stock at Frith Street before the war were still in stock – the cabriole-legged upholstered chair, the coat of arms in the carved frame, and a *torchère* candlestand. Maybe it shows how patient dealers had to be in those dark days. Other objects illustrated included an upholstered wing chair, walnut and mahogany dining chairs, a walnut bureau bookcase, a mahogany tripod table, a mahogany sideboard, two hinged cutlery boxes, glass wall sconces, a neoclassical carved mahogany side table and, like a trademark, a grand eighteenth-century chandelier, which also looks as if it were the one in stock at Frith Street. Perhaps he didn't really want to sell it.

Trade was not easy during the war, or immediately after it. The market in the finest pieces was spasmodic, and Kern had to bolster turnover by exporting lesser furniture such as sofa tables and butler's trays to American dealers. He hunted for stock in the company of Sam Wolsey, the dealer in oak furniture, sharing petrol coupons on their regular visits to dealers in the country: it was Wolsey who, after the war, found the new premises for Hotspur at 14 Lowndes Street (left), near Belgrave Square, when in 1951 Kern wanted to move back into London. The house in Richmond was compulsorily acquired by the local council, demolished, and replaced with flats.

Robin Kern, Rob's elder son, joined the firm in 1956, aged seventeen, which seems to be the genetic tradition of the family. He then served with the Royal Army Pay Corps during his national service and, after discharge in 1960, travelled in Europe with John Blairman and to America with Jerome Phillips, both of whom were the sons of established furniture dealers, to learn where, what and how to buy.

Co-operation with other leading dealers has been a mark of the firm's business, and they have often shared particular pieces with others. They have also assiduously cultivated friendships in the trade – illustrated by the last paragraph of a letter to Robin from Reginald Lumb of Harrogate in 1967, in which he said: 'I must go to prayer now, and I will put one

ABOVE & OPPOSITE
8. First floor gallery at 14 Lowndes Street, 2003.

in on the quiet for Hotspur's. And if anything comes of it, the Lord said I was to have ten per cent.'

Rob's younger son, Brian, joined in 1963 after an engineering apprenticeship with de Havilland.

In the 1950s and 60s the economy was recovering from the ravages of the war and the burden of debt incurred during it. Britain remained in a fragile economic state, not helped by the massive intervention in business by the postwar socialist government, but entrepreneurs were reappearing and it became clear that the idea of collecting antique furniture was not dead. Prosperity in America also brought American collectors to London, where the prices of antique furniture seemed very favourable. Hotspur took full advantage of these trends. Their files reveal several important American collectors, not least Jon Gerstenfeld, whose collection was the subject of a book published by Christie's in 1998, Fred and Kay Krehbiel, John Bryan, who has written for this volume, and Larry and Lori Fink. British collectors have included the Bulmer, McAlpine, Muller and Sainsbury families.

Among the many British collectors who have benefited from the firm's expertise, two particularly stand out. The first was Samuel Messer, who had made money from real estate and was intent on building a fine collection of eighteenth-century furniture. Charles Cator writes of his collection, to which Hotspur supplied many fine pieces, elsewhere in this volume (pp. 48–67). Sam's first purchases were in 1946, when he told Rob Kern that he wanted to buy six objects in the showrooms at Richmond. Since he also said that he only wanted the finest pieces in his collection, Kern would only sell him four of the six. The other two he rated as only 'good'. The second notable collector was Noel Terry, whose fortune came from the Terry's chocolate business. Terry bequeathed his collection, many of the pieces bought from the Kerns, to Fairfax House in York, where it is displayed today. It is one of the most distinguished collections of English furniture in the country and not as well known as it should be.

Not surprisingly, Hotspur was a hunting ground for museums eager to strengthen their eighteenth-century collections. The firm sold pieces to many American museums, including the Metropolitan

Museum in New York, the Huntington Gallery in California, the United States Department of the Interior (rather an apt name for a building in which Hotspur installed a chandelier), and museums in Boston, Chicago, Houston and Philadelphia. They also enriched museums in Adelaide and Melbourne in Australia, in New Zealand, and in Denmark and Israel. In Britain, there are pieces in the Victoria and Albert Museum, Kenwood, Marble Hill House and the Geffrye Museum in London, and, in the regions, in Birmingham, Bristol and Leeds. The collection at Temple Newsam House, Leeds, about which James Lomax writes in this volume (pp. 26–47), was a particular beneficiary of Hotspur's taste, the late keeper, Christopher Gilbert, being a distinguished furniture historian and an avid hunter of objects for the Temple Newsam collection.

The firm celebrated its fiftieth anniversary in 1974 with a remarkable display of the ormolu ornaments of Matthew Boulton. It was a reminder of the speciality that the firm has built up in the decorative work of Birmingham's leading eighteenth-century manufacturer.

Tragically, Rob Kern and his wife, Betty, died in a car accident in Norfolk in 1977. It was a blow to everyone, to friends and clients (they became one and the same) and particularly to the family. But the business continued on its distinguished way, steered by the now experienced Robin, and the methodical administration of Brian. Brian retired in 1999, but returns each year to man the stand at Grosvenor House, looking for all the world as if he never left. Robin, who has now been joined by Christopher Payne, remains the linchpin of the business. Since his father died, and for some time before, he has been the leader in the acquisition and sale of stock, and has shown all the taste, charm, zeal and friendliness of his father. I know that he would (and does) welcome the next generation of enthusiastic furniture historians with the same sympathetic friendship that his father showed to me. That, backed up by the utmost integrity, is the key to the firm's success.

NG

Hotspur and Temple Newsam House:
two eightieth anniversaries

JAMES LOMAX

PREVIOUS PAGE
(Detail from p. 41, Fig. 8)
The front door panel of the Bellot cabinet, a mahogany cabinet on a stand, c.1745–50.

ON NEW YEAR'S Eve 1946, the Director of Temple Newsam and Leeds City Art Gallery, Ernest Musgrave, received a letter typed on elegant pale blue wove paper (surely a great rarity at such a time) heavily embossed with the address – HOTSPUR Ltd, ANTIQUE GALLERY, Streatham Lodge, Sheen Road, Richmond, SURREY. The writer, Mr F. E. L. Kern, stated (with correct formality) that he had just seen illustrated in the current issue of *Country Life* a pair of finely carved seventeenth-century swags belonging to Temple Newsam.[1] This prompted him to enclose a photograph of a magnificently carved frame then in stock and for sale at £350. It was attributed to Grinling Gibbons because of the presence of his (then) reputed 'signature' – a split peapod. It came from Syston Court, Gloucestershire, where Gibbons is said to have worked, and contained a portrait of the Earl of Craven.[2]

Mr Kern could not have chosen a more auspicious moment or a more sympathetic curator with whom to correspond. Ernest Musgrave had recently been appointed Director of Temple Newsam and Leeds City Art Gallery in place of Philip Hendy, who had moved on to become Director of the National Gallery in London. In complete contrast to his predecessors' backgrounds, he had – through his flair, charm, good looks and social ambition – 'risen through the ranks' from his humble origins as a museum attendant. One of his first tasks had been the difficult one of returning to the City Art Gallery all the (mainly twentieth-century) paintings and sculpture which had been evacuated to Temple Newsam for the duration of the Second World War. With that job completed, he was now looking forward to creating a great museum of fine and decorative arts within the empty interiors of the great Tudor–Jacobean mansion.

Temple Newsam, which lies just four miles to the east of Leeds and is surrounded by a 1,200 acre park designed by Capability Brown, had been inherited in 1904 by its last private owner, the Hon. Edward Lindley Wood, later Earl of Halifax, from his aunt the Hon. Mrs Meynell Ingram. It contained a magnificent complement of country house treasures and works of art, including: paintings by Titian, Rubens and Claude Lorrain, and by all the

1. *Country Life*, 27 December 1946, letter from G. Bernard Wood of Rawdon, Leeds. The pair of swags he illustrated is in fact a mid-nineteenth-century example signed by W. G. Rogers.
2. Alastair Laing has suggested the portrait may represent Prince Rupert.

British masters; and furniture by William Hallett, James Pascall, Thomas Chippendale senior and junior, and the Linnells (among many great makers). It also had a famous collection of English and European porcelain; magnificent family silver built up over 300 years; as well as textiles and tapestries, supposedly 'the gift of royal hands'. All of this had been either removed or sold in 1922 when, after the collapse of morale among the aristocracy following the First World War, Lord Halifax had decided to hand over the building and parkland to the Corporation of Leeds for a nominal sum. After essential repair work had been done on the structure, the doors were thrown open to receive the first visitors on 19 October 1923. Thus the season 2003–4, when the house will reopen after three years' closure for major repairs, marks the eightieth anniversary of public ownership of this great place and the continuous growth of the collections for the enjoyment and benefit of the whole community. It is a charming coincidence that this same anniversary should be shared with Hotspur, one of the firms of dealers through whom some of the most memorable works of art now in the collections have been acquired, and with whom we continue to enjoy the most cordial relations.

In 1923 the Corporation was delighted to receive the historic park as a ready-made recreational amenity for the inhabitants of the new suburbs, which were spreading relentlessly westwards. They were less sure about the future use of the vast mansion with its seventy-five rooms now left virtually empty. The house was most famous for its associations with Lord Darnley, the husband of Mary Queen of Scots, who had been born here in 1545, although for exactly 300 years – since 1622 – it had been owned by the Ingram family (Viscounts Irwin) and their descendants. For the first few years under the City's ownership, the large numbers of new visitors were herded around the empty interiors by guides delivering barely credible ghost stories and anecdotes, handed down from generations of backstairs staff (for want of anything else to speak of). But in 1938 Philip Hendy had persuaded the Corporation to merge the management of Temple Newsam and the Art Gallery under a single Committee, and to offer him the job as curator of both.

He explained his plan in a highly perspicacious memorandum. First, he pointed out the extraordinary potential of the house as a future museum of fine and decorative art. Each generation of owners had left its mark on the different interiors and thus every period in the history of style and taste was represented within its walls – from early Tudor to Edwardian baroque – including a particularly fine series of mid-eighteenth-century rooms, notably the Saloon or Picture Gallery. He argued that collections of furniture, ceramics and silver, as well as paintings and tapestries, could be built up again in a systematic way and displayed within these indigenous 'period rooms' in a natural 'country house' context and to the best possible advantage. American museums were paying huge sums to acquire historic interiors for this purpose and here was an ideal purpose-built example on their doorstep. Furthermore, he implied that, as the price of antiques and works of art was actually falling at this time, there should be no delay in beginning a task that might become increasingly difficult in the future. To the eternal credit of the Corporation of Leeds, Hendy's ambitious scheme was accepted in principle. No time was lost, even during the war years, to put this new policy into effect.

So, a few months after Musgrave's and Kern's original correspondence (after a generous discount had been agreed and having been given six months to pay), the frame arrived at Temple Newsam. What would have attracted Musgrave would have been the virtuoso quality of the carving, its association with a famous craftsman, its good country house provenance and the fact that it was coming from a distinguished and highly reliable firm of dealers. Nevertheless, he was obliged to obtain a second opinion from Ralph Edwards at the Victoria and Albert Museum for the purpose of securing a grant-in-aid. Edwards was obviously cautious of the attribution to Gibbons, but nevertheless recommended a grant-in-aid, suggesting that the layer of treacly brown paint should be removed so as to expose the lime wood beneath.

For many years the frame was given pride of place in the various displays and room arrangements, and was illustrated in a number of early guidebooks.

Inevitably, as research developed and the attribution continued to be questioned, the frame lost something of its original glamorous aura; scholars have commented on its similarities to and differences from Gibbons's documented work and to the work of other followers. Parallels with the work of Jonathan Maine (fl. c.1680–1709) in the Consistory Court Chapel in St Paul's Cathedral, and of William Emmett (fl. 1641–1700) at Chelsea Hospital, have been cited, but a definite attribution is unlikely to emerge because of the lack of documents. Its art-historical significance lies in showing, in the words of David Esterley, 'how thoroughly other carvers digested and freely expressed Gibbons's style in their own work'.[3] In recent years, as restoration work has been driving much of the thinking behind the new displays in the house, it became one of a small number of important pieces which were nevertheless 'difficult to place'. However, it has at last found a splendid new home in the Crimson Bedroom, where it hangs against the replicated Regency red flock paper and is surrounded by other late seventeenth- and early eighteenth-century Ingram family portraits.

The year 1947–8 was something of an *annus mirabilis* for Musgrave, for that was the year in which Lord Halifax returned over a hundred heirloom paintings to the house as a gift. Other gifts that year included the Hollings Collection of English earthenware, the Oxley Collection of continental silver, mounted hardstones, rock crystals and ivories, and Lord Allendale's gift of the Early Renaissance interior from Bretton Hall. Musgrave's campaign to create a great decorative art museum was gathering momentum.

One of Musgrave's weaknesses, with which his successors have all had to live – albeit without undue difficulty – was for gilt marble-top side tables. During his regime the house acquired a splendid group of them, many with great provenances: a now famous pair attributed to Matthias Lock from Ditchley; a Palladian pair from Wentworth Woodhouse; a fine Irish rococo pair; and a splendid example, perhaps by Linnell, from Bramshill. These were to be joined much later by the pair (with their accompanying mirrors) designed by Robert Adam for Croome Court – perhaps the *ne plus ultra* of the genre.

3. Gilbert, *Furniture at Temple Newsam House and Lotherton Hall*, Vol. 1, pp. 240–1, Vol. 3, p. 727.

One of the most stylish examples is the one that Hotspur proposed to Musgrave in 1950, three years after the Syston Court frame (Fig. 1).[4] Its strongly Palladian form is softened by the double scrolling legs with their vigorous relief carving, and the carved apron with fronds of acanthus leaves. Most memorably of all, garlands of naturalistic flowers trail around the front of the legs and continue around the sides. Perhaps it is not too fanciful to suggest that the table is in fact a pagan altar prepared for a special fête in honour of Flora. But the great feature of this table is the miraculous survival of its original gilding due to its having been covered in a coat of brown paint for most of its life. Its removal by Hotspur had exposed the subtleties of texture and finish, and especially the contrast between burnished and mat surfaces.

4. Ibid., Vol. 2, p. 353; and Luff, 'Marble Top Tables in England', *Antique Collector*, April 1964, figs 1, 2.

OPPOSITE
1. A carved gilt wood marble-top side table,
c.1735.
H: 34½" (87 cm); w: 54" (137 cm);
D: 27" (69 cm).
This important marble-top side table
with cut corners was made by Benjamin
Goodison (fl. 1727–67) who was among the
finest cabinet-makers of his age, supplying
furniture to the Royal Palaces of Hampton
Court, Kensington Palace, Windsor Castle,
Buckingham Palace, Holkham Hall,
Longford Castle, Devonshire House
and Chatsworth.

5. Ibid., Vol. 2, pp. 256–7, 445.
6. Ibid., Vol. 1, pp. 76–8.

Three years later Musgrave found the table's perfect room-mates via Ronald Lee, another notable London dealer: a pair of carved gilt wood sconces, displaying many of the same Palladian motifs and probably made in the same workshop, under the supervision of the royal cabinet-maker James Richards or Benjamin Goodison. The resulting ensemble is a textbook example for students of design history and fine craftsmanship.[5]

Musgrave died tragically in a motoring accident in 1958, leaving the young Geoffrey Beard – his newly appointed assistant – temporarily in charge. Within a year, Robert Rowe was appointed to the new post of Director of Leeds Art Galleries, with his main office at Temple Newsam, and so the main energies for collecting continued to be focused on the decorative arts. If Musgrave's regime had been about quantity, Rowe's was surely now about quality, and he brought a critical connoisseur's eye to every proposal for new acquisitions. His relationship with Hotspur began somewhat tentatively in 1961 with the purchase of a set of four walnut chairs of the 1730s (Fig. 2).[6] At this time there was a considerable dearth of seat furniture in the house apart from the Gallery suite by James Pascall, which had been bought back from Lord Halifax in 1939. The new chairs had their original upholstery with half-stitch needlework backs and seat covers, in a wide arabesque design worked in red, white and purple wools. The forelegs have relatively conventional carved shells on the knee, but terminate in somewhat unusual trefid feet, perhaps suggestive of their Scottish provenance since they were traced to Brahan Castle, Ross-shire. The settee which accompanied the suite had also been acquired by Hotspur and had been sold to the Auckland Institute and Museum in New Zealand.

By 1965, the year in which the Chippendale Harewood Library writing table was purchased – achieving a world record price of 41,000 guineas at Christie's and establishing Temple Newsam in the forefront of decorative art museums – Christopher Gilbert had been on the staff at Temple Newsam for some four years. He was to become one of the most prominent furniture historians of his generation and Thomas Chippendale's modern biographer. For

2. One of a set of four walnut side chairs with their original needlework covers, c.1735. H: 42½" (107 cm); W: 25" (64 cm); D: 23" (59 cm).
The four side chairs were originally part of a suite consisting of a settee and six side chairs. The settee was purchased from Hotspur by the Auckland Institute and Museum in New Zealand.

OPPOSITE
3. A satinwood secretaire cabinet, c.1798. H: 92½" (235.5); W: 37½" (95 cm); D: 23¼" (59 cm).
The cabinet forms part of a group of furniture that consists of twenty-three pieces, fifteen of which conform to the design of this cabinet, known as the Weeks's cabinet, over which there has been much speculation about the identity of the cabinet-maker. The question of the date of the Weeks's cabinets has been helped by the silver-capped glass bottles that appear in one of the dressing drawers (the Edward James Foundation cabinet) and which are dated 1798 with the stamp of William Chawner.

34

35

Temple Newsam he pursued a vigorous campaign for research and acquisitions of all kinds, publishing the first two volumes of the furniture catalogue in 1978, and a third volume entirely devoted to his subsequent acquisitions twenty years later. His publications, including those on vernacular furniture, remain a benchmark for research and presentation.

An early major acquisition with which Gilbert was connected was the cabinet inscribed on the enamel clock face 'WEEKS'S / MUSEUM / TITCHBORNE STREET', one of a well known group of similar pieces dating from the late eighteenth century and emanating from this luxury emporium (Fig. 3).[7] The Temple Newsam example is one of the most complete, despite the loss of the barrel-organ behind the lower cupboard doors, which connected with the striking mechanism of the clock. However, the rest of the fittings are still remarkably intact: the lower drawer is elaborately equipped for *toilette*, with a sloping ratcheted mirror and numerous beautifully fitted boxes, while the upper drawer opens as a desk and is backed with a set of drawers. The glazed upper section resembles a Venetian window (or triumphal arch), containing shelves for china or books, and the whole is surmounted by ormolu candle vases at each of the corners and a circular clock in the centre, following closely the design of the façade of the Weeks's Museum in Titchborne Street. Veneered in satinwood, with shaped sabicu panels framed by rosewood cross-banding, and with its elegant fitted boxes and drawers enriched with ivory and silver handles, it could be described as the quintessence of *fin-de-siècle* refinement. Curiously, it has a number of parallel features with the contemporaneous 'Temple' clock by Vulliamy (Fig. 5) and the two are usually displayed in close juxtaposition at Temple Newsam in Lady Irwin's New Terrace Room. It distantly recalls a design dated 1791 in Thomas Sheraton's *Drawing Book*.

Weeks's Museum of 'mechanical curiosities' was established in Titchborne Street in about 1797, and included a showroom probably intended for potential buyers to view merchandise, which could be made to order. There would clearly have been a number of specialist craftsmen employed on a piece such as the Temple Newsam cabinet, which may nevertheless

---

7. Ibid., Vol. 1, pp. 55–8, Vol. 3, p. 716. The whole group was discussed at length by Christopher Gilbert in 'Some Weeks's Cabinets Reconsidered', *Connoisseur*, May 1971, pp. 13–21.

have been masterminded by Weeks himself. A trade label with the name of George Simson, upholder and cabinet-maker of St Paul's Churchyard, has been found on a related lady's secretary in satinwood, which suggests that he may be the principal craftsman responsible for this highly distinctive group.[8]

Robert Rowe revealed his own personal enthusiasm for exquisitely made neoclassical works of art, especially objects that combined white marble and gilt bronze, by buying the fine bracket clock inscribed by the well known maker Jean-Baptiste Lepaute, 'H'GER DU ROI', in the mid-1960s.[9] It is one of a group of clocks with identical cases dating from around 1785, including one formerly at Clumber Park, but all with movements by different French makers. Its purchase might have seemed an aberration at the time, since it has never been a high priority to buy continental works of art for Temple Newsam, except for very particular reasons.[10] However, since the Harewood Library writing table had just been acquired, it seems very likely that Mr Rowe – with his connoisseur's eye always keen to explore stylistic themes – wanted to draw some parallels between English and French neoclassicism.

He was able to do this even more effectively with the group of marble and ormolu objects he acquired from Hotspur over a number of years in the mid- to late 1970s. The *neo-grêc* 'Burgoyne' candle vases are discussed elsewhere by Nicholas Goodison (p. 107) and they are rightly considered masterpieces of the Soho workshops.[11] Robert Rowe also bought a 'Narcissus' clock case by Matthew Boulton (Fig. 4) similar to the one illustrated in this volume by Nicholas Goodison on p. 121.[12] At Temple Newsam they fulfil perfectly the curatorial imperative to consider works of art both from the aesthetic and contextual points of view. Thus, for many years the Boulton pieces have been displayed in their 'natural' context as a garniture on top of the Harewood Library writing table. Here, visitors and students can consider the different ways in which Chippendale and Boulton used the neoclassical repertory of ornament, and also the different ways in which ormolu was employed as a decorative medium. Other neighbouring works of art displayed in Lord Halifax's former library (recently restored to

4. 'Narcissus' clock case by Matthew Boulton, c.1780.
H: 17" (43.5 cm).
This clock case is similar to the one at Soho House in Birmingham described by Nicholas Goodison on p. 120. This model has a marble base fringed with a chased ormolu border. The obelisk is decorated with a medallion of Ceres or Plenty.

8. A remarkable combined musical automaton, clock and *nécessaire*, inscribed 'Thomas Weeks', was accepted in lieu of taxes by H. M. Treasury and allocated to Temple Newsam in 2000.
9. *Horlager du Roi* (Clockmaker to the King). A group of clocks by the Lepaute family is discussed by Morton and Stroube in *French Clocks*, p. 44.
10. For example the *bureau plat* by Bernard van Riesenbergh from Allerton Park, or the *lit à l'anglais* by Jean Baptiste II Tilliard.
11. Gilbert, Ibid., Vol. 2, pp. 385–6; and Goodison, *Matthew Boulton: Ormolu*, pp. 297–300.
12. Gilbert, Ibid., Vol. 3, pp. 630–1; and Goodison, Ibid., pp. 220–2.

5. Ormolu-mounted white marble 'Temple' clock by Vulliamy, c.1791. Numbered 246.
H: 19½" (49 cm); W: 11¾" (30 cm).
The circular white enamelled dial with its original pierced gilt metal hands lies within a white marble case topped with a gilt metal urn finial. This is flanked by four gilt metal urns standing on a temple of four Doric columns with the figure of Euterpe playing her flute. The Muse leans on a truncated pillar that stands on an ormolu plinth engraved 'Vulliamy LONDON No. 246'. The brass back plate is engraved 'Vulliamy London No. 246' and the pendulum also bears the number 246.

6. A carved close stool, c.1755.
H: 17" (43 cm); W: 21" (53 cm); D: 15½" (39.5 cm).
The rectangular upholstered hinged top sits upon plain rails with deep aprons that are elaborately carved in the rococo taste, with 'C'-scrolls and acanthus foliage, linking four boldly carved cabriole legs terminating in scroll toes in the French taste.

BELOW
7. A mahogany triple shell-back settee, c.1745. H: 38" (96 cm); W: 63" (160 cm); D: 21" (53 cm). This settee of triple chair-back form has carved and pierced splat-backs which represent shells contained within a carved and moulded framework with interlaced slats below. The outflowing arms have carved acanthus supports. There are six legs; the cabriole front legs carved with acanthus decoration, terminating in claw and ball feet. This settee was originally part of a large suite of seat furniture comprising two settees and six side chairs. A similar set of chairs repeating the unusual shell-back design are at Stourhead; a payment of £64 for chairs in 1746 to Giles Grendey may relate to these chairs.

OPPOSITE
8. The Bellot cabinet, a mahogany cabinet on a stand, c.1745–50.
H: 81" (206 cm); W: 42" (106 cm); D: 25" (64 cm).
This cabinet, with a break-pediment top centred by a carved cartouche, is supported on a finely carved mahogany stand with bold claw and ball feet; the claws being pierced around the ball feet, the knees carved with shell motifs with large open brackets to a central shell in the frieze. The cabinet has a central door and side panels enriched with brilliantly coloured panels of chenille in cotton and silk, and the front-facing corners have freestanding columns and Corinthian capitals.

13. Gilbert, Ibid., Vol. 1, pp. 171–3.
14. Williams, *Sophie in London*, p. 101.
15. Benjamin Vulliamy was Royal Clockmaker to George III and the Prince of Wales. Records for his clocks start in 1797, when the firm had reached clock number 296. Clock number 25 was made for the Emperor in 1792–3, indicating that this example can be accurately dated to 1791. Fascinating details exist for the breakdown of costs for Vulliamy's clocks. Clock number 304, for instance, a 'small temple clock', lists the prices for each part: Bullock, the movement, £5 15s. 6d; Culver, engraving the hands, 5s. 0d; and Crockett, the gilding, £8 18s. 0d.
16. Gilbert, Ibid., Vol. 2, p. 307.

Lenygon's green and gold scheme of 1912) complement this centrepiece and further enhance a uniquely cerebral and aesthetic experience. They include the lyre-back chair from Brocket Hall and the marquetry side table from the Circular Dressing Room at Harewood House (both by Chippendale), the superb *Duchesse de la Ferté* by François de Troy, Roubiliac's *Bust of Alexander Pope* and, nearby, a larger marble *Narcissus* by William Theed.

The fourth object of this white marble and ormolu group is the 'Temple' clock inscribed 'Vulliamy LONDON No. 246' which was acquired in 1977 having been sold at auction slightly earlier from Malahide Castle, Co. Dublin (Fig. 5).[13] It celebrates the Triumph of Love with the figure of Euterpe, in Derby biscuit porcelain (modelled by J. J. Spangler), who, having passed through a triumphal arch (engraved on the back plate), now pauses to play her flute between the Doric columns of the portico. Like the Weeks's cabinet, with which it resonates so strongly, the clock is the epitome of that 'noble simplicity' which Sophie von la Roche commented on after her visit to Vulliamy's showrooms in 1786, and which she found so congenial compared to the 'luxury and magnificence' of his stock of French clocks.[14] Although the Vulliamy records do not survive before 1797, other evidence supports the date for this model to be about 1791.[15] Other examples are known, including one at Buckingham Palace.

But by this date (1979) Hotspur had also supplied Temple Newsam with a remarkable group of carved mahogany furniture from the mid-eighteenth century. The earliest was a handsome close stool (Fig. 6) with deep shaped aprons carved in low relief with leafy rococo 'C'-scrolls.[16] An unexpected point of interest for curators was the discovery of some remnants of a Regency gothic red flock wallpaper used as a lining before the original internal box was removed. The stool's bedmate now (so to speak) is the spectacular rococo State bed from Aldby Hall, and together they form part of an ensemble of bed and dressing furniture in the Gothick Room at Temple Newsam, where every piece dates from within five years either side of 1755.

Earlier, in 1969, came the triple shell-back settee (Fig. 7) of a well known pattern, long since attributed

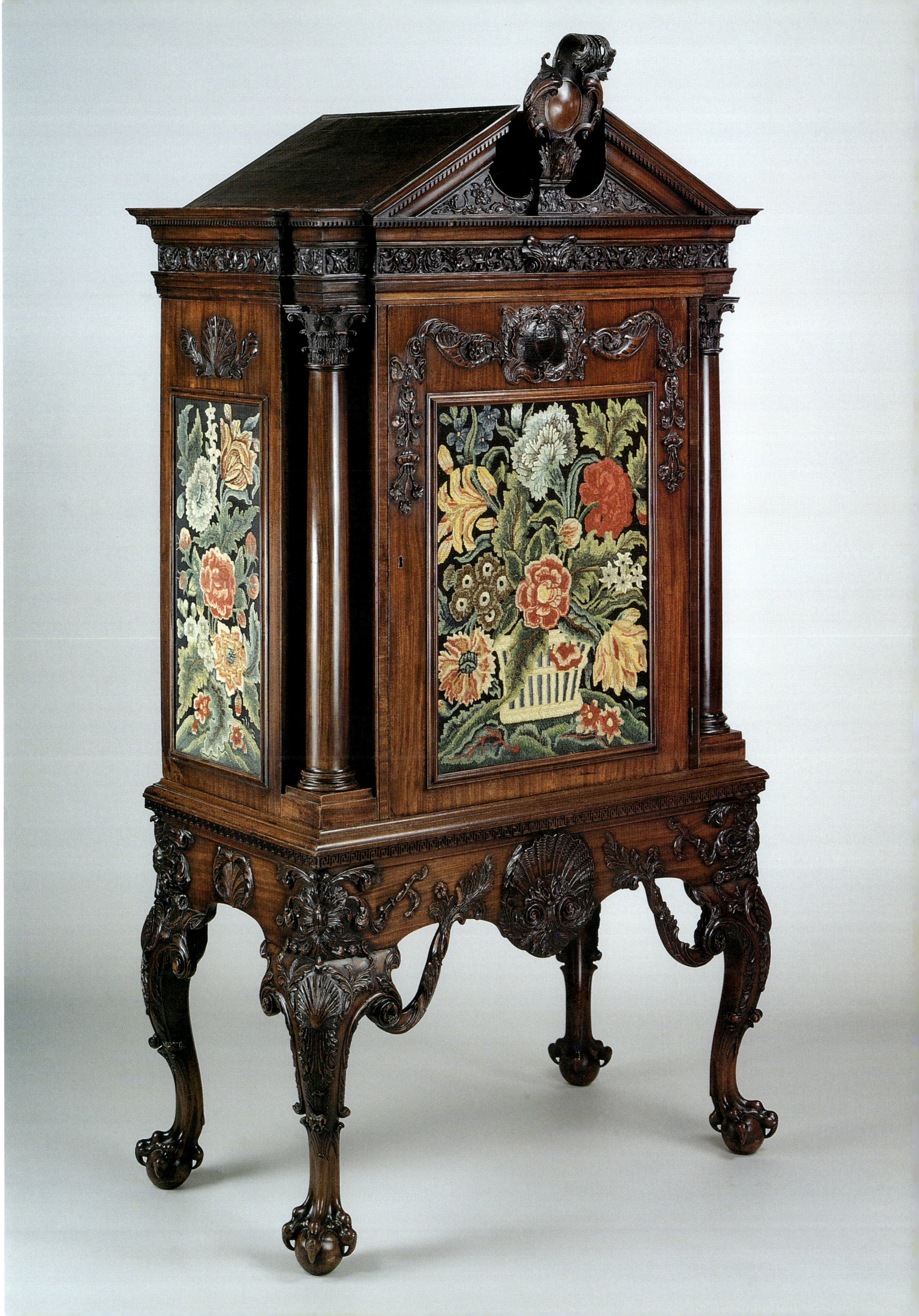

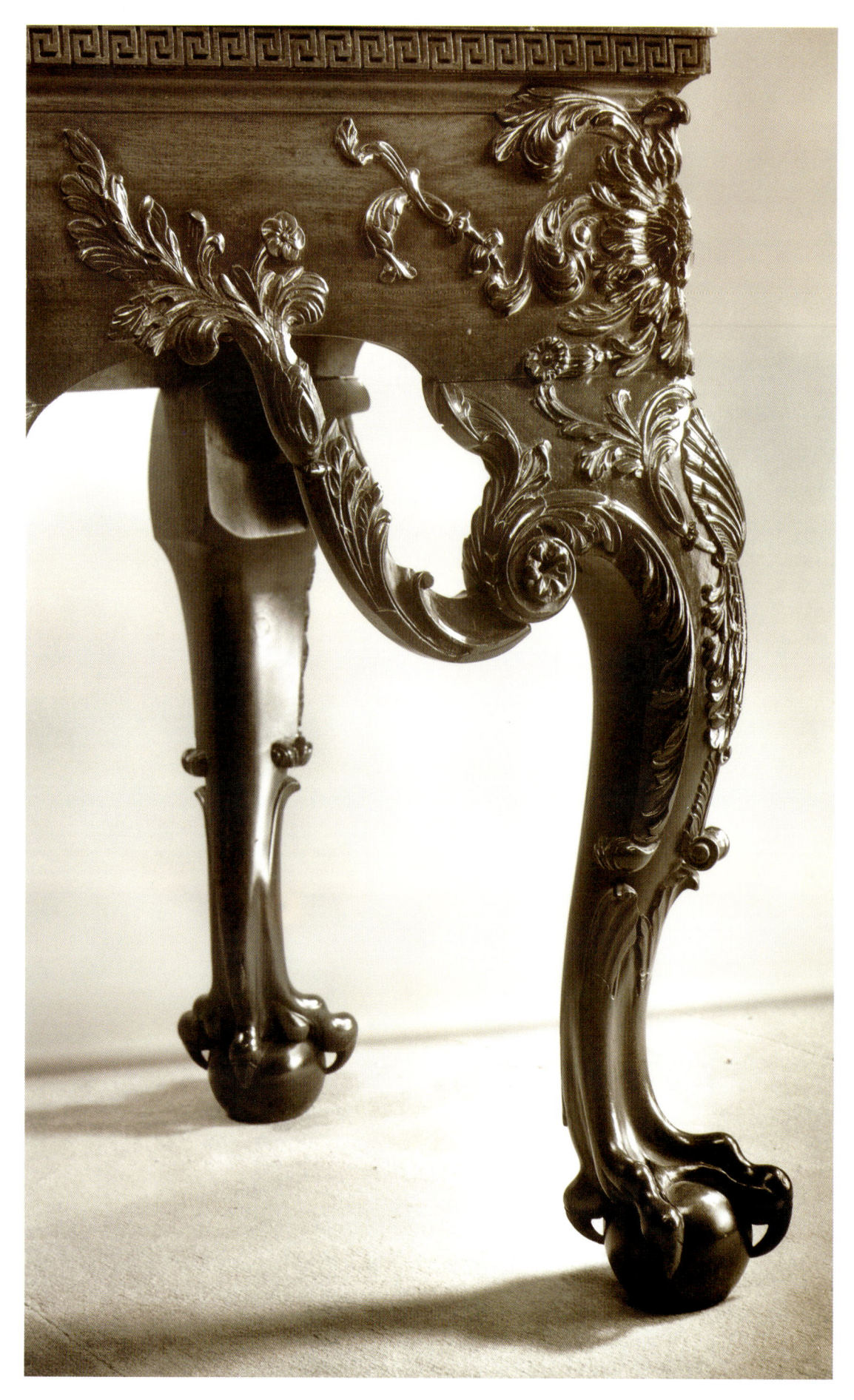

ABOVE & OPPOSITE: Details of Fig. 8.

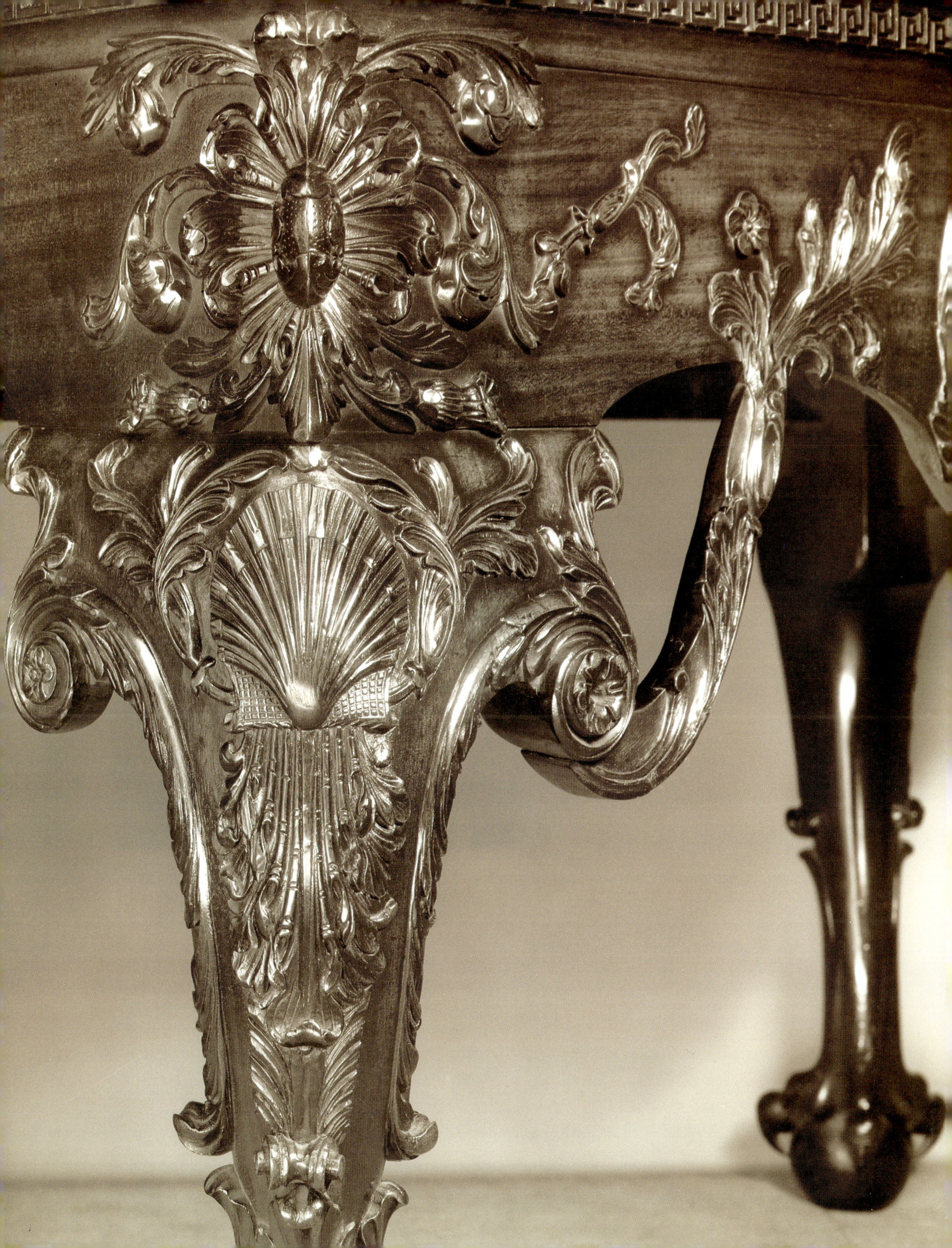

to Giles Grendey on the basis of a documented suite at Stourhead.[17] Grendey was one of the few English masters who allowed his journeymen to 'sign' their work with incised initials, and although none are found on this example, the letters 'TT' have been noted on other chairs of this model. 'TT' also used his initials on the suite of scarlet japanned furniture bearing Grendey's trade label and made for the Duke of Infantado, of which six chairs are at Temple Newsam. Another handsome walnut splat-back chair attributable to Grendey is also in the collection, thus giving a good representation for this prolific London furniture-maker.

Perhaps the most interesting piece from this group is the cabinet on a stand, the Bellot cabinet, now datable to around 1760–5 and attributed to Gillows of Lancaster (Fig. 8).[18] The strongly architectural design of the upper part, perhaps based on a manual such as Batty Langley's *The Builder's Director and Bench-Mate* (1746), serves as an aedicular frame for panels of chenille-work at the front and sides, worked in cotton and silk. The interior reveals two tiers of twenty-two ogee-shaped side drawers, flanking five long and short drawers faced with exquisite panels of floral sprays, butterflies and birds in silk embroidery on a satin ground in the Chinese taste, while above there is a mirror-lined niche with Ionic columns. The lower section has four massively carved cabriole legs and is enriched with shells and rococo foliage.

The key to the Gillows attribution is fourfold: first the undoubted provincial style of the carving; secondly its reliance on a published source; thirdly its provenance with the Bellot family of Stockport, Cheshire; and fourthly its affinities with other contemporaneous pieces attributable to Gillows, and which continue to come to light. It remains a remarkable piece of furniture, much loved by general visitors and scholars alike.

Christopher Gilbert's tragic early death in 1998 brought to an end a remarkably productive period in the history of collecting at Temple Newsam. At least two attempts had been made to nominate Gilbert for an Honour during his lifetime (one instigated by the partners of Hotspur), but to no avail. Nevertheless, soon after he died the perfect opportunity to make an appropriate memorial for him appeared in the form

---

17. Gilbert, *op. cit.*, Vol. 2, pp. 326–7.
18. The Bellot family were from Lancashire and the attribution of Gillows of Lancaster as the firm responsible for this magnificent cabinet on a stand is a strong one; one of the Bellot family's executors, Mrs Kathleen Taylor, remembers putting the relevant evidence into one of the cabinet's drawers prior to selling it at Sotheby's in 1969. See Gilbert, *op. cit.*, Vol. 1, pp. 50–5.

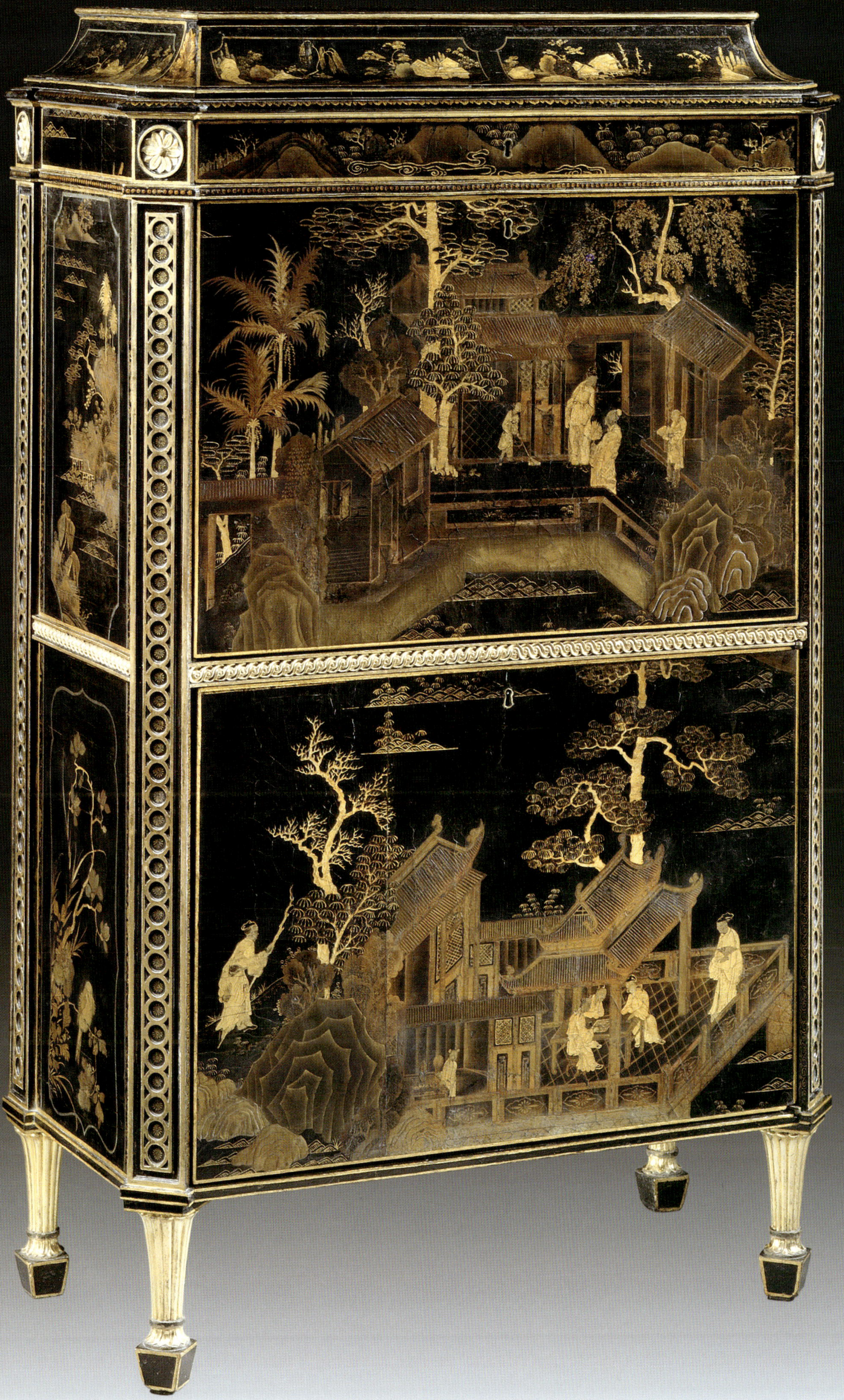

of the 'Lady's Secretary', made by Chippendale for the State Bedroom at Harewood in 1773 (Fig. 9). Hotspur, Mallett and Partridge had acquired it jointly at auction and it was destined for a transatlantic client. An export licence was applied for, and – not unexpectedly – this was deferred for three months (extendable for another three) on account of its pre-eminence, and to enable a museum in Britain to raise the equivalent sum (£650,000) to save it from export. It was the kind of challenge that Christopher Gilbert had relished and at which he had excelled in the past. Here was a perfect opportunity to provide a permanent memorial to him among the collections at Temple Newsam.

The story of the 'Lady's Secretary' has been told many times and space does not permit it to be told again at length.[19] Suffice to say that it formed part of the ultra-luxurious furnishings of the State Bedroom at Harewood, in which all the case furniture (pier commode and two cabinets) was of the finest oriental lacquer. Chippendale's bill shows it to have cost just £26 because his client, Edwin Lascelles, had provided the necessary materials in the same way that Lascelles had provided the green silk damask for the State bed, the seat furniture and the wall hangings. Evidently, there was enough lacquer left over for Chippendale to make another identical example for a second client, Robert Child of Osterley (a rare example of Chippendale's business efficiency), as discussed by Anthony Coleridge on pages 236 and 237. The model itself, derived from a French *secrétaire à abattant*, was sufficiently chic for another 'twin' of exactly the same size to be made for the adjoining State Dressing Room, and which is still at Harewood: the difference is that this second example is veneered in satinwood with marquetry decoration. It formed a suite with the 'Diana and Minerva commode' and probably the 'Three Graces commode'. The two secretaires were finally re-united at Harewood for *The Art of Thomas Chippendale* exhibition in 2000. When it was found that the key for the lacquer secretaire had been inadvertently left behind at Temple Newsam, Terry Suthers, the Director of the Harewood House Trust, was quite unperturbed and produced the key for its satinwood sister to find that it fitted the other perfectly!

19. For example, Coleridge, 'An Addition to Chippendale's Oeuvre', *Antiques*, Vol. CXLIX, No. 6 (June 1996), pp. 862–7 (discusses the Osterley secretaire); and 'A Tale of Two Secretaries', *Christie's International Magazine*, June 1997, pp. 44–6.

The campaign to save the Harewood secretaire was a monumental one, undertaken by Anthony Wells-Cole, in effect Christopher Gilbert's successor at Temple Newsam. He succeeded because of the generosity of so many benefactors, headed by the three vendors themselves who made substantial donations, together with the Heritage Lottery Fund, the National Art Collections Fund, the Monument Trust and many other grant-giving bodies. In addition, many individual members of the Furniture History Society and the Leeds Art Collections Fund wanted to be associated with this memorial to someone who had been such a champion, with one particular anonymous admirer providing a six-figure sum. Its arrival at Temple Newsam was truly a red-letter day in the history of collecting at the 'Hampton Court of the North'.

JL

An historic British collector: Sam Messer

CHARLES CATOR

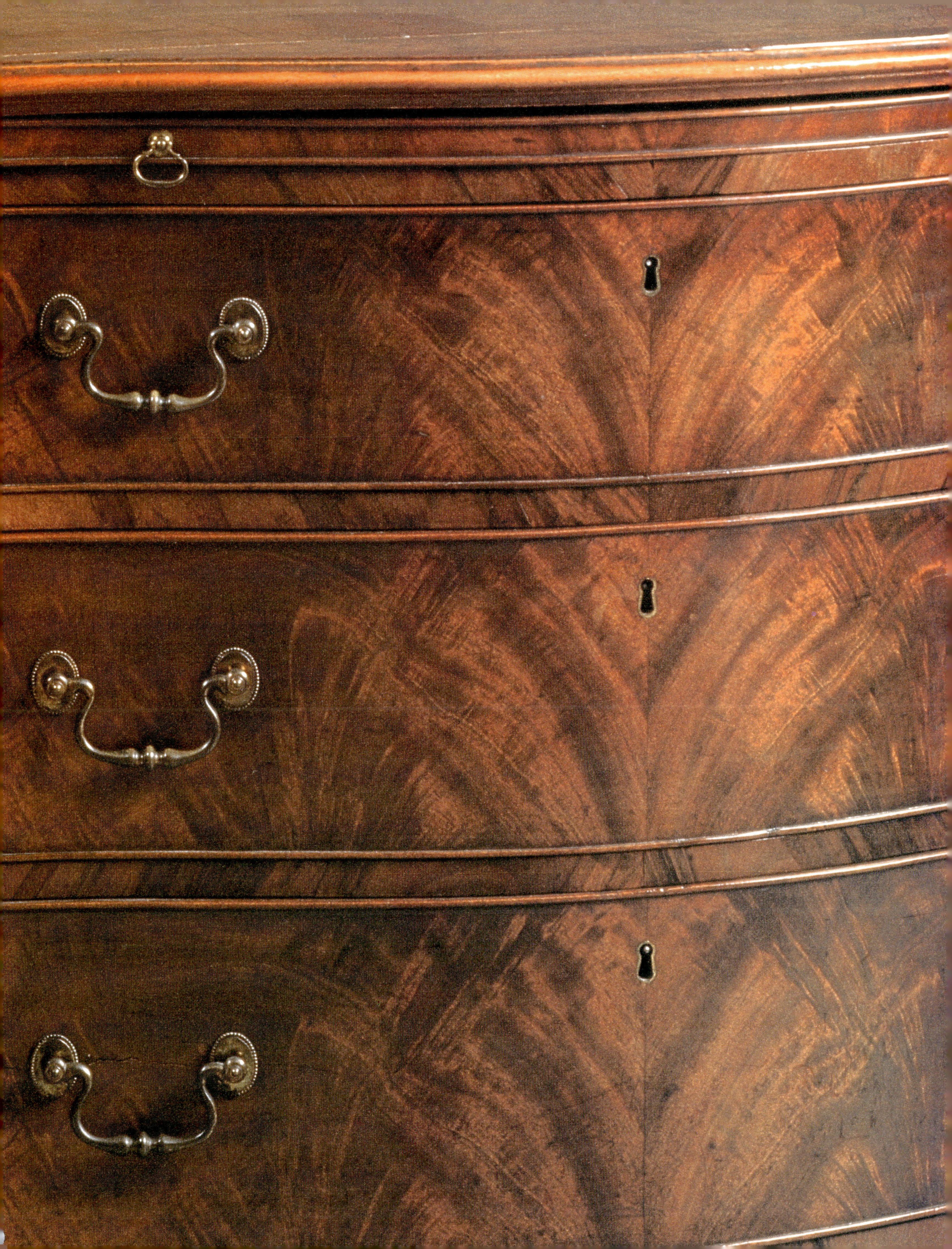

PREVIOUS PAGE
(Detail from p. 53, Fig. 2)
Mahogany serpentine commode, c.1780.

AN HISTORIC BRITISH COLLECTOR

THE PROCESS OF collecting is one of the most fascinating aspects of the art market – indeed it is the very lifeblood of the market. It is endlessly intriguing as to why collectors collect in the first place: what captures their passion and enthusiasm, what they see in particular objects, how they assess the relative values of design, provenance, condition and colour. Over the years it is the aspect of my job that has most interested me and the one that I have most enjoyed.

The wonderful friendships that develop through it bring the very greatest pleasure – and that process of understanding and appreciating together is a bond that endures. However varied the joint interests, somehow inevitably the discussion always returns to the subject we all enjoy the most, and in any English furniture collecting conversation it is never long before the name of Hotspur comes up. Hotspur has played a seminal role in the creation of many of the most distinguished twentieth-century collections. This is not just through providing the opportunity for emerging collectors to acquire spectacular and interesting works of art – but through the whole process of encouragement, friendship and, above all, wise advice.

The nurturing of collectors and, therefore, collections has become one of the leitmotifs of Hotspur's style. Since my earliest days at Christie's, I have always been struck by the warmth and generosity with which Robin, Brian and, before them, their father, have welcomed all enthusiasts – scholars, curators, fellow members of the trade – and even the salerooms and, of course, collectors. And that encompasses the whole range of collectors, from those with the largest budget to those with equal passion but more modest means. Anyone with a genuine interest will never find the dazzling display of treasures on offer at Lowndes Street intimidating because they are immediately received into that happy world of knowledge, passion and friendship.

Of the many distinguished collections with which Hotspur has been closely involved, one of the most remarkable was that of Sam Messer. With its unerring quality and very concise focus, in many ways it encapsulated the 'Hotspur style', and for Robin it has always represented the *ne plus ultra* of collections. The definitive group of mid-eighteenth-century carved mahogany that Sam assembled has exercised a strong influence on Robin and he has always considered it to be the example of what new collectors should aspire to. In a typically generous gesture, he would often take enthusiastic collectors at the beginning of their collecting cycle down to Pelsham to meet Sam and look at the collection with him. It was a brilliantly effective way for Robin to show them what they could perhaps create and, above all, what great pleasure they could derive from the process. Sam hugely enjoyed showing his furniture and certainly those fortunate enough to have made the expedition will never forget the experience.

Sam Messer had worked all his professional life in property – and had been a partner of Jack Cotton. His burgeoning interest in English furniture was transformed by a chance meeting with the legendary R. W. Symonds in the early 1950s. Sam later referred to it in a letter to Symonds as 'in a lift at Grosvenor Square', so it was almost certainly on the way up to the flat of J. S. Sykes, another celebrated Symonds collector. Symonds advised Sam Messer from then until his death in 1958, and it was in this period that Sam formed the nucleus of his collection. Under his guidance, Sam learnt to assess those qualities in a piece by the exacting criteria that Symonds had established over the years: untouched condition, original patination and fine quality timber, combined with good proportion, an elegant line and a balanced use of crisply carved ornament. These were Symonds's guiding tenets to which he adhered throughout his remarkable career, advising on the creation of almost all of the great private collections of English furniture formed in the first half of the twentieth century, as well as helping to create the splendid collection at Colonial Williamsburg. His advice was sought by a formidable range of collectors whose names have become so familiar among the provenances of many of the very finest examples: J. S. Sykes, Geoffrey Hart, Alfred Jowett, Frederick Poke, Geoffrey Blackwell, E. Guy Ridpath, Lord Plender, Sir Harold and Lady Hague, Guy Charrington, Sir John Prestige, General and Mrs Micklem, the brothers Eric and Ralph Moller, and

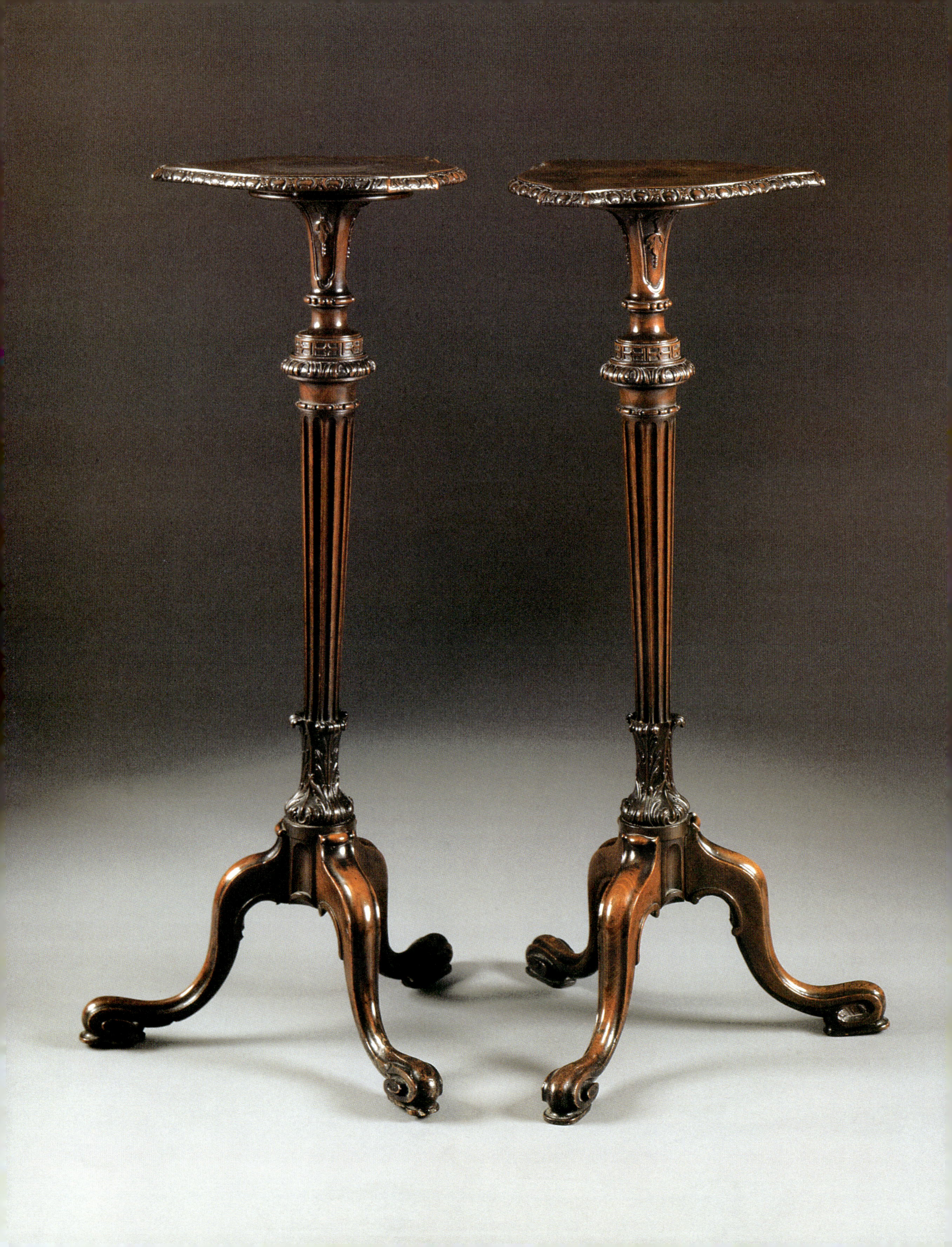

OPPOSITE
1. A pair of mahogany candle stands, c.1765.
w: 18" (46 cm); H: 44¾" (113.5 cm).
One of three pairs of triangular-top candle stands of this model in the collection; this pair was bought in 1953 for £725 on the advice of R. W. Symonds.

2. A mahogany serpentine commode, c.1780.
w: 43" (109 cm); D: 24½" (62.5 cm); H: 33¾" (85.5 cm).
Acquired in the mid-1950s, the elegant serpentine form of this commode is enhanced by the choice of superbly figured mahogany.

AN HISTORIC BRITISH COLLECTOR

Claude Rotch, whose collection was bequeathed to the Victoria and Albert Museum in 1962. But best known of all, of course, was Percival Griffiths, whose collection at Sandridgebury first became widely appreciated in 1929 with the publication of *English Furniture from Charles II to George II*[1] which Symonds illustrated entirely with Percival Griffiths's pieces, making the collection the *locus classicus* for many subsequent collectors.

Symonds had first met Percival Griffiths in 1911, and in a charming *Country Life* article, 'Portrait of a Collector',[2] Symonds described Griffiths's approach to furniture, stressing how different it was from that of the collectors at the turn of the century. It was this concentration on colour, patination and line that Symonds communicated so brilliantly to the collectors who followed Griffiths, and one of the great glories of the Messer Collection was the superb colour of almost every piece, with a particular focus on the close and straight-grained, hard-textured mahogany that Symonds so admired.

Those special qualities sought out by Symonds have always been emphasised very strongly by Hotspur; it is no surprise that some of Sam's purchases through Symonds were made at Hotspur, with Symonds endorsing the invoices, as was the case for the pair of triangular-top candle stands acquired in June 1953 for £725 (Fig. 1). All collectors tend to develop themes within their collections and Sam was no exception, so within the very concise confines of his mid-eighteenth-century mahogany he concentrated on particular types.

Thus there were eventually three pairs of these very distinctive and rare candle stands in the collection, all acquired from Hotspur, the second pair in June 1959, the year after Symonds's death, for £880. Another significant purchase from the Symonds years was a mahogany serpentine commode (Fig. 2), which illustrates perfectly how colour and figuring of the timber can transform a handsome piece into an exceptional one. Symonds had included it in an article on 'Provincial Cabinet-Making in the Eighteenth Century'[3] and he proved to be typically prescient as the commode belongs to a group that has recently been attributed to Henry Hill, who carried on an extensive upholstery and cabinet-

---

OPPOSITE
3. A mahogany stool, c.1765, bought in 1960 at the Grosvenor House Fair.
W: 24" (61 cm); D: 18" (46 cm); H: 17½" (44.5 cm).

4. A mahogany stool, c.1765, bought in 1971.
W: 25" (63.5 cm); D: 20¾" (52.5 cm); H: 17¼" (44 cm).

---

1. Symonds, *English Furniture from Charles II to George II*.
2. Symonds, 'Portrait of a Collector', *Country Life*, 13 June 1952, pp. 110–12.
3. Symonds, 'Provincial Cabinet-Making in the Eighteenth Century', *Antiques Review*, June–August 1981, p. 22, fig. 17.

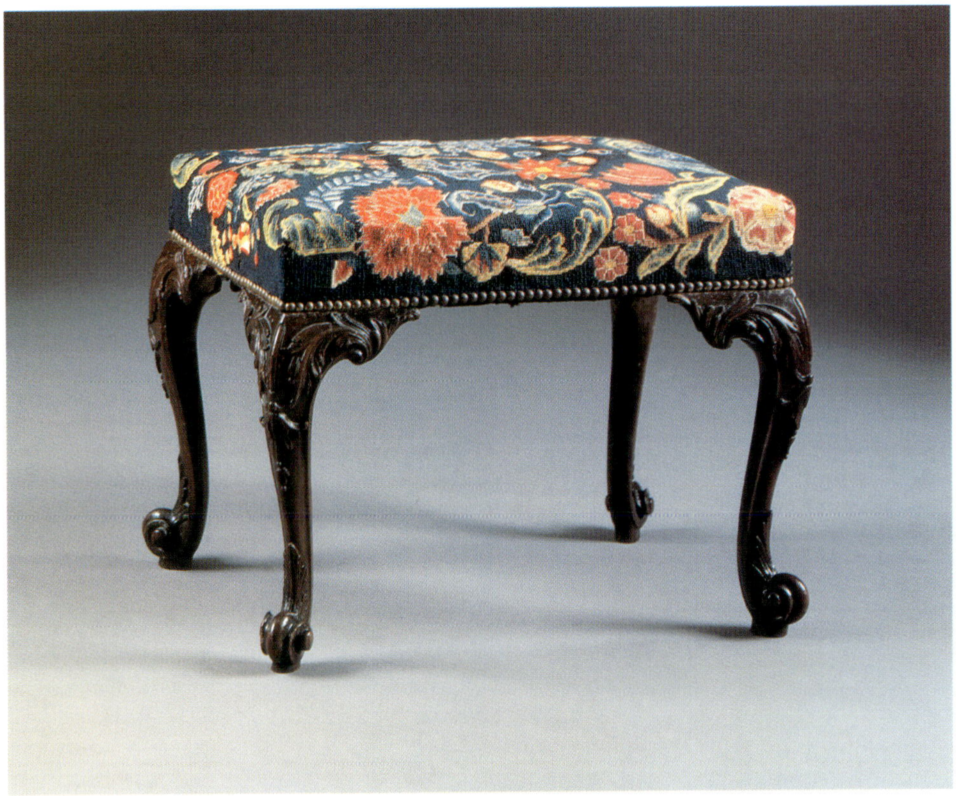

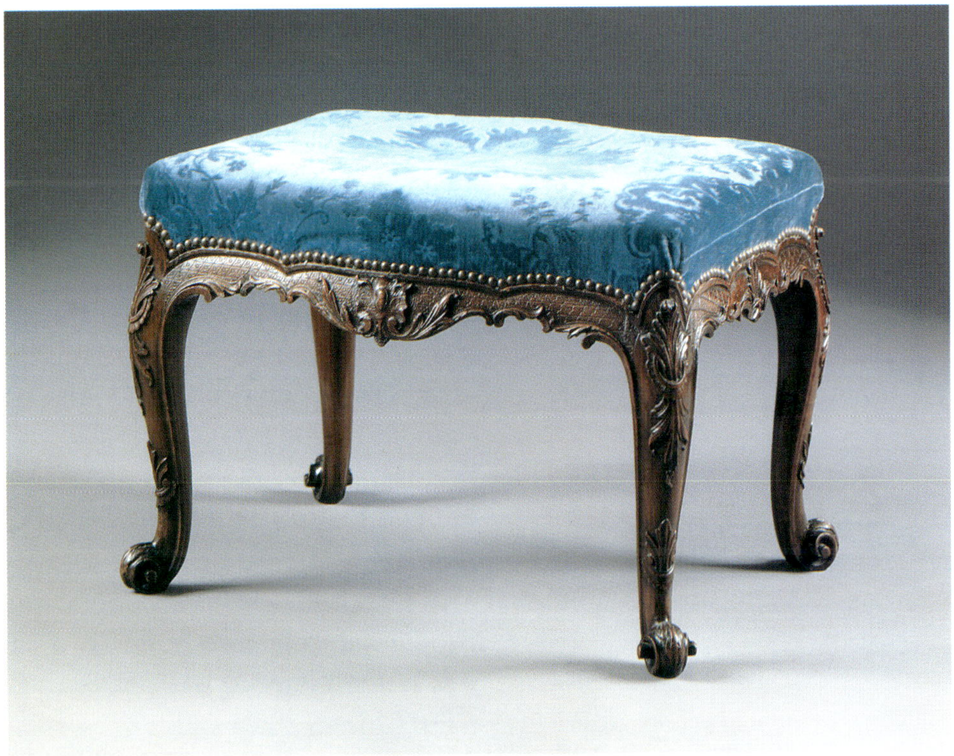

OPPOSITE

5. A mahogany 'goldfish-bowl' stand, c.1765. The stand. w: 22¼" (56.5 cm); H: 26¼" (67 cm).
The bowl. Diam: 11" (28 cm); H: 13" (33 cm).

6. A mahogany tripod caddy stand, c.1760. The stand. D: 9" (23 cm); H: 23¼" (59 cm); including the silver caddy, 4¼" (11 cm); H: 4½" (11.5 cm); Weight: 14 oz.
The silver caddy associated with this stand is by William and Aaron Lesturgeon, made in 1777.

4. Symonds, 'The English Tea Table', *Antiques Review*, March–May 1951, p. 11, fig. 13.

making business for over forty years in Marlborough, Wiltshire.

As with so many collectors, space became a problem for Sam even after the move to Pelsham, near Rye, in the early 1960s. He was as passionate about collecting as ever, so through the later 1960s and 70s he tended to concentrate on smaller pieces, many of which he acquired from Hotspur, and on refining his superb group of clocks and barometers. Most of the spectacular seat furniture had been acquired by the early 1960s, but stools are something the furniture collector can always add. Sam found two fine examples at Hotspur, both carved with crisp acanthus sprays; one with an immensely elegant profile bought at the Grosvenor House Fair in 1960 (Fig. 3); the other, acquired in 1971, is slightly earlier in date and has a richly ornamented seat frame (Fig. 4). The remarkable series of stands are particularly striking as supports for silver tea kettles, silver tea caddies, Chinese dishes, and even a glass goldfish bowl (Fig. 5). This often led Robin to go in search of an appropriate silver, porcelain or glass utensil to set the piece off to perfection. Nothing is ever too much trouble and Hotspur always comes up with something exactly right, such as the cylindrical tea caddy by William and Aaron Lesturgeon for the eye-catching caddy stand supported by a hierarchy of delicately balanced 'C'-scrolls (Fig. 6). If the search for the ideal proved unsuccessful, as with the richly carved tripod stand originally intended to support a Chinese dish, then Hotspur commissioned a modern silver example from Garrard, but only after a two-year wait (dish not shown, Fig. 7). In 1951 Sam had acquired his first triangular-top kettle stand from Hotspur – discussed and illustrated by Symonds in 'The English Tea Table' in *Antiques Review* in 1951 (Fig. 8).[4]

Continuing on this same theme, a series of candle stands followed, the first pair bought in 1953; it was one from this pair that found its most unusual expression in the goldfish-bowl stand and is traditionally associated with William Vile on the basis of the pair supplied by him to Queen Charlotte. Sam's exceptional triangular stands, which are rarities seldom seen on the market, had been designed to support silver tea kettles and he was

57

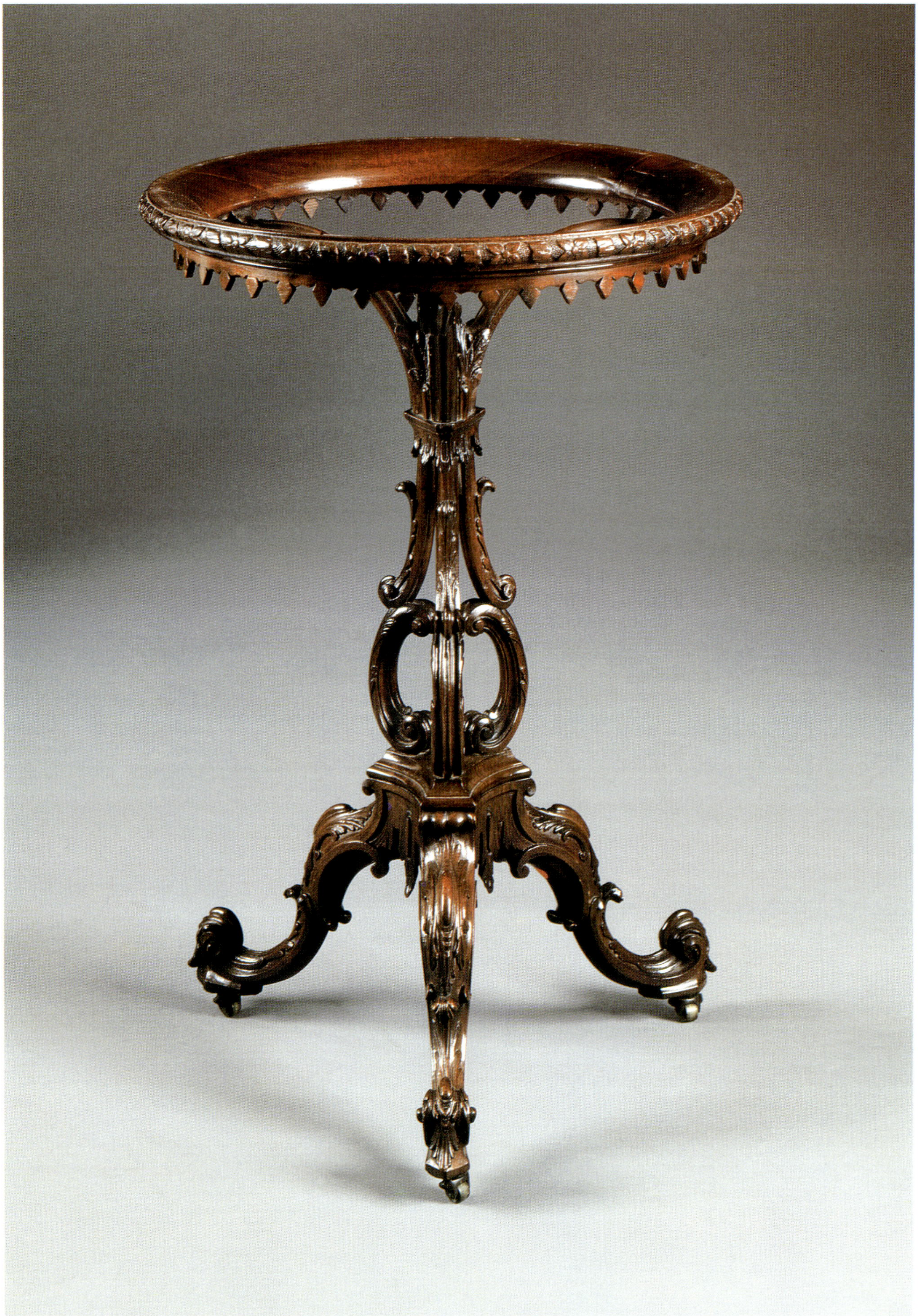

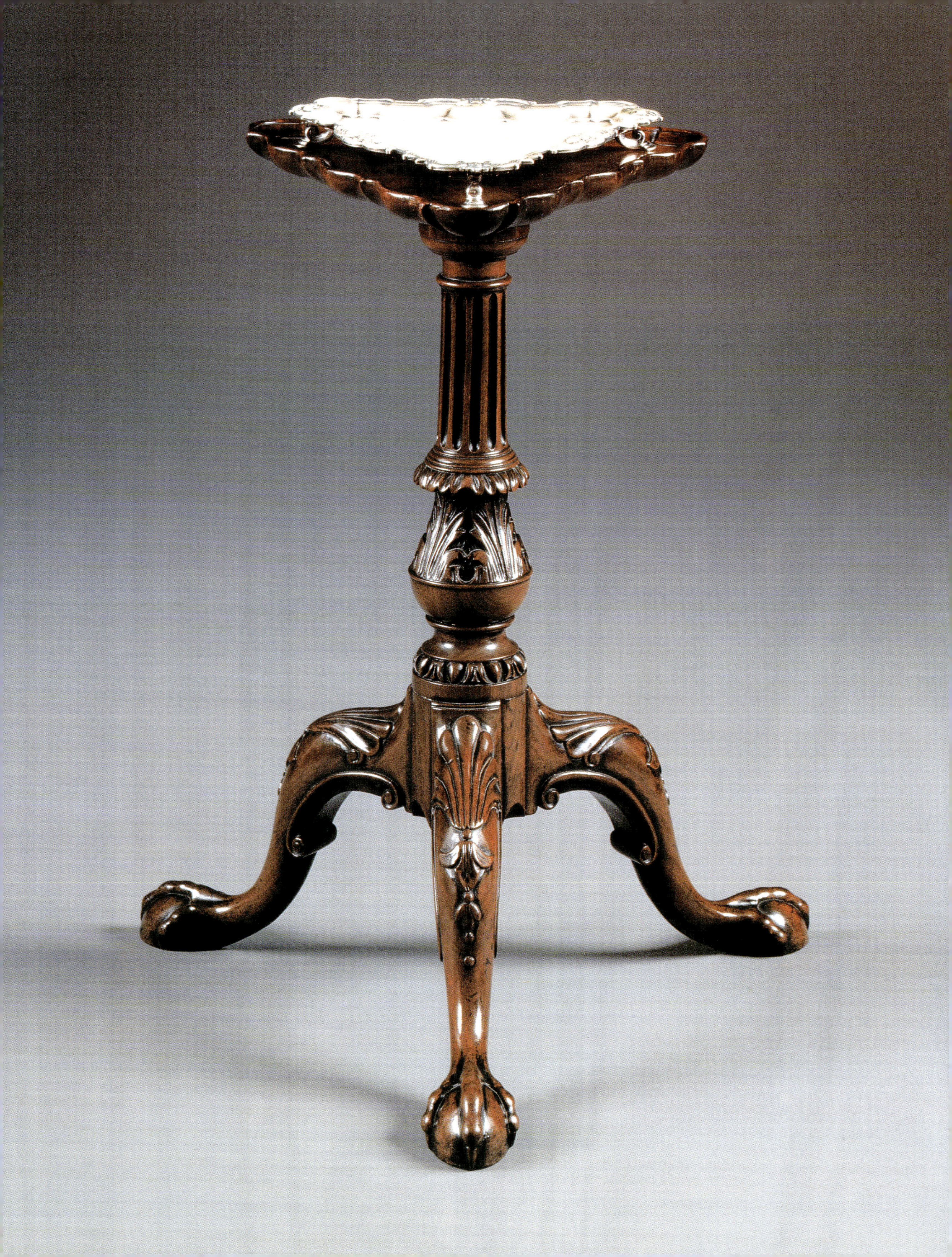

PREVIOUS PAGES
7. A mahogany tripod stand, c.1760.
Diam: 22" (56 cm); H: 31" (78.5 cm).

8. A mahogany kettle stand, c.1750,
purchased in 1951.
W: 12½" (32 cm); H: 22" (56 cm).

OPPOSITE
9. A mahogany kettle stand, c.1755,
purchased in 1975.
W: 13" (33 cm); H: 19" (48.5 cm); with a silver
tea kettle, stand, lamp and triangular stand
by John White.
The triangular stand, 1734.
H: 14¾" (37.5 cm).

10. A mahogany kettle stand, c.1750.
W: 11½" (9 cm); H: 21" (53 cm).

5. C.I.O.N.A., *International Art Treasures Exhibition Catalogue*, Assembly Rooms, Bath, 1973, no. 66, fig. 48.

assiduous in acquiring appropriate silver pieces to complement them. Robin found a tea kettle for him, complete with its triangular waiter, for the stand with an elaborately complex profile that had been exhibited in the *International Art Treasures Exhibition* at the Assembly Rooms in Bath in 1973 (Fig. 9).[5] This was acquired from Hotspur in 1975, in the same period as another, plainer kettle stand – more robust in character with crisply carved shell corners – that was one of my favourite pieces in the collection (Fig. 10). Hotspur's role even extended to helping Sam's wife, Pam, look for a suitable wedding anniversary present; together they found the mid-eighteenth-century bottle stand (Fig. 11) – which demonstrates all the qualities Sam so admired: an unusual and distinctive form, precise carved detail and, above all, a superb colour. How thrilled he must have been.

Colour was also the defining characteristic of the mahogany centre table (Fig. 12) with a gadrooned border and edge to the serpentine frieze. With its combination of lustrous timber and an elegant profile, enhanced by sparely used, crisply carved detail, it nobly fulfilled the Symonds criteria.

So Sam continued to build on the collection selectively, and with great enjoyment, throughout the 1960s and 70s. He almost always bought from his established and trusted sources – Moss Harris (in the early years), R. A. Lee (especially for the clocks and barometers), Partridge and, of course, Hotspur. He followed the market closely right up to his death in 1991, always dropping in at Lowndes Street when he was in London to catch up on the collecting news. After his death in the summer of 1991, Christie's were instructed by his executors and family to sell the collection. As soon as I received the news, I wanted to make sure that his two oldest friends in the furniture world – Robin Kern and John Partridge – knew before anyone else, so I dropped in on Robin early one morning: it can never be too early for Robin. We spent an hour happily reminiscing – above all on the extraordinary pleasure Sam's collection had given him.

The sale of Sam Messer's collection at Christie's in 1991 remains one of the great landmarks in the history of English furniture collecting. It was one of the most thrilling periods of my career. We had

61

11. A mahogany bottle stand, c.1745.
w: 26¾" (68 cm); d: 17½" (45.5 cm);
h: 20¼" (51 cm).

12. A mahogany centre table, c.1745.
W: 33¼" (84 cm); D: 21" (53 cm);
H: 27½" (70 cm).

OPPOSITE
13. A mahogany tallboy, c.1755.
w: 47¾" (121 cm); D: 26" (66 cm);
H: 60½" (153 cm).

very little time to prepare the catalogue, less than two-and-a-half months from late August. Hardback catalogues need an additional three weeks to allow for the binding so it was close-run to ensure publication in early November. Fortunately I had already worked quite extensively on the collection, and so I knew it well. I had first met Sam in May 1978 with Anthony Coleridge and John Partridge at my first major house sale: Jim Joel's immaculately kept estate near St Albans, Childwick Bury. Sam had come to look at the superb, small mid-eighteenth-century mahogany commode originally from Serlby Hall and most probably commissioned by the second Viscount Galway in about 1750. The Childwick Bury commode was part of a very distinctive group of commodes on a stand, which illustrated the development from a chest or coffer on a separate stand to the fully unified commode of the later eighteenth century. Sam had already acquired a splendid pair of related commodes from the Eric Moller Collection in 1958 and another single example from Partridge in 1963 – hence his interest in the Childwick piece, which he subsequently acquired through Partridge. Later on, and continuing on the theme, he managed to acquire a tallboy, again part of the same group, from Hotspur (Fig 13).

Anthony Coleridge had suggested that Christie's should prepare a catalogue of his collection of furniture, clocks and barometers that would become a lasting record of the provenances and would also include the most current research; at one stage there was an idea that this might be published. In the end this was never developed as Sam was such a private person and he was understandably concerned about the publicity. So I spent many happy days at Pelsham with Sam, discussing the furniture he so loved, and, as I learnt to look with his eyes, it was fascinating to imagine the unbroken thread of collecting knowledge passed down from Percival Griffiths and Robert Symonds.

In his essay on the Gerstenfeld Collection,[6] another collection he admires enormously, Robin discusses Symonds's continuing influence on succeeding generations of collectors. One feature that comes across very clearly is the intense appreciation of the skill of the craftsman and the technical ability of

6. Lennox-Boyd, *Masterpieces of English Furniture: The Gerstenfeld Collection*, pp. 52–64.

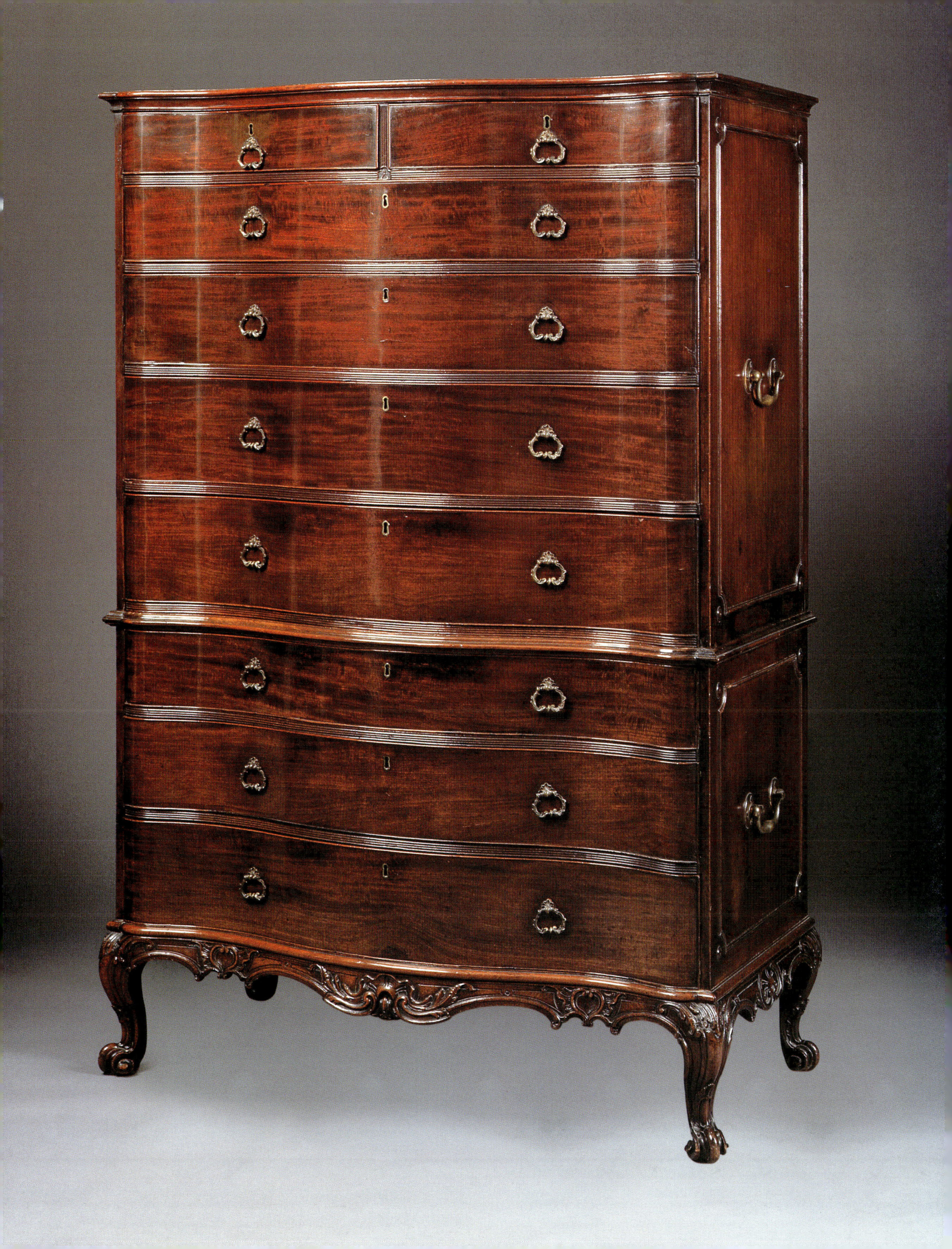

the cabinet-maker to achieve the desired end result that would stand the test of time. Perhaps it is in his balanced understanding of both the aesthetic and the practical that Symonds's enduring appeal to today's market lies. For collectors like Sam Messer, understanding the construction of a piece is an essential element in the overall enjoyment, and this approach has always been part of the Hotspur ethic – as Robin describes it: 'the way the inside of a piece of fine furniture speaks on the outside'.

Sam's acquisitions from Hotspur cover a period of more than twenty-five years from the first purchase of an early eighteenth-century silvered wood and walnut girandole (Fig. 14) in 1951, and spanned the period of Rob, Brian and Robin Kern. The close bond established in those years ensured that the friendship continued after Sam's days of active collecting were over, through the 1980s until his death. Those forty years of mutual trust and confidence are an exemplary illustration of what can be achieved between dealer and collector – but then the dealer was Hotspur.

C C

OPPOSITE
14. A silvered wood and walnut girandole, c.1710. H: 34" (86.5 cm); W: 23¼" (59 cm). This is the first piece that Sam Messer acquired from Hotspur in March 1951 on the advice of R.W. Symonds.

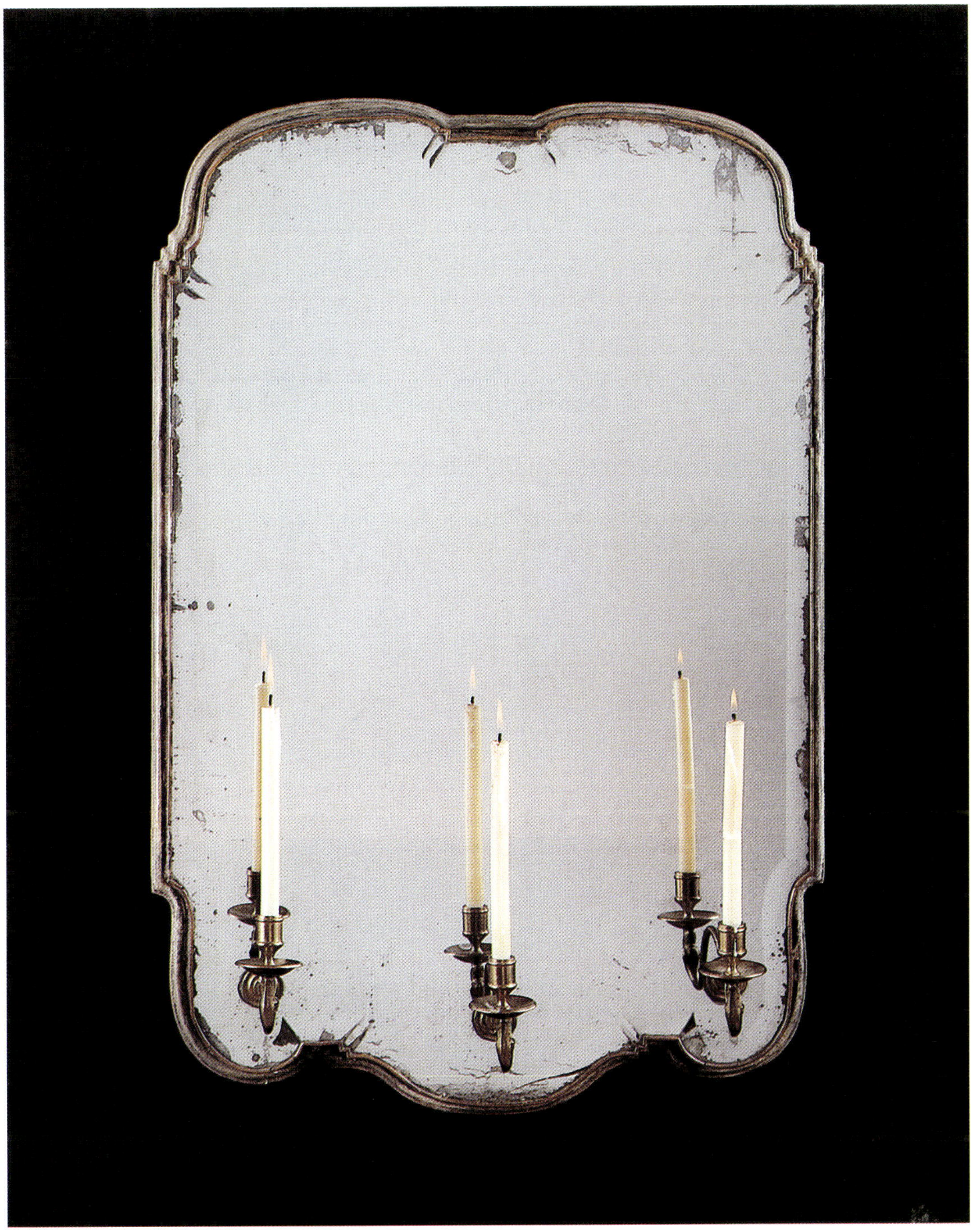

A contemporary American collector

JOHN BRYAN

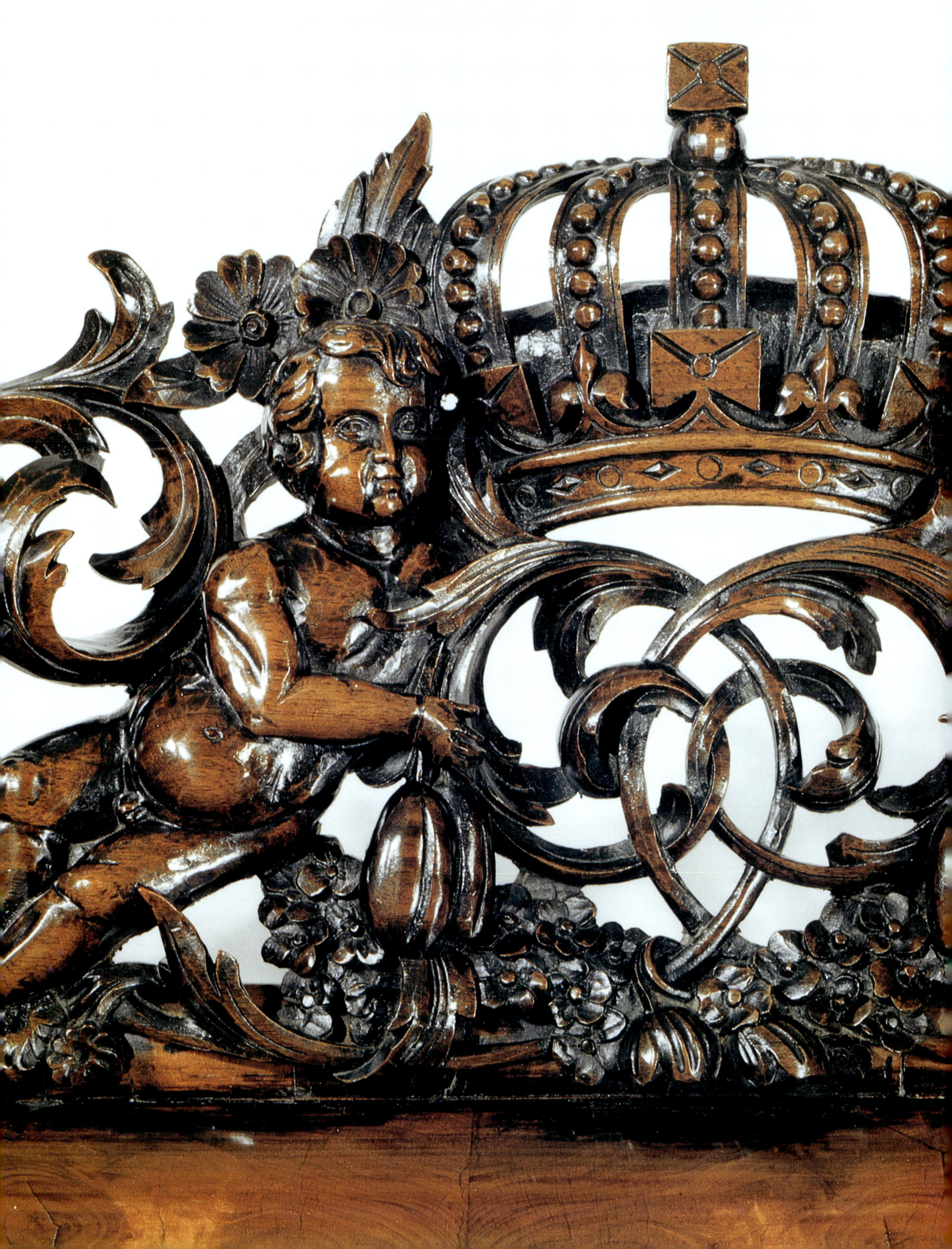

A CONTEMPORARY AMERICAN COLLECTOR

THROUGHOUT MOST OF recorded history, the collecting of art and antiques has been an activity pursued by pharaohs, royalty and merchant princes. In today's more egalitarian age, collecting is enjoyed by a much wider range of people and even includes ordinary business people such as myself.

For the purpose of this commentary, it is useful to divide collectors into two separate groups. There is the professional collector, primarily associated with museums, and the amateur collector, for whom collecting is only an avocation. As a life-long businessman whose occupation has been reasonably demanding, I most certainly belong to the amateur category. Thus, it is from that perspective that I am offering a few comments on the collector of today.

To define the amateur collector of English antiques, i.e. English decorative arts, we really should exclude those whose interest is purely decorative and who most often make their purchases through intermediaries, usually called decorators. That is a very important part of the market and these individuals purchase serious pieces of decorative art, but they are not really collectors.

The title of collector, albeit amateur, is one that I eschewed for many years. It is a term that imparts a sense of purpose. It also demands at least a modicum of knowledge, some commitment of time and, above all, a passion for collecting. Some have it; some do not. I, today, must admit that I do.

Is there a collecting instinct? Most assuredly, the answer is yes. I have it, and my wife does not. It is probably a vice and a virtue at the same time. However, it is surely a condition necessary to being a collector.

For me, it all started back in the late 1960s when I was on a trip to England. I bought a truckload of furniture in the Cotswolds, having spent two days visiting shops there. The truckload, mostly country oak and walnut furniture, cost me £1,000 in those days, and the shopping trip was a lot of fun. I was hooked!

A few months later, when the truck arrived at my home in Mississippi, my father was not impressed. I overheard him using some rather strong expletives to describe all of that rotten furniture that I had bought in England. At any rate, that journey to England began over thirty years of interest in the early English decorative arts.

What is the appeal of collecting? As you can imagine, it varies enormously. For some, it is very much like a sportsman on a hunt – searching out and finding objects can offer great thrills. For others, it is the love of the deal – the negotiation. In fact, I know one collector whose primary motivation is to collect bargains. Each piece in his collection is an anecdote, an acquisition story that ends with his successful purchase of the piece at an absurdly low price.

The emergence of the auction house as a major source of antiques has produced buyers who are, obviously, quite attracted to the 'rush' they get from victory in the auction room. I know of collections exclusively built by purchases at auction. The stirring of one's competitive juices adds a psychic value to objects bought in the salerooms. Also, some buyers at auction are comforted by knowing there is an under-bidder – a person who is willing to pay about as much as the successful bidder.

Some collectors, including myself, really enjoy receiving new pieces and placing them in their collections. But this is not true for everyone. There are collectors who simply buy, store their pieces, and never even uncrate them.

There is occasionally commentary about the investment opportunities afforded by collecting. Of course, some collectors are just traders or investors disguised as collectors, but they are rather rare. The majority of collectors of antique furniture are not, in my judgement, thinking about reselling the pieces when they acquire them.

I suspect that for collectors the greatest satisfaction is derived from simply owning and displaying, learning about and talking about the objects themselves. Antiques stir our interest in history. They feed our aesthetic senses. They give us intellectual and academic challenges! So, whether one is collecting just to occupy and amuse oneself, or one is creating a major collection with great vision and purpose, it really does not matter.

How does one decide what to collect, once bitten by the bug? It depends, of course, on circumstances. One's experiences, family and friends are very influential, as are the dealers one may meet from time to time. The collector develops a taste, but often it is just a chance encounter that germinates that taste.

For me, I so vividly recall seeing a few pieces of early eighteenth-century furniture in the home of an architect friend of mine when I was a newly married fellow in my twenties. I liked the look. My friend gave me the names of a few country dealers in England. A few months later, I made the trip to England. I expect most collectors have a similar story about how they began collecting.

The wide range of circumstances that influences the amateur collector inevitably produces unexpected – even peculiar – and highly personal collections. Amateur collections, obviously, reflect the resources and time that collectors may have. They also reflect, quite often, the influence of dealers, other professional advisers or other collections. It has often been noted that the recreation of Colonial Williamsburg had an enormous impact on a generation of American collectors.

Amateur collections are, perhaps, most interesting when they simply reflect the personality of the collector. Some collections are highly focused with clear definition; others are quite eclectic. Some are carefully edited with great attention to connoisseurship; others just expand without being upgraded. Some are displayed in beautiful settings and with great attention to detail; others are effectively stored. Some are quite academically inclined; others are primarily decorative.

Collections are occasionally built with a view that some day they will be part of an institution. Notable American examples are the Bayou Bend Collection, developed by Ima Hogg in Houston, Texas, and the collections of Henry Francis du Pont at Winterthur, near Wilmington in Delaware. As their collections grew in size and importance, the collections became house museums. These examples remind us that it is the amateur collector who has provided most of the decorative arts housed in museums throughout the world. Without amateur collectors, we would hardly have these great institutions to instruct and inspire successive generations about the decorative arts.

The significant influence of the established,

traditional antiques dealer on antiques collectors cannot be overstated. There are, of course, people who acquire without advice or the influence of others, but they would be exceptions. Most of us amateur collectors are constantly asking and listening to all sorts of people associated with the trade in order to make judgements about what is worthy and what is not. That is how we learn. Among the advisers to collectors are saleroom specialists, freelance consultants and museum professionals, but the most important adviser is the dealer.

Dealers are the advisers with, perhaps, the most inherent conflict of interest in that they own these items and have chosen them with care. Nonetheless, they surely are a very strong force in influencing collections. They are major teachers and mentors to many collectors.

To us collectors, dealers are really personalities more than they are businesses. Inevitably, we like some of them and not others, and I assure you that we give great preference to dealers we like. Occasionally, collectors make their purchases from only one dealer or just a few. In my judgement, that will somewhat inhibit the building of a notable collection.

As a collector in other fields, I do find the English antiques trade particularly genteel and, on the whole, rather straightforward in its dealings. Many dealers have become genuinely good friends.

Certainly standing among the pre-eminent dealers in my time is my friend Robin Kern, whose beautiful Lowndes Street shop, called Hotspur, is the eponym of the the honourable and brave Shakespearean character. Like a few other such establishments in London, it is beautifully appointed and immaculate in its appearance. The experience of visiting there is always exciting.

After touring three floors to see the stunning new pieces that have been assembled since our last visit, we usually adjourn to Robin's inner sanctum on the top floor for tea and conversation. We might occasionally discuss some current events, but mostly we talk about what is going on in the trade and what new pieces are about to come on the market. Like most long-time dealers, Robin has a great library, and he remembers every piece that has passed through his hands. A dealer's great store of knowledge is very important for collectors.

Robin has a number of characteristics that are, in my judgement, quite distinctive. They are traits that inspire great confidence and have helped him build important client relationships. First, he is the most assiduously polite person I think I have ever known. Never is he ruffled. And he is eternally thoughtful in all that he says and does. This, of course, is from the perspective of a customer.

Robin has another remarkable quality: he is disarmingly candid when discussing the pieces that he has for sale. No facts are edited out of his commentary. It is a trait that makes purchase decisions much easier, and it inspires confidence in the man. Robin also has an impeccable 'eye'. Many dealers have beautiful pieces, but it is rare to see a gallery with so many appealing objects. There are no awkward pieces of furniture. There are no pieces for which apologies must be made.

As I have visited Hotspur hundreds of times in London, Robin has on occasion come to stay with us in America. For me, it is exciting to have another 'eye' to look at things, do a little editing and move furniture around. On one occasion, my wife returned to the house one afternoon to find that Robin Kern, and I had reordered the furniture in several rooms. Her shock at seeing what we had done rattled Robin's sensibilities so much that he began to apologise immediately. Fortunately, my wife ultimately approved of our changes.

Robin is a seriously good businessman, but he never appears mercenary in his approach to business. Because I have seldom for most of my career been able to attend auctions, it has been my *modus operandi* to ask someone to view auctions and bid on my behalf. It is, of course, customary to pay a commission for such a service, but Robin insists that he do this work for me on a gratis basis. This is, frankly, unique in my experience, though probably a good strategy on his part. Once Robin alerted me to a major bureau bookcase that was coming up for auction. He researched the piece, viewed it several times, and successfully bid for me at auction. Then he refused a commission when I proposed it. And so I guess I remain indebted to my friend, Robin Kern.

75

76

OPPOSITE
2. A gilt gesso armchair covered with contemporary needlework, c.1750.
H: 36¾" (93 cm); W: 26½" (67 cm); D: 19" (48.5 cm).
The small size of this chair is very unusual for this style.

I should now like to tell you about a few of the pieces that I have acquired from Hotspur over the past twenty years. As you will see, they are mostly early pieces.

My first purchase from Hotspur was a pair of walnut needlework sconces (Fig. 1) that I bought in the 1980s. I admit to a weakness for English needlework. It adds a great measure of warmth and, I think, aesthetic appeal to any piece of furniture. These sconces had once been in the collection of Jim Meers, someone whose taste I particularly admire. They were made in around 1700, and each has a moulded cross-grained frame that encloses under glass panels, petit-point needlework depicting Daniel in the lions' den and Saint Francis of Assisi. At the bottom, each sconce has a shaped brass candle arm. The sconces are particularly colourful and add much charm to my collection.

My next purchase from Hotspur was the carved gilt wood armchair (Fig. 2), which I saw one day sitting in the ground floor gallery in Lowndes Street. At first it did not look very English, but I was soon reminded that eighteenth-century English furniture-makers often adopted a French foot for high-style chairs. What immediately attracted me to this piece was its decidedly small size. This type of chair is quite often made in a large size in order to accentuate its grandness. The small scale, which is difficult to appreciate from the illustration, is very charming. Today, this chair resides in a very small-scale space alongside other pieces of eighteenth-century English furniture, designed when we human beings were smaller people. I was also drawn to this piece because of its glorious needlework cover. No needlework is more beautiful than a piece with green ground that over time has turned slightly blue: we now know that fugitive yellows fade somewhat, resulting in this almost teal-like colour.

The chair is transitional and dates to around 1750. It is remarkably well detailed in its carving and enjoys cabriole legs, both back and front, that are linked by elaborately carved aprons. This armchair gives me great satisfaction, and I treasure the fact that most of the original gilding is intact. It came from the collection of Contessa Mona Bismarck.

This next purchase from Hotspur is probably the

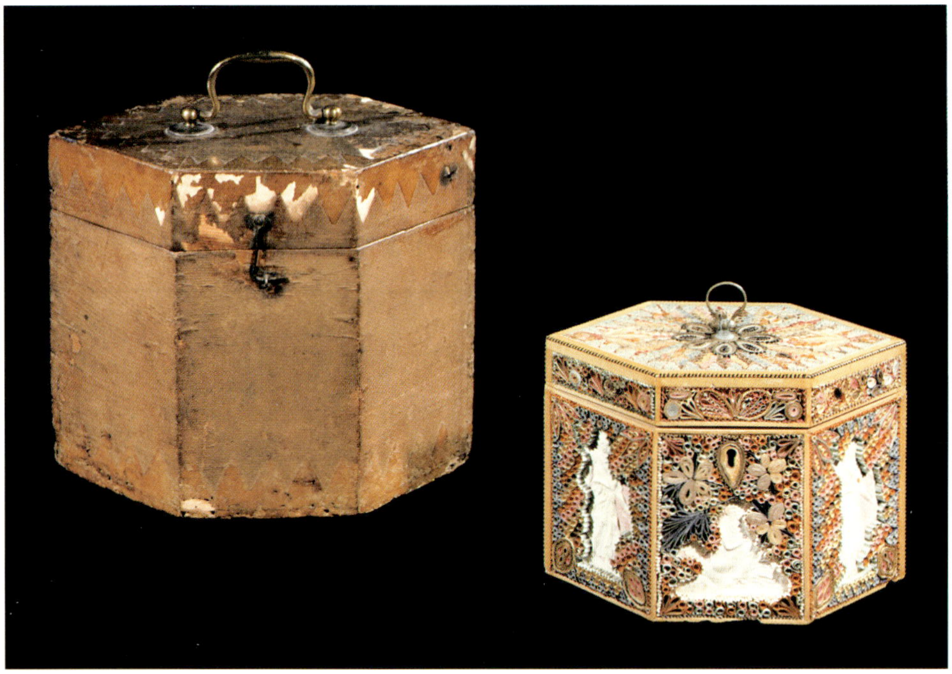

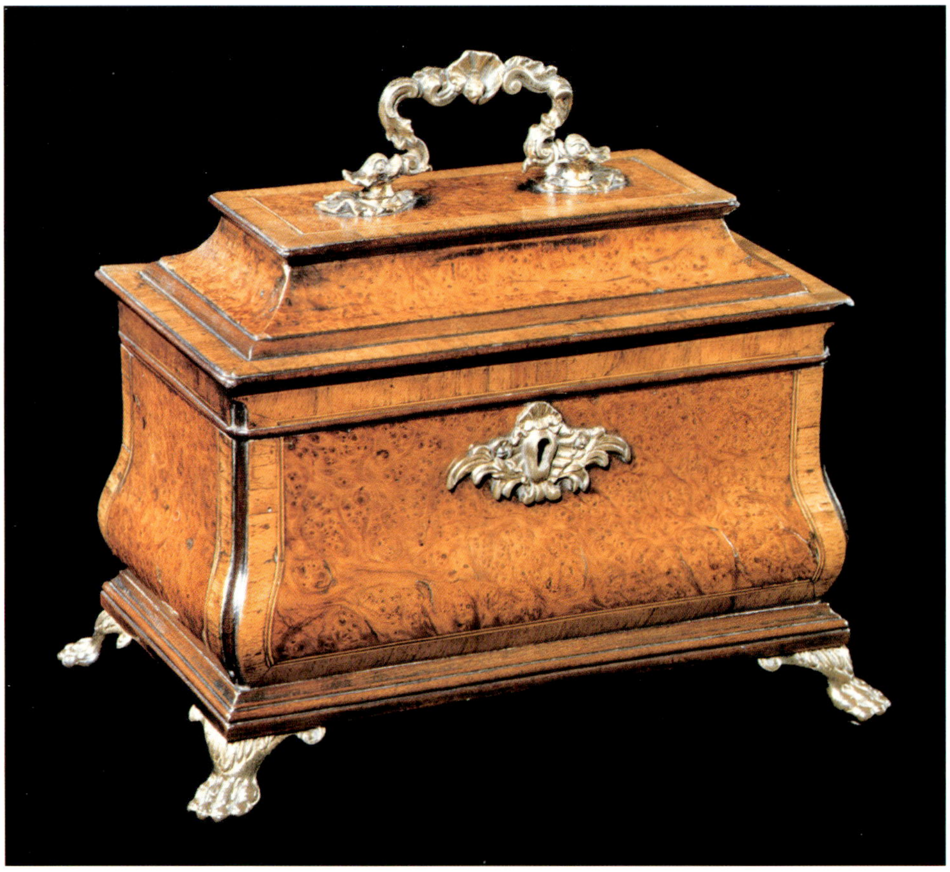

OPPOSITE
3. A tea caddy decorated with paper filigree work and with its original case, c.1790.
H: 7" (18 cm); W: 9" (23 cm); D: 6" (15 cm).

4. A tea caddy with a *bombé*-shaped body veneered in burr yew, c.1750.
H: 9½" (24 cm); W: 10¼" (26 cm); D: 6¼" (16 cm).

latest piece that I have ever purchased from them. A tea caddy (Fig. 3) from the late eighteenth century, it is accompanied by its original case, which has preserved both its immaculate condition and its original colouring. Paper filigree work was a favourite recreation for ladies in the eighteenth century, and in 1786 the *New Ladies Magazine* describes paper filigree-work as 'A profusion of neat elegant patterns and models of ingenuity and delicacy suitable for tea caddies, toilets, chimney pieces, screens, cabinets, frames, picture ornaments, etc., etc'. Another tea caddy purchased from Hotspur is this earlier one dating from the mid-eighteenth century (Fig. 4). I particularly like this one because of the beautiful burr yew veneers to the unusual *bombé*-shaped body of the caddy. It also has interesting gilt metal dolphin handles. We know, of course, that these tea caddies were quite important household objects in the eighteenth century. Imported tea was a highly prized product and very much a part of the everyday ritual of upper-class British families.

Today, tea caddies and other such small boxes are very desirable collector's items. They are often well designed and do not require a lot of display space. I have a small collection of tea caddies, and have perhaps been attracted to them, in part, because the company for whom I worked for many years has a large tea and coffee component to its business. At any rate, these two tea caddies are part of a small collection that I particularly like. The filigree-work caddy is distinguished by its condition. It was discovered by my co-author in this volume, Simon Redburn, and worked its way through Hotspur to me. The burr yew piece is extremely interesting in spite of it being a little late for my collection.

Mirrors are another favourite item to collect for many of us. This particular eighteenth-century overmantel mirror (Fig. 5) has three main bevelled glass plates, the tops being delightfully shaped and contained in a frame of multi-bevelled glass borders so typical of this period. When I first saw this overmantel I imagined it above the fireplace in the drawing-room of my home. So, I noted the measurements and checked them as soon as I returned back to the United States. The fireplace wall in our drawing-room has a conventional opening surrounded by

A CONTEMPORARY AMERICAN COLLECTOR

5. An arched-top overmantel mirror with multi-bevelled glass borders, c.1700. H: 35″ (89 cm); W: 62″ (157.5 cm).

a King of Prussia marble slip and decorative moulding. There is a mantelpiece. Above the opening are two rectangular raised panels, one of which is larger than the other. The overmantel mirror was a perfect fit in one of the panels, but alas, not the one at the top, and the mirror was much too high above the fireplace opening. Then I had an idea: I would reverse the raised panels, and after doing so the mirror would fit perfectly. It looks as though it were made for the spot. It is fortuitous indeed that such a mirror, which started life in the early part of the eighteenth century, has survived with its original looking glasses.

As a needlework collector, I was immediately attracted to this magnificent stump-work casket (Fig. 6). Although Hotspur is not a notable needlework dealership, I suspect that Robin saw this piece and thought of me. This incredible workbox was made in about 1680, and its size is particularly impressive. Another feature is that the whole structure is outlined with mouldings of tortoiseshell veneer laid over gold. It is finished on all four sides, and the top opens to reveal a mirror on the underside with pincushions, pen trays and ink-bottles. The front consists of a pair of doors that open to an interior

6. A stump-work box of large proportions with tortoiseshell decoration, c.1680.

fitted with numerous drawers, and there is an upper section with a landscape painting entitled SEVILLA, with mirrored walls in which it is reflected. The brilliant colours, superb condition, and general size of this stump-work box define it as a superior example that gives me enormous satisfaction. A few years earlier I had bought from Cora Ginsburg a stump-work travelling mirror, which is also outlined in tortoiseshell. These two happily reside today alongside one another.

Many years ago, I purchased from Mayorcas (an important needlework dealer in St James's) a set of needlework that had once belonged to an eighteenth-century wing chair. In addition to the beautiful colours and condition of the needlework, it was especially notable that the covering had panels that had been on the outside of the armchair's wings. This is rather unusual, in fact, and so I commissioned my friend Robin Kern to find the chair upon which this needlework had originally resided. Not an easy task, but with great tenacity Robin found it – a walnut wing chair of about 1720 (Fig. 7). We cannot, of course, be absolutely sure that this is the original needlework for this particular chair, but it fits! Robin found the chair at the shop of his good friend, John

82

OPPOSITE
7. A walnut wing chair covered in
contemporary floral needlework, c.1720.

8. A gilt gesso side table, c.1715.
H: 30¼" (77 cm); W: 36" (92 cm);
D: 21¾" (55 cm).

Keil, a dealer of whom I have also been an occasional customer.

The gilt gesso side table (Fig. 8) is iconic of the early part of the eighteenth century. Its rectangular top is decorated with gilt gesso strap-work that is supported on a shaped frieze, which has similar decoration to the top, and is centred by a shaped apron carved with a strong shell motif. The four cabriole legs are carved with acanthus decoration and with inverted scroll feet. It replaced a lesser example, which Robin arranged to sell for me at auction. Gilded furniture is not my wife's favourite.

The walnut stick barometer (Fig. 9) dates from about 1690. The arched top with three gilt wood finials sits above a pierced fretted panel, flanked by twisted columns. The brass face of the barometer is unsigned, and the cistern cover at the base has shaped and pierced ears. Barometers, like their cousins the clocks, appeal to people with mechanical inclination, as well as to furniture collectors. Like them, I too have a small group of classic barometers, this being the earliest.

The walnut settee (Fig. 10) is particularly elegant, dating to around 1714, with an upholstered back contained in a thin walnut frame. The piece is distinguished by fine seaweed marquetry panels that decorate the tops of the cabriole front legs, the shepherd's crook arms and the turned stretchers that link the front legs to the back cabriole legs. This settee was in the E. B. Moller Collection and is recorded by R.W. Symonds.[1] It is now covered in contemporary blue-green damask.

The late seventeenth-century walnut mirror with cresting is a particular favourite of mine (Fig. 11). One of my very first purchases of English country furniture was a cushion mirror, which was missing its crest. This piece not only has its original mirror plate but also its glorious original crest. It is highly detailed, and the carving is of an extraordinary quality and complex design, centred by a carved and pierced crown and flanked by two *putti*. The cushion frame that surrounds the original bevelled mirror glass is veneered in oysters of olive wood so typical of the 1690s. It is most fortunate that such a delicate and elaborate frame has survived to this day.

Dr Samuel Johnson, the compiler of the first

OPPOSITE
9. A walnut stick barometer, c.1690.
H: 50" (127 cm).

1. Symonds, *Furniture Making in Seventeenth and Eighteenth Century England*, pp. 88–9, figs 133, 134.

10. A walnut settee, c.1714.
H: 42" (107 cm); W: 55½" (138.5 cm); D: 26" (66 cm).

85

ABOVE & OPPOSITE
11. A walnut cushion mirror with elaborate cresting, c.1690.
H: 38″ (96 cm); W: 29″ (79 cm).

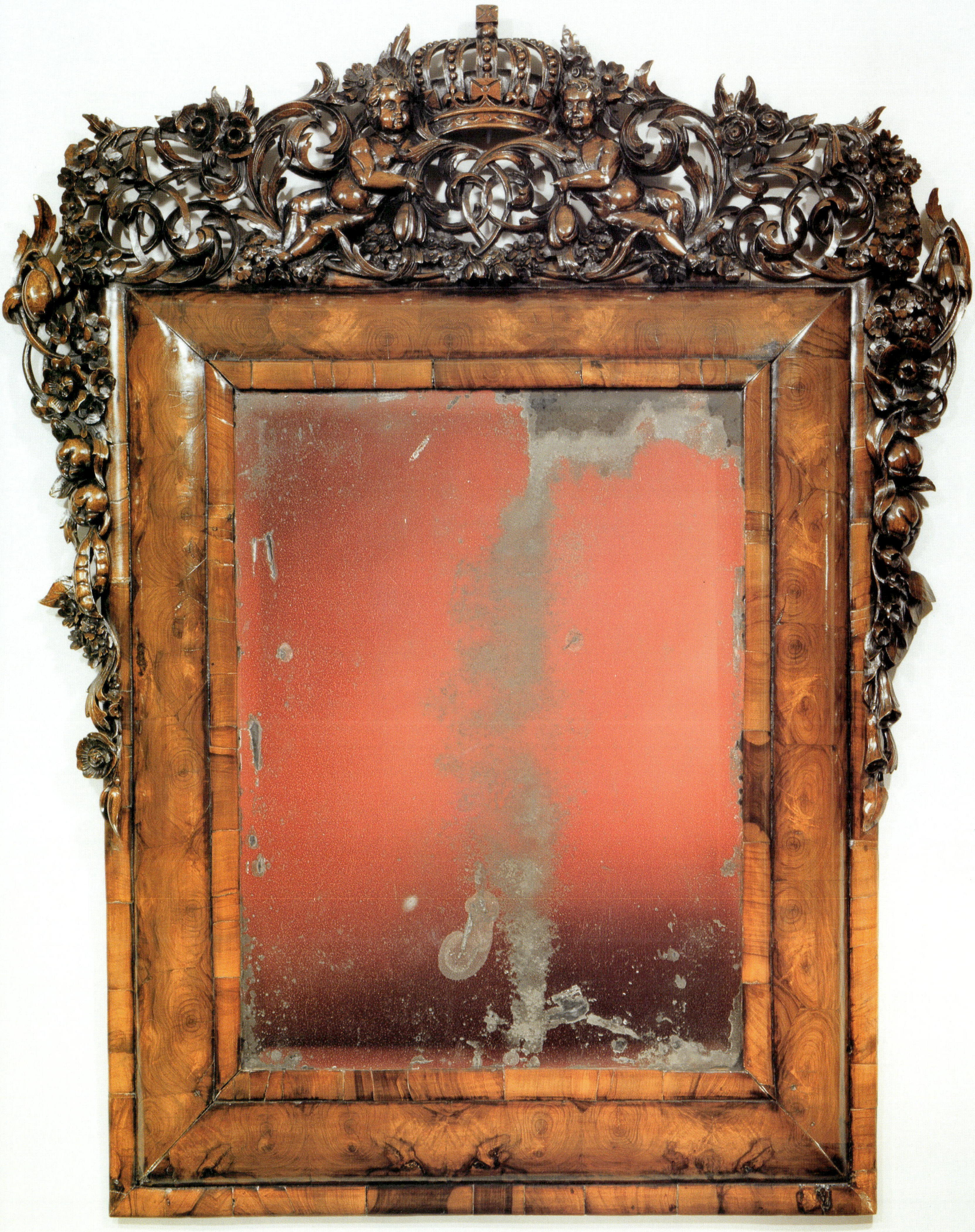

OPPOSITE
12. A walnut 'X'-frame armchair, c.1715.
H: 38½" (98 cm); W: 26½" (67.5 cm).

English dictionary, was one of England's greatest literary figures, and this chair (Fig. 12) is provenanced to him by repute. The remarkable under-framing is both complicated and bold in design for a chair of its period, circa 1715. It forms around an 'X' frame, back and front, with its upholstered seat and back now covered in contemporary floral needlework. It would originally have been covered in leather. Notice how the support to the seat front is in two stages, the lower part with cabriole legs of great elegance. For strength, shaped stretchers unite the legs. Dr Johnson was a heavily built man, and this chair has a particularly interesting form. The 'X' stretcher was a prominent feature of important early chairs. This chair is illustrated in *Christie's Season*, 1928, and recorded in a sale of 12 July 1928, lot 86, where it fetched 560 guineas.

The early seventeenth-century walnut kneehole desk is perhaps my all-time favourite piece from Hotspur (Fig. 13). It has the conventional kneehole form, but it is fitted out for an architect. It is a very masculine piece and looks so very useful. One distinguishing feature is the fact that the desk is veneered on all four sides, indicating that it was meant to stand in the middle of a room. Unfortunately, I do not have a place where it can be shown as a centrepiece, so it is alongside a wall in the library in my home. What I value most about this piece is that it is in its original pristine condition, enjoying original colour and patination with cleverly matched figured walnut veneers. The drawers retain their original engraved, lacquered brass handles. I first saw this desk in a photograph that Robin sent to me. Dealers often send photographs. I was on the phone immediately and bought it. Sometimes we collectors agonise and debate, but this is a piece I knew I wanted immediately.

Looking glasses, as I have mentioned, form an important part of many a collection of decorative arts, and none more so than my final choice from the pieces that have come from Hotspur. This mirror (Fig. 14), which is circa 1720, illustrates the virtuosity of the carver and gilder at this time, and uses the unusual feature of pewter decoration in place of the normal gesso work. I do not know if the pewter enrichments would have been gilded to match or

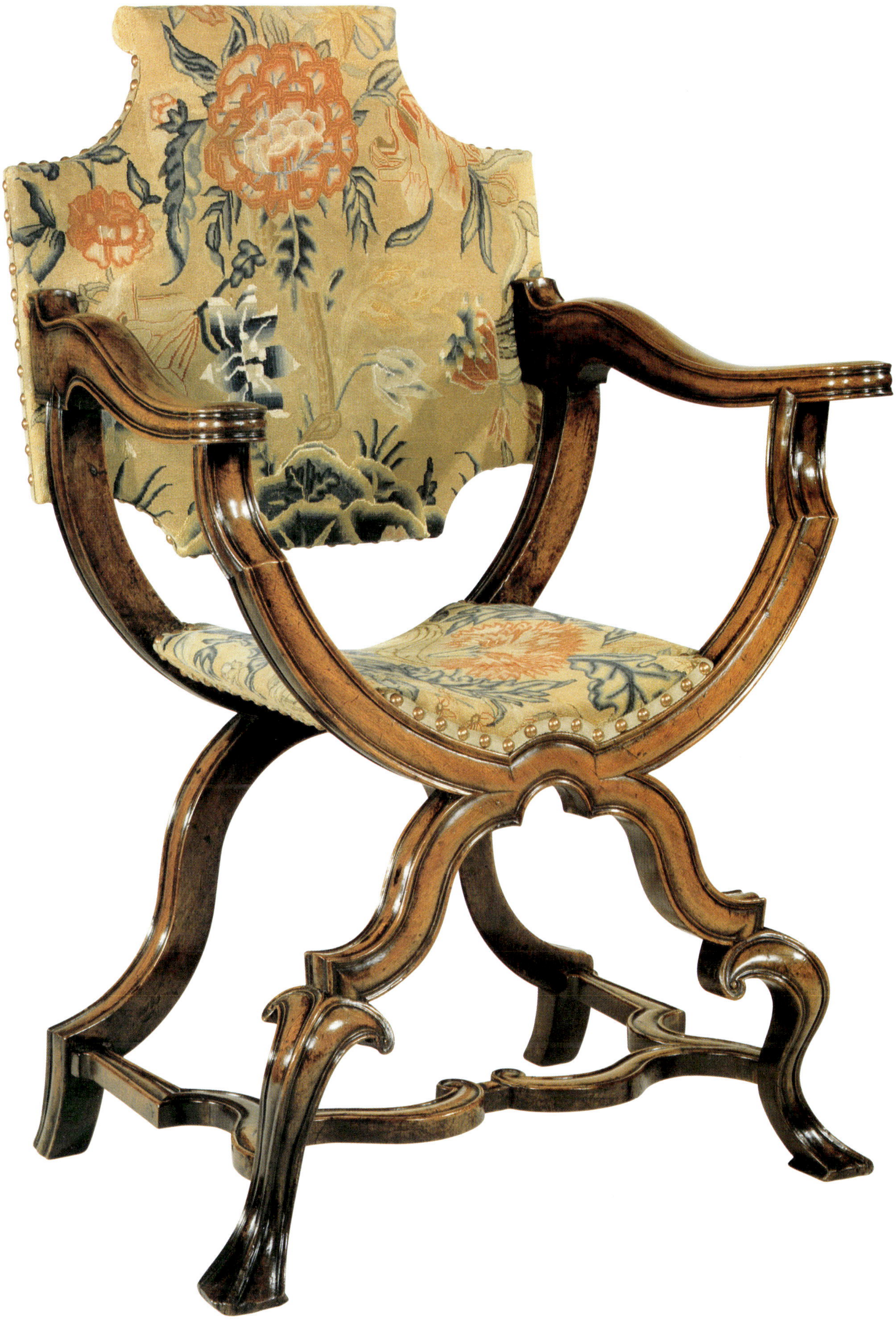

ABOVE & OPPOSITE
13. A burr walnut kneehole architect's desk,
c.1715.
H: 30½" (77.5 cm); W: 37" (94 cm);
D: 22" (56 cm).

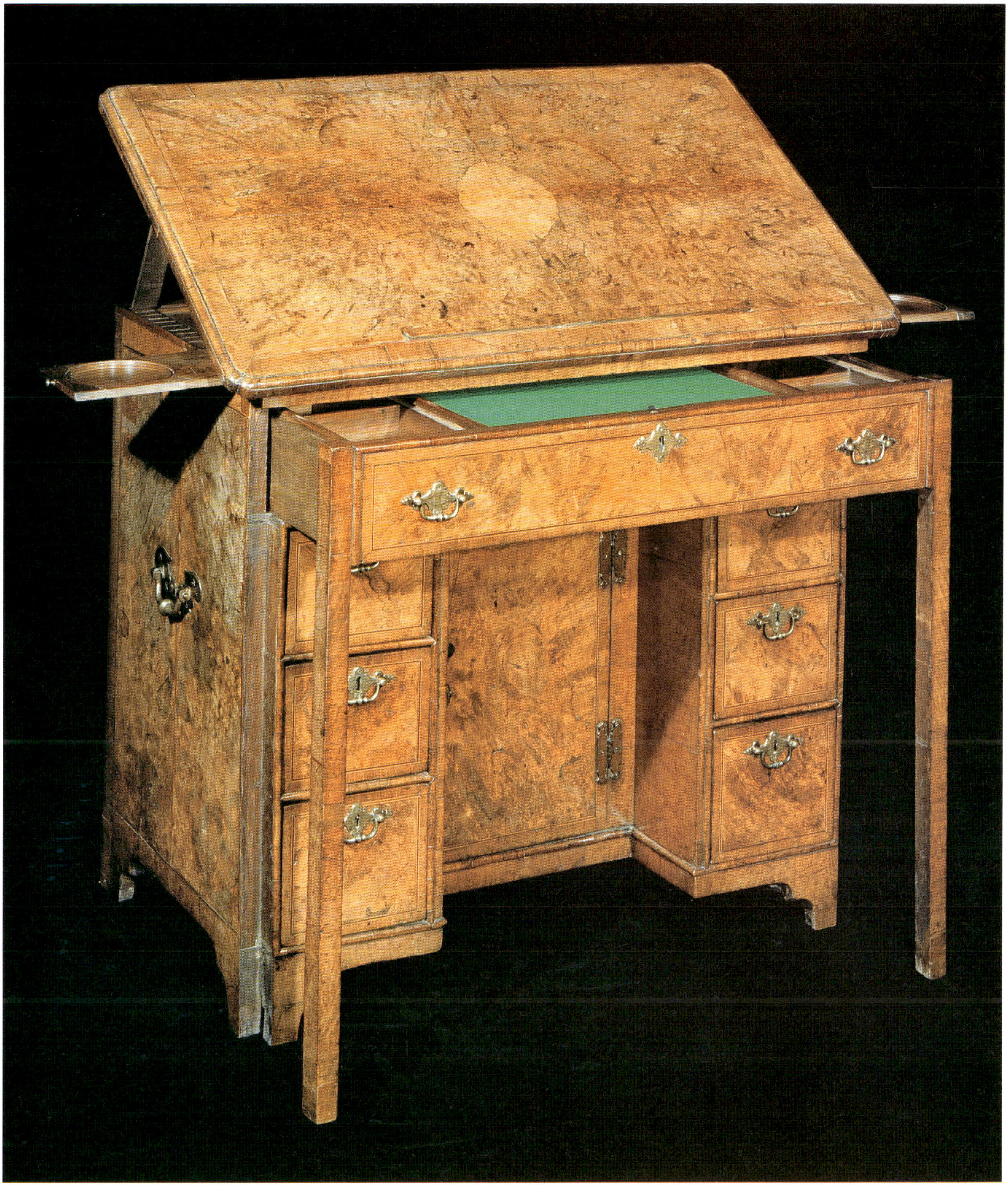

would have been left as a contrast to the gilt background. Either way, I believe this to be a most interesting format. The design of the mirror is full and very detailed, with a broken arched pediment centred by a pewter shell above an arched, moulded frame that surrounds the original bevelled mirror. The apron below is similarly enriched, again with a shell, acanthus and scrollwork all in pewter. It is an extraordinary piece that gives me great pleasure.

I was recently talking to a collector friend of mine who has just become an octogenarian. His quite successful professional and business career is long behind him, and he says he is now too old for golf. His greatest pleasure in life, perhaps in all his life, has come from his collecting.

Testimonies like that should, I think, give the greatest satisfaction to longtime successful dealers such as Robin Kern of Hotspur.

JB

Matthew Boulton: ormolu

NICHOLAS GOODISON

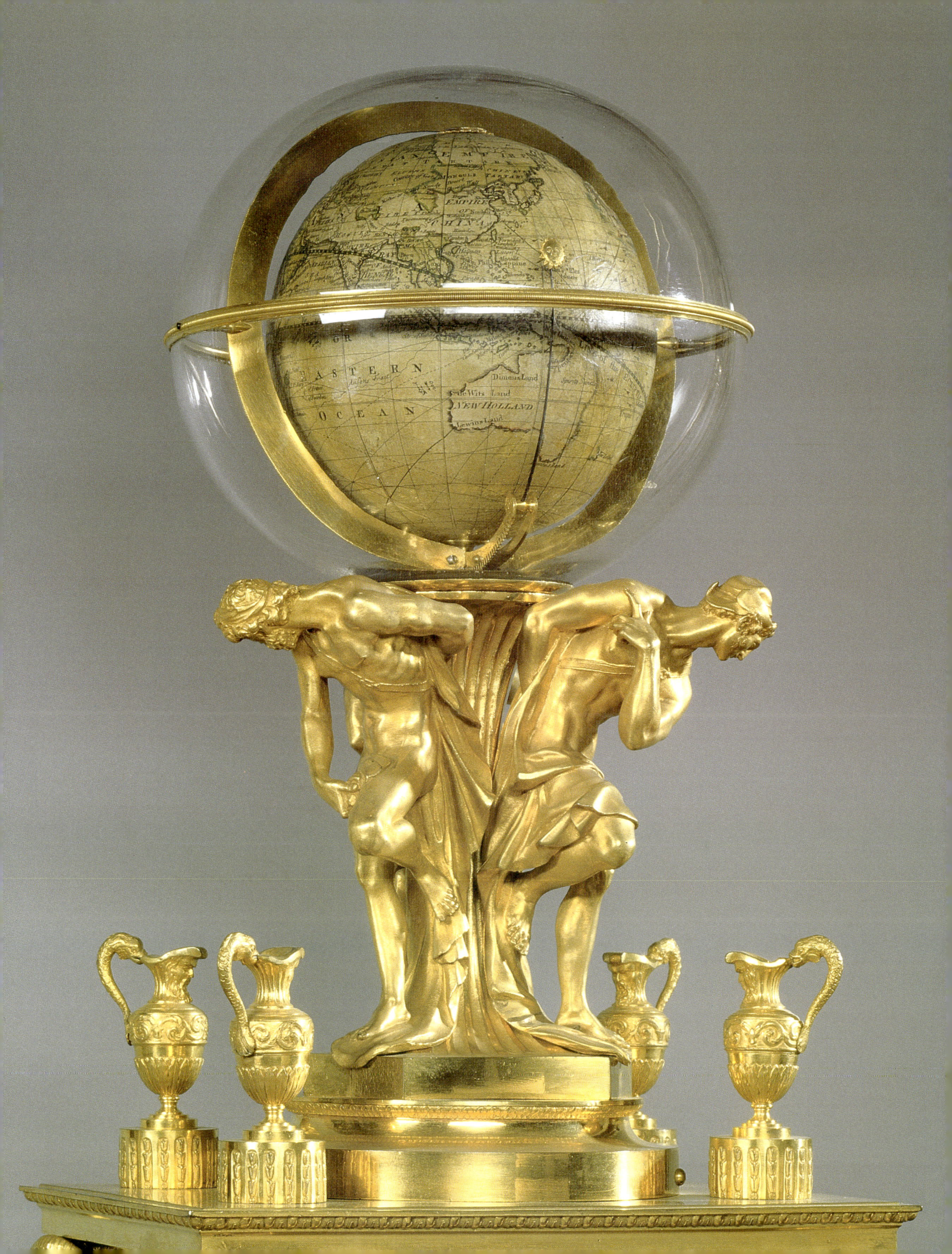
NEW HOLLAND
OCEAN
CHINA

PREVIOUS PAGE
(Detail from p. 115, cat. no. 11)
Two of the three figures that support the
globe on top of the Geographical clock,
1771-2.

SINCE THE 1960s Hotspur has been one of the principal dealers in the ornamental ormolu vases and clock cases produced by Matthew Boulton at his manufactory at Soho, near Birmingham, in the 1770s; all the objects discussed here have passed through Hotspur. Boulton and his partner John Fothergill established the manufactory, but it is Boulton who commonly gets all the credit for the ornaments – not surprisingly – because he was the moving spirit in the partnership and in the design, production and marketing of the ornaments.

Boulton was a towering figure in the metalworking trade in Birmingham, indeed in the whole of England. Josiah Wedgwood, his friend and rival, called him the 'most complete manufacturer in England in metal'. His manufactory was one of the wonders of the industrial world. Visitors came to see it from far and wide and marvelled at the industrial processes employed in it. The manufactory was a major producer of buttons, buckles, 'toys', silver and plate, and became the leading producer of ormolu ornaments in England, in hot competition with the French metalworkers. The ormolu business failed financially because the ornaments were too expensive and relied heavily on handcraft. It was a short-lived business, but despite its commercial failure, Boulton achieved a reputation for the production of ormolu that has never faded.

Boulton, like Wedgwood, was trying to cash in on the fashion for the antique (known today as neo-classical) taste and in particular the craze for vases that prevailed in the 1760s and 70s. Vases could be fashioned into candle vases, candelabra and perfume burners or be used as decorative motifs on clock cases and watch stands. After flirting with various materials for vase bodies, he decided that the most suitable were the marbles (cat. nos 2, 6) and fluorspars, particularly blue john (cat. nos 1, 3, 5), which he bought from the stone-workers of Derbyshire. But he also used glass bodies produced by his friend James Kier at Stourbridge (cat. 7), and in many cases he used gilt (cat. 13) or enamelled copper vase bodies.

His sources of design were many and various. He copied ornaments from books (especially the great source books of classical ornament), he borrowed ornaments from their owners, he imitated

French designs, he bought ornaments and plaster casts in London, he derived designs from leading architects such as James Stuart and William Chambers, he copied cameos made by Wedgwood. Many of the components of his ornaments were used for both ormolu and for silver and plate.

Boulton was an entrepreneur, an engineer, and a natural philosopher. He had prodigious energy and an enquiring mind that some might have found tiring. He is best known today for his crucial role in the development and sale of James Watt's improved steam engine, which did so much to transform factory and mining production in the last quarter of the eighteenth century. He is also known for what was perhaps his second greatest achievement, the foundation of the Soho Mint, which became one of the biggest producers of coins and medals in the country. In the context of his total achievement, the ormolu business seems almost a sideshow. But it was important not just because his products are highly prized today; through it he made many contacts among the leaders of society, which greatly helped him during the later development of his businesses.

He was not an academic classicist. There is sometimes little consistent logic in the motifs chosen to decorate his vases. But he gleaned enough classical learning to satisfy the thirst for classical allegory. His clock cases and watch stands, for example, convey messages about mortality or the transience of beauty or worldly success. They often incorporate a funerary urn or a memorial obelisk. The watch stand illustrated in catalogue number 14 shows Narcissus admiring his own image in the pool, and we all know what happened to him. The clock case of catalogue number 13 shows Minerva, the Goddess of Wisdom, pointing to the fleeting hours, while the boy seated on the books holds a scroll on which are inscribed lines from Virgil about the brevity of life.

The ewers of catalogue number 9 are based on a classical shape for a wine jug, although they have a cavity far too small to hold more than a few thimblefuls. In deference to Bacchus, the God of Wine, they are decorated with satyrs' masks, a motif common in French ormolu ornament connected with drinking. The cutlery urns of catalogue 10 are each decorated with a medallion of Ceres, the Goddess of Plenty, and were made to stand in a dining-room. Unfortunately these two urns, which were almost certainly once at Matthew Boulton's own home at Soho, are now separated from the mahogany stands on which they once stood. The urns are now abroad, and their stands remain in this country. I do not understand to this day why the export of the urns was not deferred to allow a British museum to try to buy them.

Other vases were decorated with more generic ornament, all gleaned from the classical repertoire. These included lions' heads (cat. no. 3), lyres, rams' heads and *bucrania* (cat. no. 5), and winged figures (cat. nos 7, 8). The vases in catalogue numbers 4 and 6 have candle branches that probably derive from a French model (the same branches appear on Boulton's 'lion-faced' candlesticks, examples of which have been on the market in recent years) and the vases (cat. nos 1, 2) probably owe some of their inspiration to the architect James Stuart.

It was William Chambers who was the most important influence on Boulton's designs. It wasn't just Chambers's Franco-Roman taste that appealed to Boulton. It was also that Chambers was George III's tutor and architect. As early as 1770 – and ormolu production at Soho only began in 1768–9 – Boulton was receiving designs from Chambers. He had breakfast with him in March 1770, and soon after was received by the King and Queen. He made a clock case and several vases for them, all to Chambers's designs, all of which survive today at Windsor. Being an entrepreneur, Boulton saw a commercial opportunity in the King's commissions. He copied the designs of these vases and of the clock case for sale to other patrons. Catalogue number 12 shows a King's clock case, many of the mounts of which are cast in the same moulds as Chambers's clock case for the King. The chief difference is the use of lacquered glass panels in place of blue john.

This particular clock case was brought into Hotspur by a go-ahead ex-police sergeant who had bought it from a dealer in Wales in 1967. He was told that the clock came from Moccas Court, Hereford. He took a gamble when he bought it. It was extremely dirty and it was not obvious that the gilding was in fine condition; also the provenance could not be proved. These problems deterred dealers who had seen it. They also found it suspicious that such an overtly grand case could house such a simple movement, with a backplate signed 'Whitehouse', which appeared to be a misspelling for Whitehurst.

I was with the sergeant when the ormolu case was cleaned in clockmaker Dan Parkes's workshop in Clerkenwell. The gilding was magnificent. I tell the tale of the identification of the movement by Dan as a product of Eardley and Norton, and of the documentation supporting the attribution, in my book *Matthew Boulton: ormolu*. The evidence that I subsequently unearthed in the Boulton archives corroborated the story retailed by the sergeant that the clock had come from Moccas Court. Rob Kern bought the clock, I believe in conjunction with Mallett's, and sold it to an American collector. More recently Robin bought it back. He sold it to the Courtauld Institute where, bearing in mind its design by William Chambers, it has found an appropriate home in Chambers's crowning architectural masterpiece, Somerset House.

Boulton used many of the same mounts on the case of his geographical clock (cat. no. 11). He made this remarkable clock, the movement of which he commissioned from his friend the Derby clockmaker John Whitehurst, in 1771–2. The clock shows the time on a twenty-four hour dial, the date on the same dial, the rotation of the earth, and the movement of the sun along the ecliptic. The case is a marriage of ornament in the antique taste, copied from Chambers's King's clock case, and the *cinque cento* figures that support the rotating globe. Boulton bought the plaster casts of these figures from the sculptor John Flaxman. The original figures decorate a silver crucifix by Gentile da Faenza in St Peter's in Rome. Boulton made a sidereal clock at the same time, which in addition to the time and date, showed the movement of the sun on the ecliptic and the movement of the fixed stars at any chosen latitude. The design, manufacture and sale of both clocks are well documented in the Boulton archives. Boulton described both of them in a letter to Lord Cathcart, the ambassador to the Court of Catherine II in St Petersburg in 1771, along with a Minerva clock, which was being made at Soho at the same time. I describe both 'philosophical' clocks in detail in my book. The sidereal clock is now at Soho House, Birmingham.

Boulton made these two clocks in the hope of a sale at Christie's in 1772. The sale comprised a glittering collection of ornaments, of which the two clocks were the highlights. Boulton was confident that the combination of antique ornament and demonstrations of the movements of earth, sun and stars would appeal to buyers. He had said, in a letter to John Whitehurst during the making of the clocks, that he was 'determined to make such like sciences fashionable among fine folks'. In the event, neither of the clocks sold. He was bitterly disappointed by the failure, and wrote to his wife about what he thought of the English aristocracy: 'I find philosophy at a very low ebb in London and therefore I have bought back my two fine clocks which I will send to a market where common sense is not out of fashion. If I had made the clocks play jigs upon bells and a dancing bear keeping time, or if I had made a horse race upon the faces I believe they would have had better bidders.'

When Rob Kern first saw the geographical clock, he suffered no such preference for horses or dancing bears. It is a pity that he couldn't have been at the auction 196 years earlier. He called me late one evening, a few days before the Grosvenor House Fair in 1967. He wanted some advice about a clock that he had seen, and said that I was the only person who had studied its movement. I knew instinctively that he must mean the geographical clock, for the simple reason that there was no other clock that he would conceivably ask my advice about: he was very experienced, while I was young and inexperienced. I did, however, know about the geographical clock. It had fired my interest in Boulton because I had seen it in the catalogue of the exhibition of the Lunar Society in Birmingham when I was interested in writing about the clockmaker John Whitehurst. I had then discovered the crucial correspondence between Whitehurst and Boulton about its manufacture (and about the manufacture of the sidereal clock) in the Boulton archives in Birmingham. So I had deserted Whitehurst and switched my literary and research endeavours to Boulton. I had written an article about the geographical clock for *Connoisseur*. By permission of the owner, Mrs Philips of Tean, I had gone to look at it in pieces in the workshop of Mr Garbe in Charlotte Street, London, where it was being restored. So I told Rob Kern that it was magnificent, but I said that I didn't think it was for sale. Mrs Philips had told me that she was having it restored and looked forward to having it back at Tean. 'Oh, but it *is* for sale,' said Rob, and the next day he called me again to say that he had bought it. He exhibited it as the centrepiece of his stand at the Grosvenor House Fair a few days later. It was bought, I am glad to say, by a private collector in England.

There is a twist to this tale, one of those twists of coincidence that must make dealing so unpredictable and exciting. There was no reason, in the ordinary course of his business, why Kern should have visited Mr Garbe's workshop. He told me that before he called at the workshop he didn't know of either Mr Garbe or his restoration business. He only visited Mr Garbe because he had sold a fan table with an ivory fan to an American client. The fan had been damaged and the client had advised him to take it to Mr Garbe for repair. He would never have seen Boulton's clock, which he knew he had to try and buy as soon as he saw it on the workbench, if he had not previously sold the fan table. He asked Mr Garbe to approach the owner of the clock, which he did. Mrs Philips told me later that she had decided to sell because she needed money for the repair of the drains at Tean.

The firm's passion for Boulton's ormolu work dates from this timely encounter in Charlotte Street. Similarly bitten by the ormolu bug, Robin and Brian mounted an exhibition of Boulton's ormolu in celebration of Hotspur's fiftieth anniversary in 1974. Boulton would have been pleased to see how the Kerns have made his ornaments 'a fashion among fine folks'.

NG

At the end of each entry I have given the pertinent pages and plate references in my book *Matthew Boulton: ormolu* (Christie's, London, 2002), in which I illustrated and discussed most of these ornaments. References to other publications that mention or illustrate the ornaments in this catalogue, or other ornaments of the same type, can be found in my book; I have not repeated them here. Nor have I given the full provenance of the objects illustrated here: if it is known it is given in my book.

CATALOGUE 1
A candle vase with three branches (one of a pair), c.1770.
H 17¼" (44 cm).
Blue john and ormolu, on an ebonised wooden base.

This is one of the earlier designs of candle vase produced at Soho. The three candle branches echo the branches used on the tea urns at Syon House and in the Royal Collection, which probably owe the origin of their design to the architect James Stuart. The spiral-fluted stem with its floral collar, the acanthus mounts to which the branches are fixed, and the anthemion frieze may also owe their origins to Stuart. The vases are lined with silvered copper bowls and the rims are pierced for the emission of perfume. This type of vase was made in some quantity at Soho, often with only two branches. Two-branched vases survive, for example, at Frogmore (Royal Collection), Blenheim, Harewood House, and the Birmingham Museum and Art Gallery.

LITERATURE
Goodison, pp. 76, 271–5, 286–7, Plates 229–31, 241–2.

PROVENANCE
Private collection.

CATALOGUE 2
A pair of candle vases with three branches. c.1770.
H: 16" (40.6 cm).
White marble and ormolu.

These vases have the same mounts as the previous vase, but the central finial reverses to become a fourth candle nozzle. The marble vase bodies are unusual for this type of vase, as are the triangular marble bases. All the other examples so far recorded have square bases, usually of ebonised wood.

LITERATURE
Goodison, p. 287, Plate 243.

PROVENANCE
David Collection, Copenhagen.

CATALOGUE 3
A pair of candle vases, c.1770–1.
H: 12″ (30.5 cm).
Blue john and ormolu.

These vases are mounted on circular blue john pedestals, or 'altars', decorated with lions' masks and laurel swags. The pedestal sits on a two-stepped blue john base decorated with pierced guilloche bands, described in an inventory taken at Soho in 1782 as the 'old round step'. The finials reverse to become candle nozzles. There is a copper lining. There are many known examples of this vase, some of which have two steps but have gadrooned caps to cover the candle nozzle – when it is not in use – in the place of the reversible finial or nozzle. Others have two or three gilt steps, some have gilt pedestals. All have blue john vase bodies.

LITERATURE
Goodison, p. 297.

PROVENANCE
Hotspur Ltd.

CATALOGUE 4
A candle vase with two branches (one of a pair), c.1770–1.
H: 15" (38 cm).
Blue john and ormolu.

This vase is similar in all respects to the previous pair of vases, but it is fitted with two candle branches. These branches appear on other candlesticks and vases produced at Soho and probably owe their origin to French designs. The pedestal stands on three blue john steps, decorated with pierced guilloche bands, instead of only two. The richly veined blue john is shown to good advantage in the pedestal and was obviously chosen with care. Other examples of this candle vase are known, all with blue john pedestals and three steps.

LITERATURE
Goodison, pp. 67, 297, Plate 262.

PROVENANCE
Gerstenfeld Collection.

CATALOGUE 5
A vase perfume burner (one of a pair) (lyre vase), c.1771–2.
H: 12¼" (31 cm).
Blue john and ormolu.

This lyre vase is characteristic of a number of vases made in about 1771–2, standing as it does on the 'old round step' of blue john decorated with a pierced guilloche frieze. The pedestal is decorated with four *bucrania*, with drapery hanging from their horns, and laurel swags. Laurel swags hang from the lyres and the rams' heads. The rim of the vase is decorated with a gadrooned pattern, and the lid, which is made of blue john and is gilt on the underside, is not pierced. The lining is gilt and made of unusually thick brass. Blue john versions of the lyre vase are rare, and this is the only pair so far recorded with stone lids. A blue john vase with a gilt lid, pierced for the emission of perfume, is in the State Hermitage Museum, St Petersburg.

Several lyre vases survive with white marble bodies and pedestals and pierced gilt lids.

LITERATURE
Goodison, p. 342, Plate 346.

PROVENANCE
Private collection.

CATALOGUE 6
A pair of candle vases with three branches ('Burgoyne's' vase), *c*.1771–2.
H: 15½" (39.7 cm).
White marble and ormolu.

I have tentatively identified this type of vase as the 'Burgoyne's' vase mentioned in the Boulton archives. The central finial reverses into a nozzle. The branches are of the same type used on the vases shown in catalogue number 4. They are fixed into the rams' head mounts, which are linked by a scrolling decorative frieze. There are three floral swags on the body. The pedestal is decorated with caryatids, drapery swags and *paterae*. There are three marble steps decorated with unpierced guilloche bands. Inside the vase is a cylindrical gilt copper lining.

Other examples of this vase with white marble bodies, pedestals and steps are recorded. Blue john versions, with the same branches, are also known. Other blue john versions carry the type of looped branches used on earlier vases.

LITERATURE
Goodison, p. 300, Plates 263–4.

PROVENANCE
Leeds Museums and Art Galleries (Temple Newsam House).

CATALOGUE 7
A pair of candle vases with two branches (wing-figured vase), c.1772.
H: 14½" (36.7 cm).
Glass and ormolu, on a white marble base.

These two-branched candle vases, with a central finial, are identical to a pair of vases at Osterley Park, except that they do not have a reversible finial. They correspond to a drawing in Boulton and Fothergill's pattern books.[1] The vase bodies are made of white opaque glass, which was supplied to Boulton from the Stourbridge works of his friend, James Kier. The two branches slot into the heads of the winged figures; there is no lining. Several other vases of this type survive: a second glass-bodied pair, mounted on square pedestals with blue john panels, is at Osterley, as is a pair with blue john bodies and white marble bases. The banker Robert Child, who owned Osterley, bought all three pairs from Boulton in 1772.

LITERATURE
Goodison, pp. 357–64, Plates 365–6, 367–8, 369, 370.

PROVENANCE
City Museum and Art Gallery Birmingham (Soho House).

1. Boulton and Fothergill pattern books, Vol. 1, p. 156.

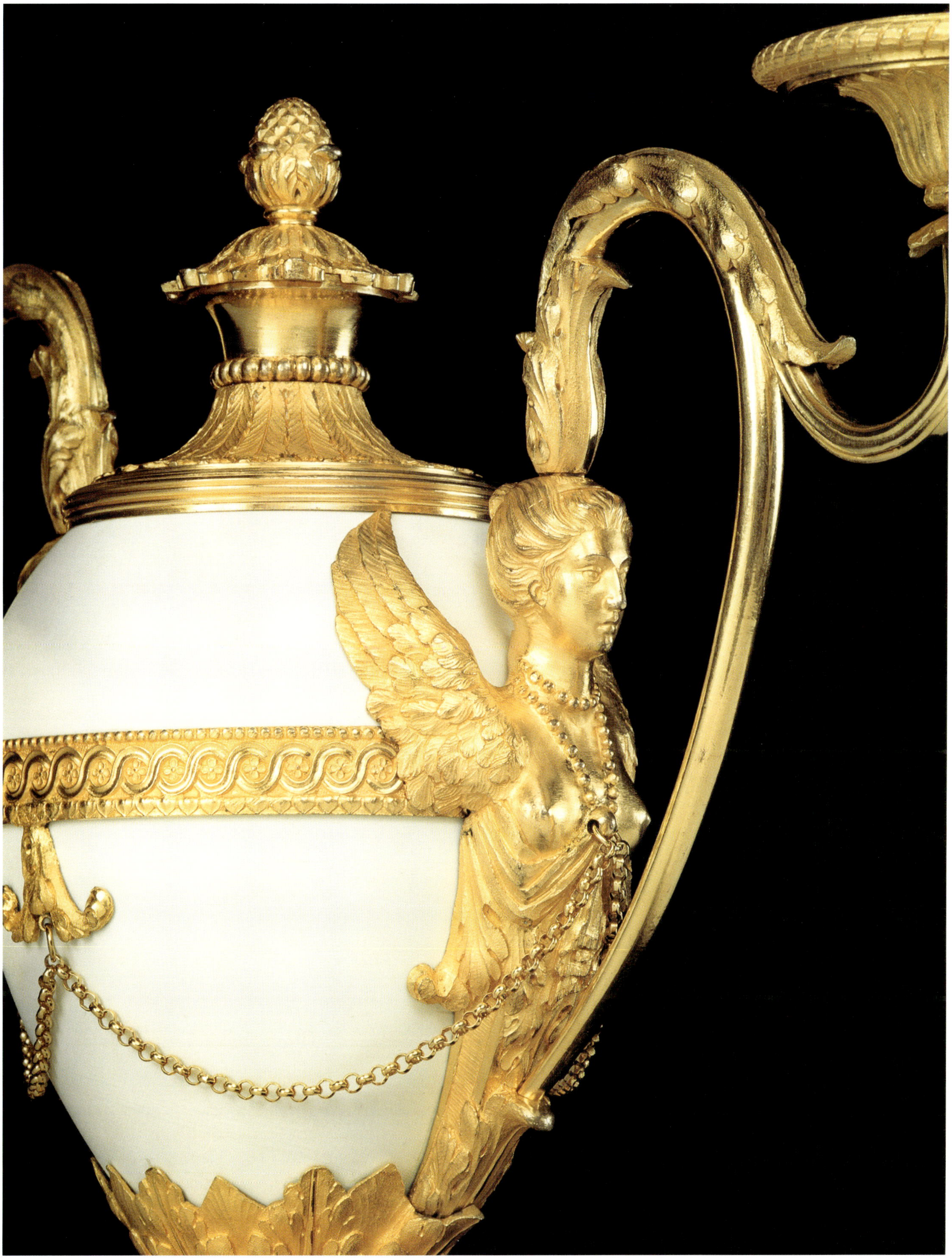

CATALOGUE 8
A candle vase with two branches (wing-figured vase), c.1772.
H: 20" (51 cm).
Blue john and ormolu, on a white marble base.

This variant of the wing-figured vase corresponds to another sketch in Boulton and Fothergill's pattern books,[1] although the mount on the body is more elaborate than the mount in the sketch. Unlike the previous wing-figured vase, the handles are fixed to the rim of the vase and not to the heads of the figures. The branches are a little more elaborate than other double branches used by Boulton, but they echo branches used on other ornaments and have some similarities to a drawing in the pattern books. The mount on the body is missing a central piece in the form of an anthemion. This type of vase was also made in white marble.

LITERATURE
Goodison, p. 364, Plates 371, 373.

PROVENANCE
Private collection.

1. Boulton and Fothergill pattern books, Vol. 1, p. 133.

CATALOGUE 9
A pair of ewers, 1772.
H: 19½" (49.5 cm) and 18½" (46.9 cm).
Blue john and ormolu.

This pair of ewers was supplied to the Earl of Sefton in 1772 at a cost of £14 14s. 0d.

A sketch of the design has survived in Boulton and Fothergill's pattern books.[1] The design echoes classical and French shapes. The device of placing a satyr's mask where the handle joins the back of the body of the jug was a feature also used by Wedgwood. The use of satyrs' masks as decoration, signalling the bacchantic use that ewers would usually be put to, might owe something to French models. The ewers have only a small cavity and their purpose was purely decorative. This pair is unusual in that it is made of blue john stones of sharply contrasting colour – one is deep purple, the other ochre and brown. There are other ewers of this type, for example a pair in the City Museum and Art Gallery Birmingham (Soho House).

LITERATURE
Goodison, p. 246, Plates 196–7, 198, 199.

PROVENANCE
Gerstenfeld Collection.

1. Boulton and Fothergill pattern books, Vol. 1, p. 83.

CATALOGUE 10
A pair of knife and cutlery urns, c.1775.
H: 22" (55.9 cm).
Lacquered copper and ormolu.

These knife and cutlery urns correspond closely to a drawing in Boulton and Fothergill's pattern books.[1] As in the drawing, the medallions represent Ceres, the Goddess of Plenty, a suitable deity for a dining-room. The lions' masks with their rings are like those on Boulton's King's vase, but they lack beards in order to make room for the *paterae* beneath them. The lids are mounted on sprung columns and are made to spring upwards when the *paterae* are depressed. The knives and forks were slotted into the inner and outer of the four rings of holes revealed when the lids are opened. The middle two rings, with their wider apertures, were for forks. They are set in red velvet, decorated with silver braid. These urns stood originally on mahogany pedestals mounted with chased ormolu borders, drawer handles and swags, one of them with drawers for spoons, lined, like the urns, with red velvet and silver braid. Josiah Wedgwood saw a 'vase to hold knives, forks and spoons on the side board' when he visited Boulton at Soho House towards the end of 1776. The drawing that he made at the time misses a number of decorative features and its proportions are wrong, but it shows that the vase he saw was similar to the drawing in the pattern book and to these knife cases and their pedestals.

His description tallies closely with these urns, except that the vase he saw had a black lacquered body. The evidence is that these urns came from Soho House, and it is possible that the urns were over-painted with simulated porphyry towards the end of the eighteenth century, perhaps when the simulated porphyry pedestal was made for the sidereal clock, which also stood in Boulton's dining-room.

LITERATURE
Goodison, pp. 262–5, Plates 215, 216–19.

PROVENANCE
Private collection.

1. Boulton and Fothergill pattern books, Vol. 1, p. 124.

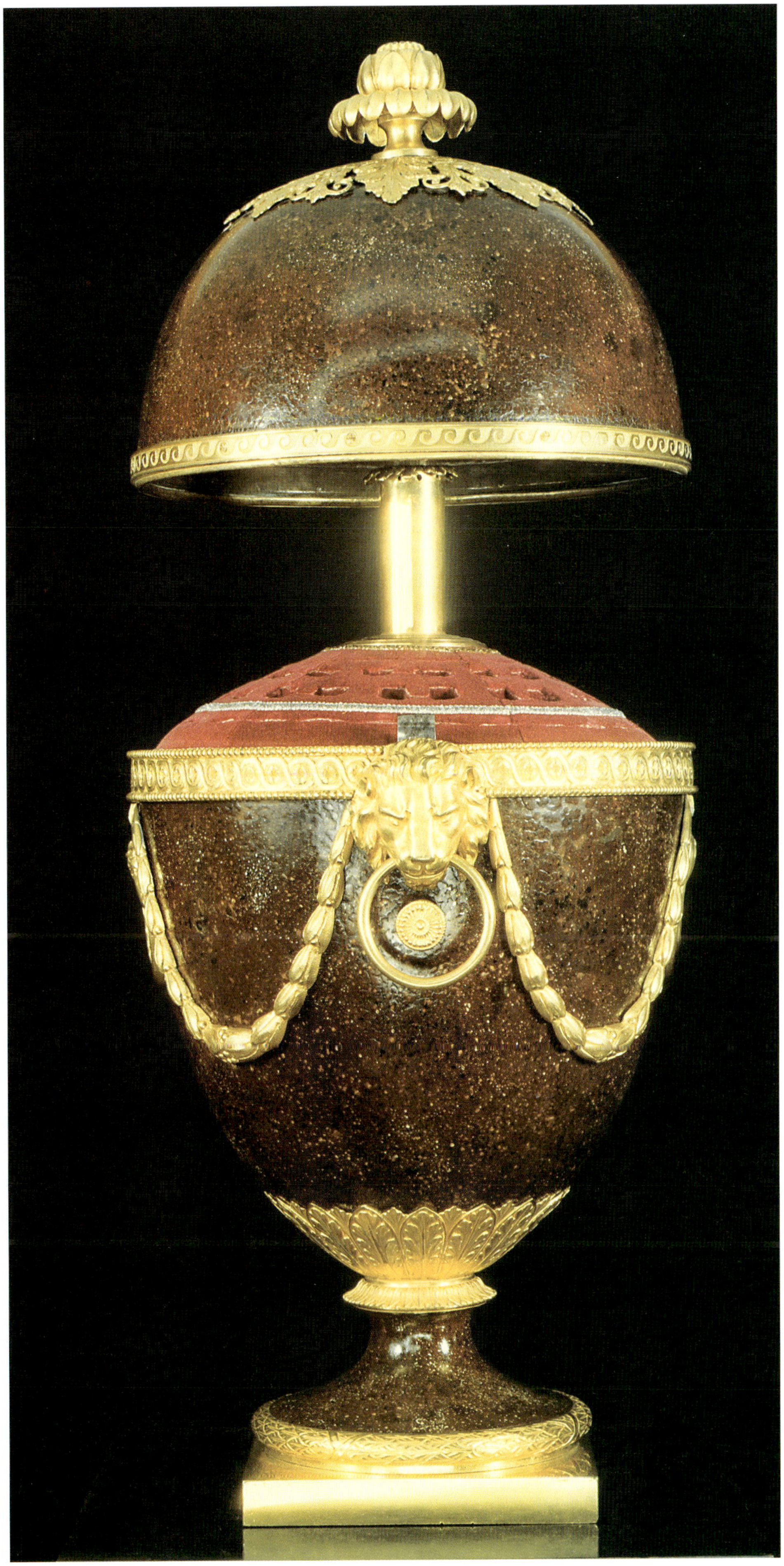

CATALOGUE 11
Geographical clock, 1771–2.
H: 30¼" (76.9 cm).
Ormolu, on wooden base
veneered with tortoiseshell.

Boulton seems to have conceived the plan of making his geographical and sidereal clocks early in 1771. He turned for advice and help to the clockmaker John Whitehurst of Derby and to their mutual friend, the travelling lecturer James Ferguson, who was actively interested in astronomical clock movements. Boulton sent the outline specification to Whitehurst early in 1771. He proposed from the beginning to copy the main features of the clock case that he was making for the King under the direction of William Chambers (see cat. no. 12). Many of the decorative features of the case – the mouldings at the top and bottom of the squared case, the rams' heads with their ribbons, the swags and the ewers with their fish or dolphin handles – were cast from the same moulds. It is also clear from his letter to Whitehurst that he planned from the earliest stage to incorporate a revolving globe on top of the clock, and that he accepted the clockmaker's observation that an annual hand would help with the adjustment of the position of the sun, which moves up and down in front of the globe along the line of the ecliptic, if they were driven by the same annual motion. It is very likely that he also had in mind at this stage the use of the three figures that support the globe. These figures were copies of three of the four figures on a silver gilt crucifix made by Antonio Gentile da Faenza in about 1582, two of which were illustrated by William Chambers in his *Treatise on Civil Architecture* under the heading of 'Persians and Caryatides'. The architect was not the source of the models for the geographical clock case. They came from the sculptor John Flaxman, from whom in December 1770 Boulton bought, among other models, a 'group of Hercules and Atlas' for two guineas. The clock is an eight-day movement. The globe turns once a day, and a carriage that runs to and fro on top of the movement operates the engraved sun. The sun is attached to a brass ring, which gives a rough idea of the extent of night and day. The dial is enamelled. The original enamelling was subcontracted to an enameller named Weston who worked in Quakers' Buildings in Smithfield, London. The globe is signed 'N. Hill' in a cartouche of classical figures. This was Nathaniel Hill, who was a well known land surveyor, mathematical instrument-maker and globe maker and who is known to have worked in Chancery Lane between 1745 and 1765. Boulton offered the clock for sale alongside the sidereal clock at Christie's in April 1772. He was hoping that it would fetch £180 but it did not sell. He thought of sending it to Russia, where he hoped that Catherine II might be a more promising buyer than the gambling English aristocracy, but he never did. Somehow it came into the possession of the Philips family at Tean, near Stoke-on-Trent. Since the family was living at Tean in the 1770s, it may well have been sold to either John Philips (1695–1777) or his son of the same name (1724–1813). The Philips family were textile manufacturers, trading under the names of John and Nathaniel Philips, and became Boulton and Watt's customers when they wanted to equip their mill at Tean with steam power.

LITERATURE
Goodison, pp. 202–7, Plates 155–9.

PROVENANCE
Private collection.

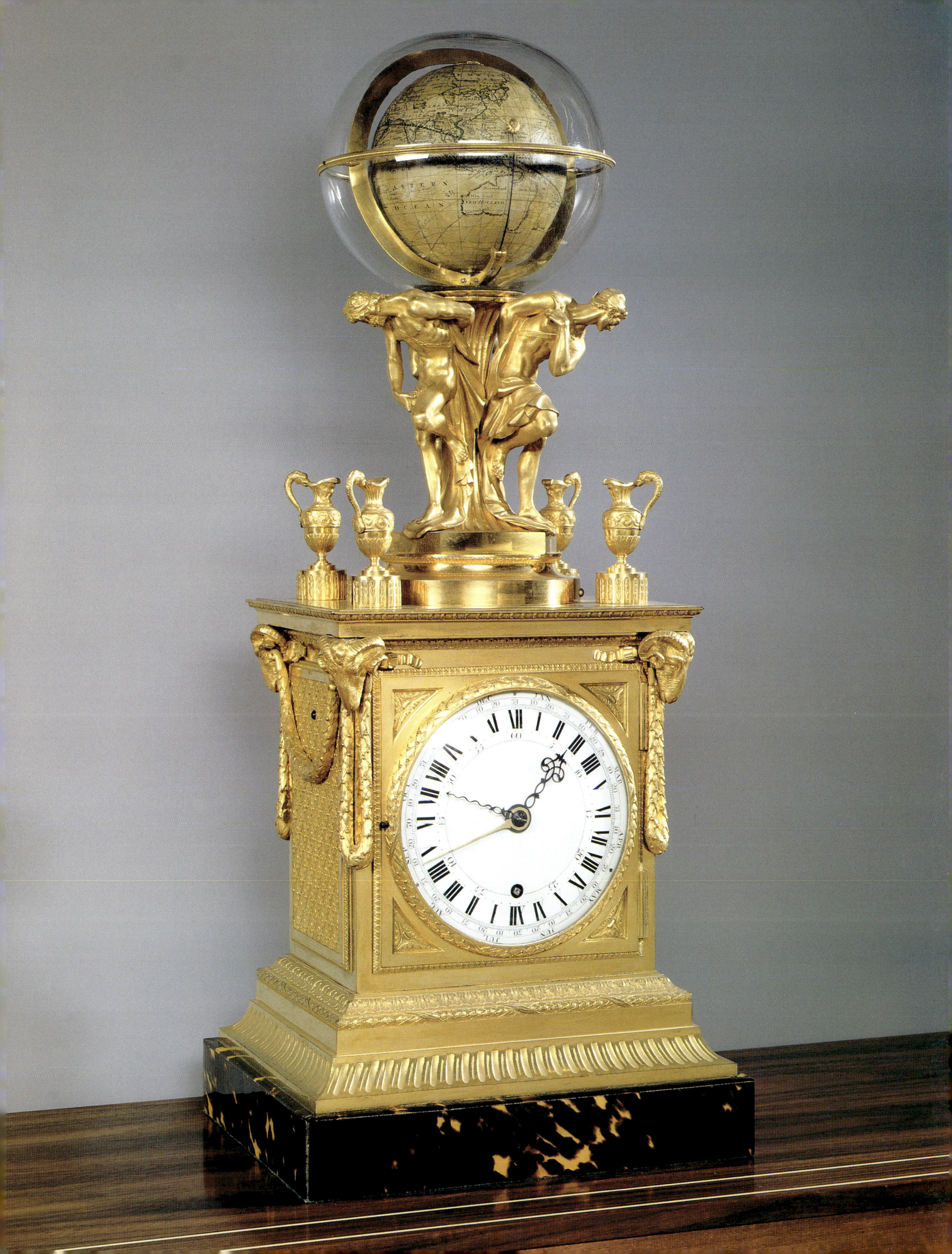

CATALOGUE 12
King's clock case, c.1771–2.
H: 18½" (46.8 cm).
Ormolu with lacquered glass panels and blue john finial.

This is a copy, with some modifications, of the clock case that Boulton made to the design of the King's architect, Sir William Chambers, for George III in 1770–1. Several features of the design can be traced to Chambers's drawings during his travels to Italy and France, and some of the mounts, such as the feet with their fluted spiral pattern, the rams' heads, the urn with its Greek fret decoration and ring handles, and the ewers with their fish or dolphin handles, are familiar motifs of Chambers's repertoire of ornament. Boulton planned to put a copy of the King's clock into the sale at Christie's in 1771, but he did not do so, and it is likely that he thought better of his plan at the last minute, having listened to the advice of his London agent William Matthews, who observed that 'your having a clock to sell at an auction of the same pattern with his Majesty's will be an affront to his Majesty as he should have given you his permission before you had copied his drawing'. It is likely that more than two of these clock cases were made, but this is so far the only one, apart from the one in the Royal Collection, that has appeared. The two cases, apart from a few obvious differences, which include the treatment of the sides and of the door at the back, and the height of the feet, are practically identical. There are differences of detail in the chasing of the mounts – for example the rams' heads and the buds on the festoons beneath the dials – but most of the decorative components were clearly cast in the same moulds. The most striking difference between the two cases is the use of blue john panels in the Royal clock, and of blue and gold painted glass in this one. The movement of this clock is a simple, eight-day striking movement, and the 'signature' on the back-plate is 'John Whitehouse, Derby'. This is probably an error. There is evidence in the archives to suggest that on occasion John Whitehurst arranged for clocks and watches to be supplied by workshops in London. It is thus possible that Whitehurst was responsible for ordering the movement of this clock and that either he, or someone at Soho, instructed the engraver to inscribe his name on the backplate. There was nothing unusual in selling another clockmaker's clock as one's own, and there are many extant clocks and scientific instruments on which the engraver has spelt the name of the 'maker' incorrectly. Instructions given by word of mouth can easily be mistaken, and 'Whitehurst' and 'Whitehouse' sound very much the same. In Birmingham, at any rate, the latter was a common enough name. The fact that there is no signature on the front of the dial supports the suggestion that the movement was bought separately. The dial was enamelled by Weston, of Quakers' Buildings, Smithfield, whose signature is on the back of it. If the clockmaker had commissioned Weston to make the dial, he would presumably have asked him to put his name on the front; it was rare for a clockmaker not to 'sign' his clocks conspicuously. It looks, therefore, as if the dial and movement were ordered separately and that, as with the dials of the geographical and sidereal clocks, which he also made, Weston was given no instructions about a 'signature'. The movement is similar to other movements from the workshop of Eardley Norton (fl. c.1760–94), who worked at 49 St John Street, Clerkenwell. When this King's clock came to light in the early 1960s it had been owned for several years by a dealer who claimed that it came from Moccas Court, Hereford, which was built for Sir George Cornewall in 1776–83.

Cornewall inherited the baronetcy from his father, the merchant and banker Sir George Amyand, in 1766. He assumed the name of Cornewall on his marriage in 1771 to Catherine Cornewall, the heiress to Moccas Court. Since the movement appears to have been supplied by Eardley Norton, the clock can safely be identified with the one mentioned in a letter from Boulton and Fothergill to William Matthews in April 1772: 'Shall also debit your account for the clock and case for Mr Amyand as agreed for £48 6s. 0d. Don't forget to see after the clock too [?]. It's from Mr Yardley Norton.' The exact identity of the 'Mr Amyand' mentioned in these letters is uncertain. One possibility is that Sir George was wrongly identified as 'Mr' in the Soho records and ordered the clock before he changed his name in 1771, but Boulton's clerks were not inclined to disregard titles, and for him to be still described as 'Mr Amyand' in April 1772 seems unlikely. Sir George Cornewall's uncle, Claudius Amyand (1718–74), and his brother John Amyand (1751–80), both died without any children. Either of these men might have bought the clock and left it to Sir George, or might have acted as his agent in London in respect of the purchase.

LITERATURE
Goodison, pp. 79–81, 213–15, Plates 160, 162–4.

PROVENANCE
Courtauld Institute Gallery.

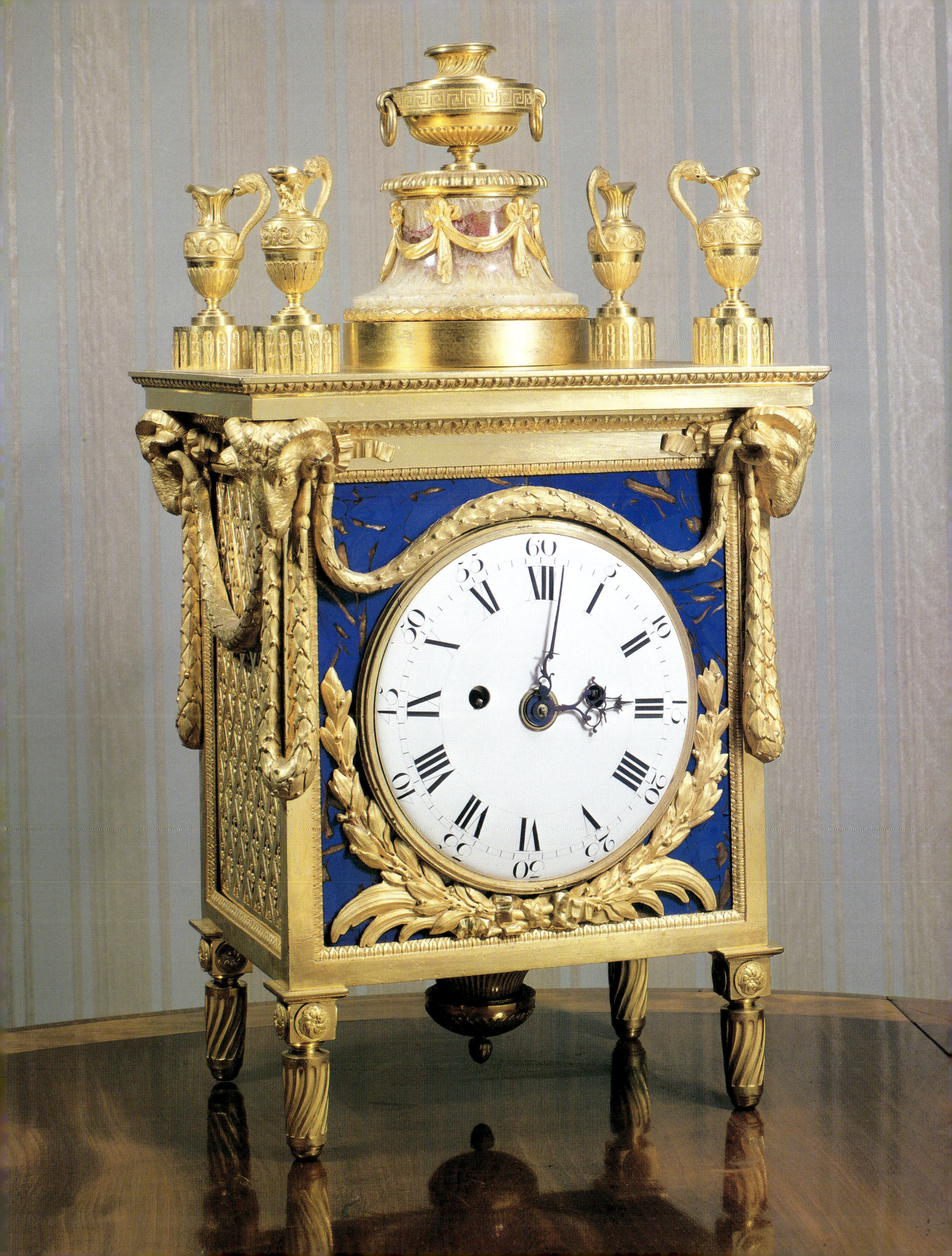

CATALOGUE 13
Minerva clock case, c.1771–2.
H: 18½" (47 cm).
White marble and ormolu.

The Minerva clock case was one of Boulton and Fothergill's earliest allegorical clock cases. A drawing of a Minerva clock survives in their pattern books[1] showing Minerva, the Goddess of Wisdom, unveiling an urn with her right hand. She wears her *aegis* – the mask of the Medusa is just visible in the sketch – and holds a spear, pointing downwards, also in her right hand. Her owl perches on the pedestal beneath the urn. The boy sits on books on the other side of the pedestal and holds a scroll. The clock face, mounted in the pedestal, is square and there is a faint outline of a chapter ring within it. The pedestal sits on a two-stepped base, which is supported by ball feet and decorated underneath with an acanthus mount. An alternative third step to the base is lightly pencilled-in, in place of the ball feet. The clock stands on a large lower pedestal, which, with its pitchers, rams' heads and tapered legs, is clearly modelled on William Chambers's designs for the King's clock case (see cat. no. 12). Presumably this version of the Minerva clock was intended to be a pendulum clock, the pendulum and possibly even some of the mechanism, being housed in the lower case. No examples of a Minerva clock with this lower case have yet come to light and it is possible that none were made. There was a Minerva clock in the sale at Christie's in 1771, and another was probably offered at Christie's in 1772.

The first of these had lines composed by the poet Gay on the theme of Time inscribed on the boy's scroll. The second was probably the clock being made towards the end of 1771 and described in a letter from Boulton to Lord Cathcart in St Petersburg, which also included descriptions of the geographical and sidereal clocks: the boy's scroll in this case was inscribed with shorter lines from Virgil about the brevity of life. This Minerva clock case conforms closely to the sketch in the pattern book. It shows Minerva unveiling the urn upon which is a plaque of Prudence making a libation to Time. She wears classical drapery, a helmet crowned with a laurel wreath (for she is also the Goddess of War) and her *aegis*, which is decorated with a Medusa mask. Peeping out from between her and the urn is her owl, symbolic of wisdom and learning. At her feet are ranged objects related to her attributes – her shield, bearing a mask of Medusa, more laurels, a book and a scroll. The boy sits on further books and reads the scroll. Two further urns are mounted at the rear of the base. The sides of the pedestal have pierced panels with a scrolling ornament. The base is decorated with a delicate scrolling frieze and grotesque heads at the corners. The feet, which look French, along with the French movement, dial and bezel, suggest that Boulton and Fothergill exported this clock case to France. Many of the ornaments and friezes appear on other vases and clock cases made at Soho. The sources of Boulton's design for the Minerva clock case are uncertain, although the ensemble has a French feeling about it. It is likely that the modeller adopted the conceit of a female figure pointing to Time and a boy (often winged in French designs) representing the Genius of Learning or Time from French models.

LITERATURE
Goodison, pp. 68, 218–19, Plates 165, 169–72.

PROVENANCE
Hotspur Ltd.

1. Boulton and Fothergill pattern books, Vol. 1, p. 76.

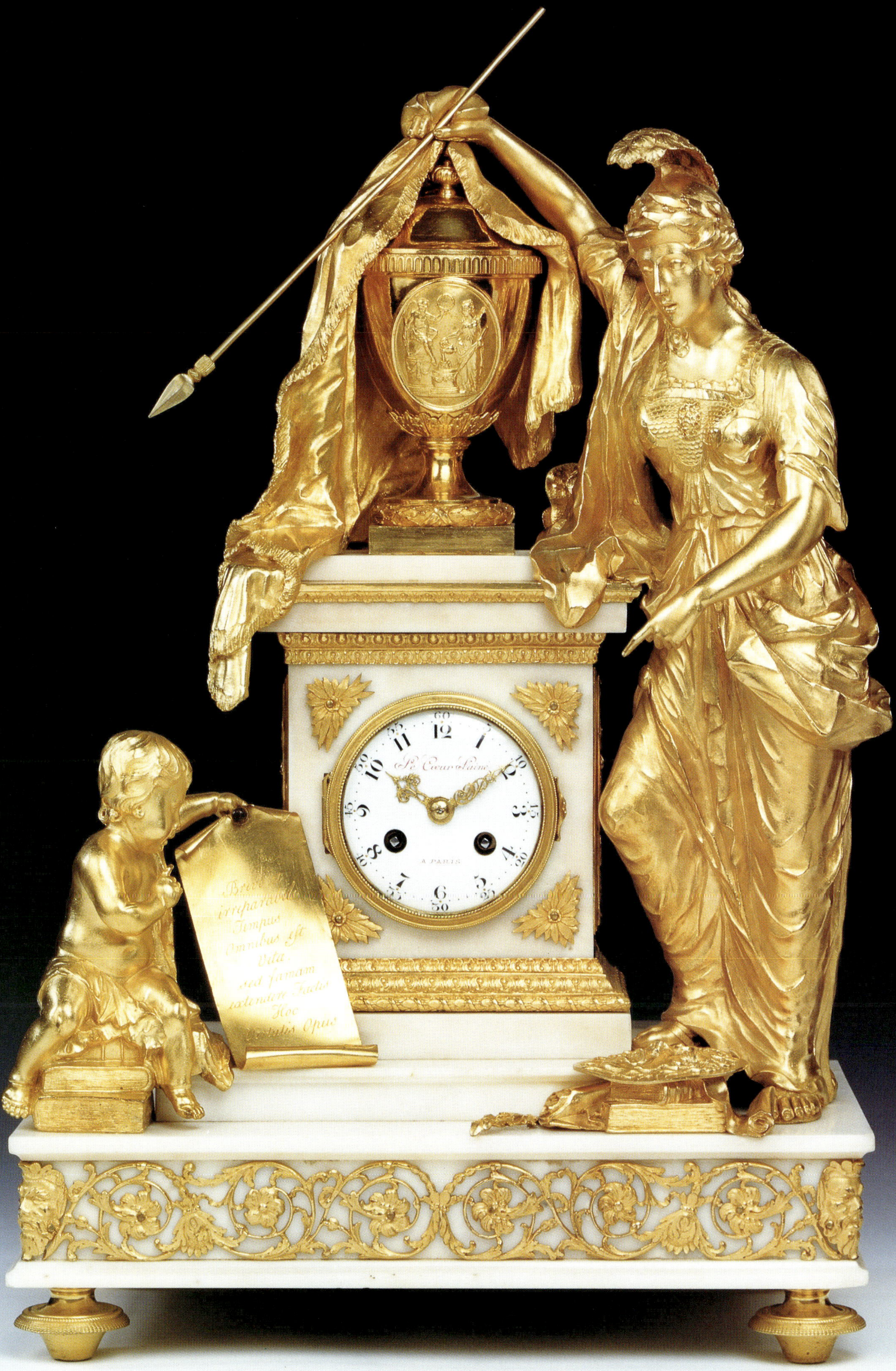

A PARIS
Tempus
Omnibus est
Vita.
sed famam
Hoc

CATALOGUE 14
Narcissus clock case, c.1775.
H: 16¼" (41.3 cm).
White marble and ormolu,
with bronzed base.

This clock case shows Narcissus gazing at his reflection, with which he had fallen in love, in a pool. The story of Narcissus, who pined away for love of his own beauty, died and was turned into a flower, was a favourite with classical authors and artists. It fitted well as one of Boulton's allegorical themes, reminding us about the futility of human vanity and the transience of human beauty. The overall design of the ornament is similar to other allegorical designs made at Soho. The figures of Narcissus and his dog are gilt. They stand on a bronzed base chased with rocks and vegetation. The pool is made of silver plate. The mounts on the pedestal and obelisk, including the swags of drapery pinned to three sides of the pedestal, are familiar from other ornaments. The medallion pinned to the obelisk probably depicts Hygieia, the personification of Health. The watch movement is fitted with an enamelled dial and gilt hands. The bezel is decorated with blue glass beads backed by silver foil, showing that the clock was intended for export (see Goodison as cited below). The ornament accords closely with a sketch in Boulton and Fothergill's pattern books.[1] The Narcissus clock case is one of several allegorical designs based on classical themes produced at Soho in the later 1770s. There were two Narcissus ornaments in the sale at Christie and Ansell's in 1778, both marble with bronzed figures, and both with vases rather than obelisks. Neither was described as a clock case, and one of them was described as a perfume burner. No Narcissus with an urn has yet come to light. A case with an obelisk and a marble base is at Temple Newsam House, Leeds (p. 37, Fig. 4).

LITERATURE
Goodison, pp. 180, 220–1,
Plates 173, 174.

PROVENANCE
Birmingham Museum and Art Gallery,
Soho House.

1. Boulton and Fothergill pattern books,
Vol. 1, p. 77.

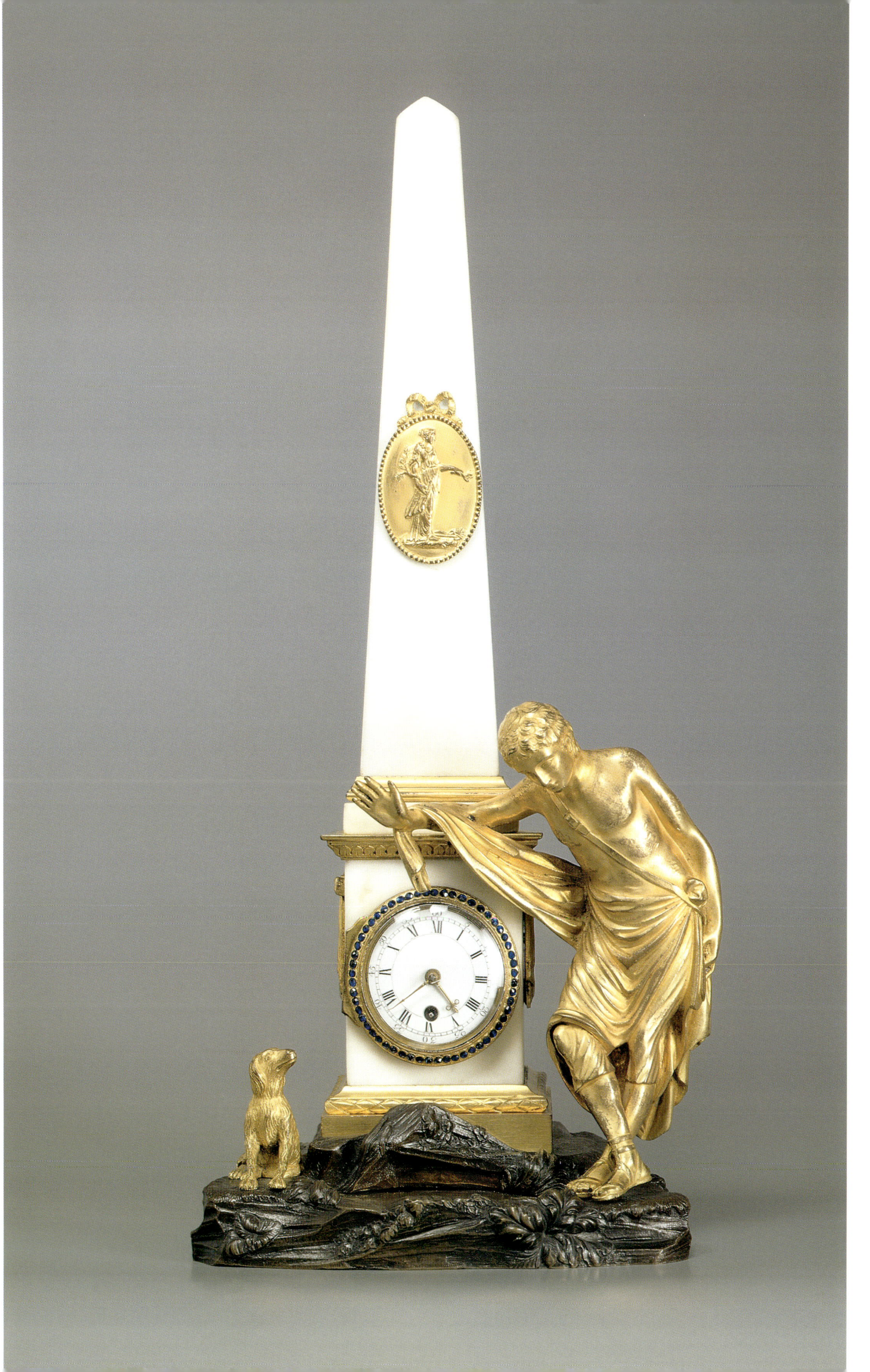

Seat furniture

SIMON REDBURN

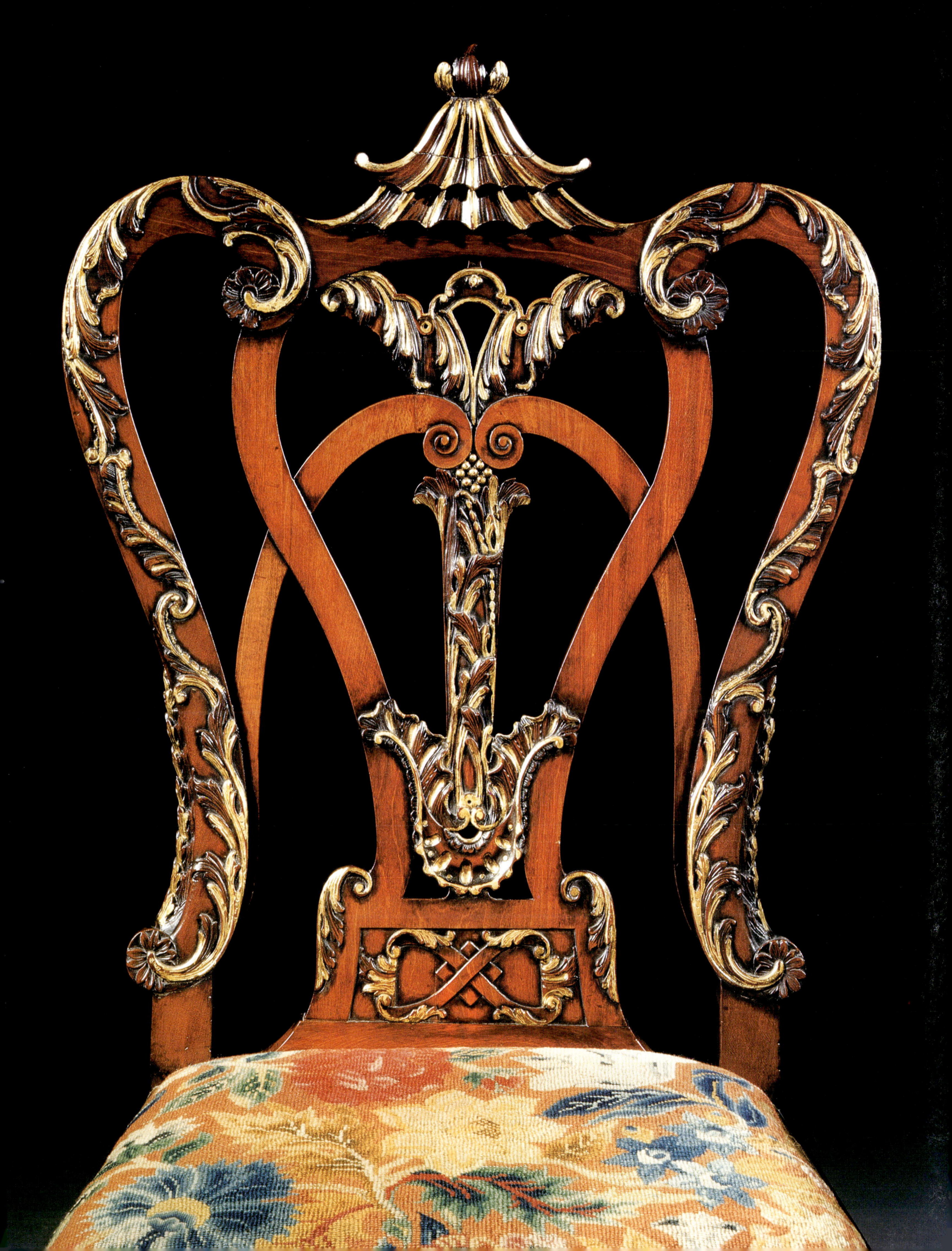

PREVIOUS PAGE
(Detail from p. 135, cat. no. 7)
One of a pair of mahogany and parcel gilt chairs with original needlework covers, c.1760.

OPPOSITE
1. A wing chair, c.1690.

1. Gwynn, *Huguenot Heritage*, pp. 74–100.

SEAT FURNITURE

ALTHOUGH I AM delighted that Robin Kern has invited me to describe and comment on a number of pieces of seat furniture that the venerable firm of Hotspur has sold during the last eighty years, it is also somewhat daunting to realise that I have known Robin and his brother, Brian, for half of this time.

They were guided in their early years by their late father, Rob, whom I remember with great affection for his friendship and warmth and for the knowledge he so freely imparted. I do have a slight suspicion that Robin has chosen for me the subject of chairs as he realises that part of my joy in visiting him in his inner sanctum at Lowndes Street is to sit in the large and comfortable Regency armchair. What a wonderful place this has been over the years to drink his somewhat strong coffee and listen to the latest news of discoveries and triumphs.

Before the accession of Charles II in 1660 most seat furniture was of very basic form, chairs being simply constructed with turned supports in naturally polished oak or beech, which was occasionally painted or gilded and in some cases covered in a textile. Upholstery was minimal; hay, wool and hair being thinly applied to the frames, comfort being provided by loose cushions filled with down and feather.

Textiles used were primarily silk velvets and damask for the more costly pieces, which were ornamented with decorative brass nailing, bullion fringe and tassels, and in some cases with applied needlework and coloured satin. The vegetable dyes produced deep, rich colours, and also ones of intense clarity. Coarser textiles made from wool were common, as was 'Turkey work' made by drawing wool through a canvas and knotting it to form a pile. This was used for seat covers and backs and occasionally table carpets. Unfortunately, textiles are by their nature fragile, and it is only in houses such as Knole and Hardwick and from studying contemporary paintings that the beauty of sixteenth- and early seventeenth-century textiles can still be appreciated.

During the next forty years, chair-makers and cabinet-makers in England rapidly assimilated the new designs and methods of construction introduced from Europe by immigrant craftsmen, many of them Huguenots.[1] These included the carvers and gilders

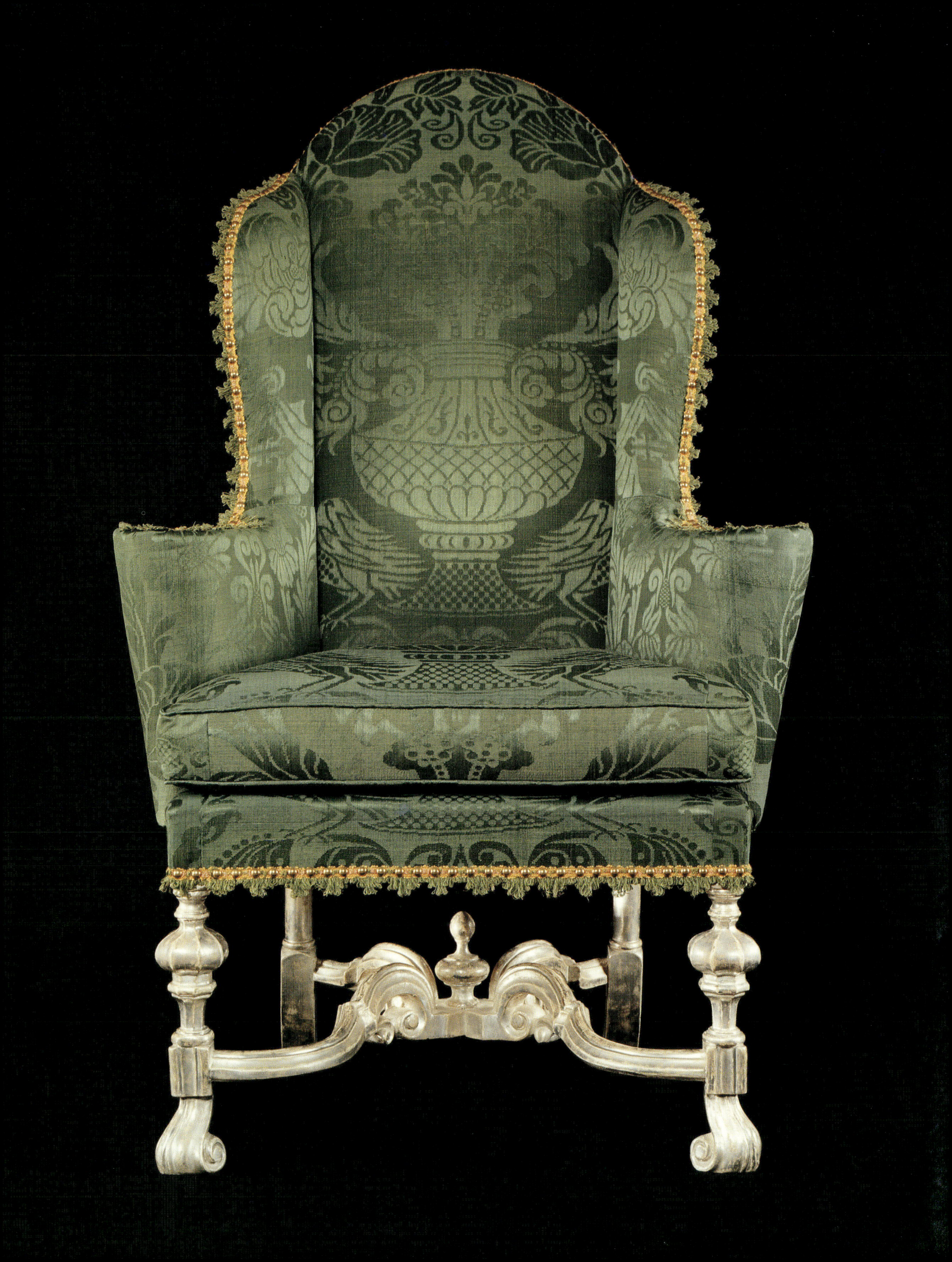

OPPOSITE
2. A walnut and parcel gilt wing chair,
c.1720, attributed to Richard Roberts.

John and Thomas Pelletier, and the upholsterer Francis Lapierre, all of whom worked extensively for the Royal Court in the late seventeenth and early eighteenth centuries. The designer and architect Daniel Marot (1662–1752) was another Huguenot who left Paris before the revocation of the Edict of Nantes, entering the service of William and Mary, first in Holland, then in London. His designs, which were first published in 1703,[2] illustrate seat furniture, beds and interior decoration similar to the furniture supplied to the Royal Court in the late seventeenth and early eighteenth centuries, including chairs with double curved 'horse-bone' legs.[3]

The earliest chair illustrated from the Hotspur archive is the rare diminutive wing chair (Fig. 1) supported on a richly carved and silvered frame. This may be compared to a less elaborate walnut example, without the wings to the back, supplied by Richard Roberts for the use of Queen Anne at Windsor. It was delivered after her death in 1714, being described as 'a large armchair', and was part of a suite which included a 'standing bed' and 'eight square stools', thus continuing the precedent of stools outnumbering chairs in State Rooms. Richard Roberts[4] (fl. 1714–29) succeeded his father Thomas (fl. 1685–1714) as carver and joiner to the Royal Household in 1714, Thomas having held the Royal Warrant since 1686. From the large quantities he supplied to the Royal Household of both utilitarian furniture and more elaborate pieces for the sovereign's own use, it is obvious that he owned one of the major workshops in London. Surviving accounts indicate that he was primarily responsible for 'moveable' pieces such as seat furniture, screens and beds, whereas the other Royal cabinet-maker, Gerreitt Jensen,[5] was responsible for supplying case furniture. This specialisation was a necessary practice in the seventeenth century through the influence of the tradesmen's guilds, but, as their influence waned, workshops were able to produce any kind of furniture they wished.

A report in the *London Journal* dated 19 October 1728 reporting a foiled robbery refers to Richard Roberts as 'Chairmaker to his Majesty', and certainly the accounts for the Royal Household indicate that the business was continued in the same manner as conducted by his father. References in the accounts

2. Marot, *Nouveaux Livres de Licts de Differentes Penssees*.
3. Bowett, *English Furniture 1660–1714 From Charles II to Queen Anne*.
4. Beard and Gilbert, *Dictionary of English Furniture Makers, 1660–1840* (*DEFM*), pp. 752–4.
5. Beard and Gilbert, *op. cit.*, pp. 485–7.

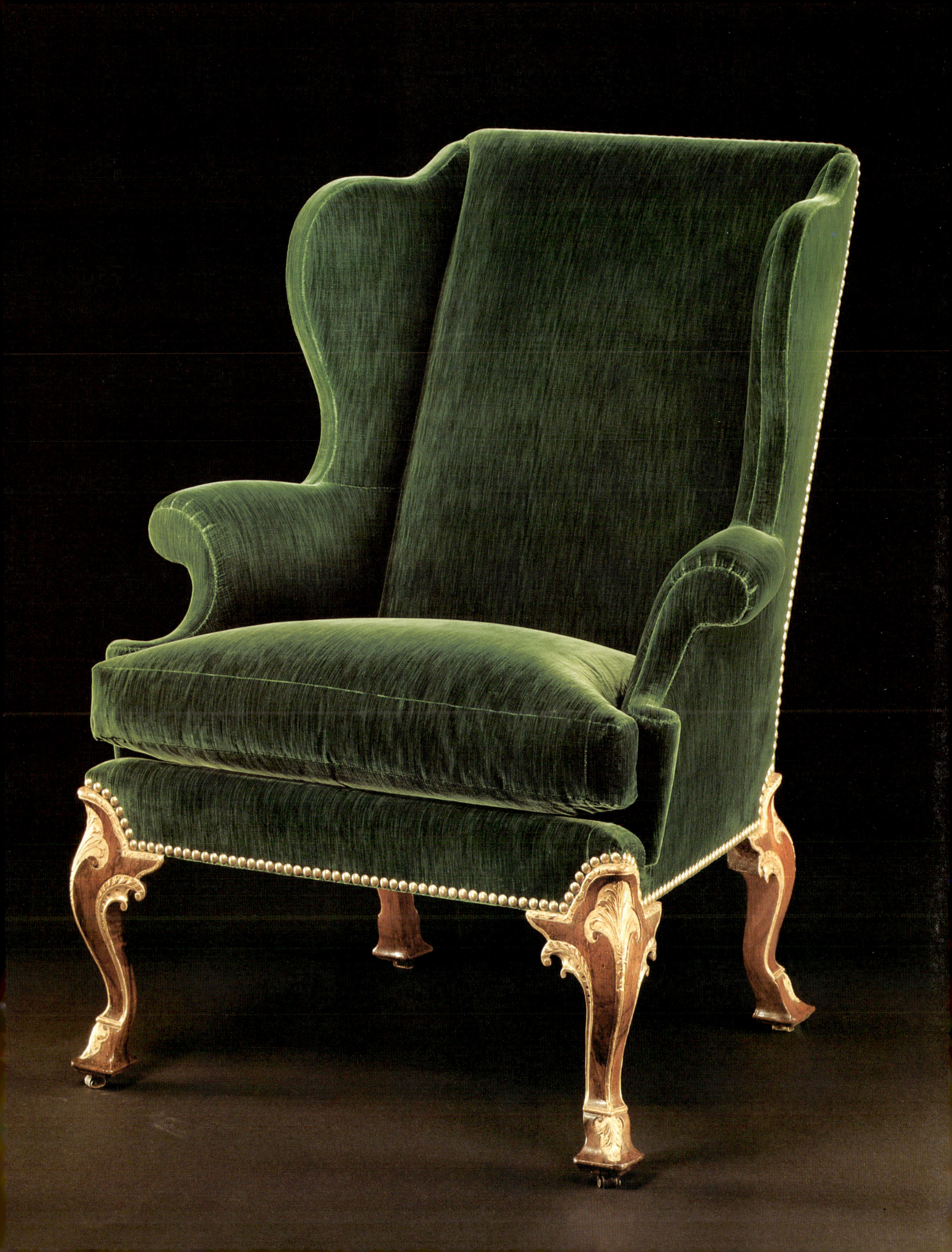

OPPOSITE
3. A carved gilt gesso side chair, c.1720, in the style of the Royal cabinet-maker James Moore.

to chairs with 'bended backs', 'cabriole legs' and 'hoof feet' certainly indicate that his designs closely followed current fashions. This is shown by another wing chair (Fig. 2), which, although stylistically completely different from the first example, can also be attributed to Richard Roberts.

Dating from about 1720, it is conceived in plain and burr walnut with panels of carved gilt gesso at the knees and toes, with gilt mouldings, and supported on distinctive spreading 'hoof' feet. It is closely related to two suites of seat furniture at Houghton Hall, Norfolk, one of 'Fifteen chairs / Two settees' and the other with 'Eight chairs' in the 'Cov'd or Wrought Bedchamber'. They were probably originally commissioned by Sir Robert Walpole for the earlier Houghton Hall which was demolished in 1722. At the time of Roberts's presumed death in 1729, the Houghton accounts indicate a debt to his firm of £1,420 8s. 7½d.[6]

Carved gilt gesso, as seen on this wing chair, is a particularly fragile medium when used as decoration on the legs of seat furniture. The side chair illustrated here (Fig. 3) of about 1720 is a particularly rare survivor. In the manner of the Royal cabinet-maker James Moore (c.1670–1726),[7] the elegant cabriole legs are decorated with acanthus leaves and are joined to the seat rail by curious open scrolled brackets. The profile and detail of this chair may be compared with other gessoed seat furniture supplied by Moore to Sarah, Duchess of Marlborough, for Blenheim Palace, and to Simon Harcourt, First Viscount Harcourt, for Harcourt House in Cavendish Square, London. The Royal collection includes a number of pieces by him which are incised 'Moore', some bearing the cipher of George I. Moore worked closely with the Duchess of Marlborough, having succeeded Vanbrugh as comptroller of works at Blenheim, Sarah referring to him as 'Her oracle'. His position at Blenheim was always thought to be somewhat curious for a cabinet-maker, but recent research in the Harcourt archives[8] indicates that he conducted similar duties for Lord Harcourt at Cavendish Square. Moore was certainly not alone in producing chairs of this form, but the aforementioned commissions mean that his work is more fully documented. The most curious part of their

6. Christie's, London, *Works of Art from Houghton*, sale catalogue, 8 December 1994, lots 126, 127.
7. Beard and Gilbert, *op. cit.*, pp. 618–19.
8. Sotheby's, London, sale catalogue, 3 July 2003, pp. 142–4.

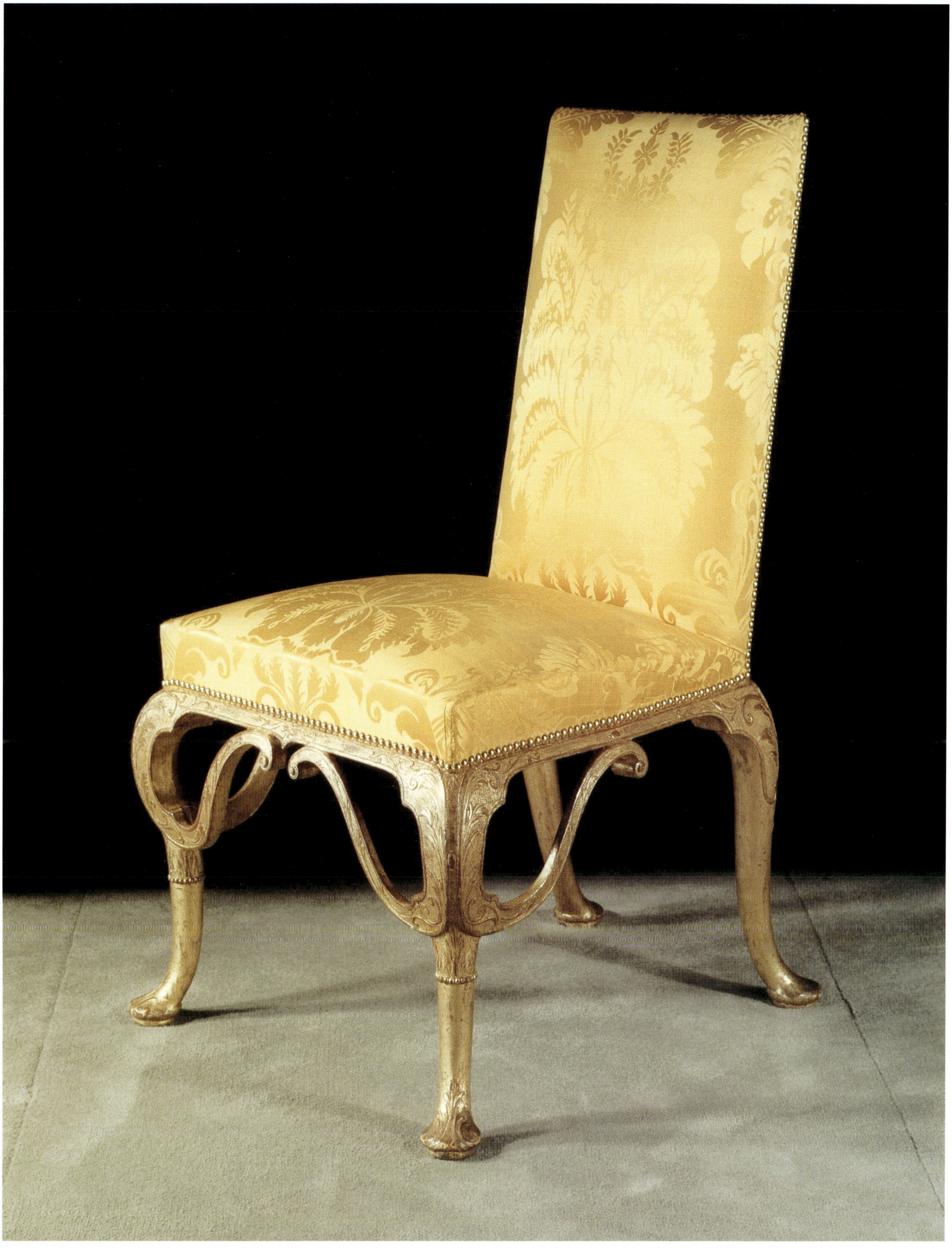

OPPOSITE
4. A walnut wing chair, c.1720. The upholstery on this chair illustrates the use of textiles in this period and was probably the work of one of the ladies of the household.

design is the arched, open scrolled brackets, which also appear on a pair of plain walnut stools, unfortunately not provenanced. These also have legs with faceted upper parts supported on turnings with pad feet, and a narrow moulded seat frame. The early eighteenth-century carved gilt gesso stool seen in catalogue 2 is also a rare survival, the claw feet being of an unusual form at this period.

One of the many delights of English seat furniture is the study of the various textiles used to cover the basic upholstery. An example illustrating this use of textiles is the needlework covers of the early eighteenth-century walnut wing chair (Fig. 4), its form again indicating the diversity of styles of the early Georgian period. They are worked on canvas with wool and silk in tent stitch, with an exuberant abundance of brightly coloured summer flowers and leaves. Intended for a small and more 'domestic' room, this chair is in complete contrast to the first three examples, which were intended for more formal and important interiors with their modern coverings of silk damask and velvet. These are historically accurate, the green velvet on the walnut and parcel gilt wing chair (Fig. 2) being based on the bottle green silk velvet, which probably dates to 1730, on the Houghton chairs. The present needlework was probably worked by one of the ladies of the household for which the chair was made, as were the covers on the pair of mid-eighteenth-century stools shown here (Fig. 5). Previously unused, their pristine and unfaded colours might appear somewhat bright to the modern eye, but illustrate the freshness and vivid hues that could be achieved with vegetable dyes.

In contrast, the needlework on the carved gilt wood chair of about 1740 (Fig. 6) is certainly professional work. The moulded cartouche-shaped back and ovoid seat of this chair are covered with needlework of coloured silks and wool in tent stitch, the back depicting Mars and Venus, the seat with sprays of flowers, all within conforming borders. It belongs to a group of five chairs that were originally at Spye Park, Chippenham in Wiltshire. One of the chairs now in the Lady Lever Art Gallery, Port Sunlight,[9] is worked with the Sacrifice of Iphigenia, another with Venus and Vulcan, and another with Europa and the Bull, the fourth in later damask. A closely related

9. Beard, *Upholsterers and Interior Furnishing in England, 1530–1840*, p. 184, fig. 181.

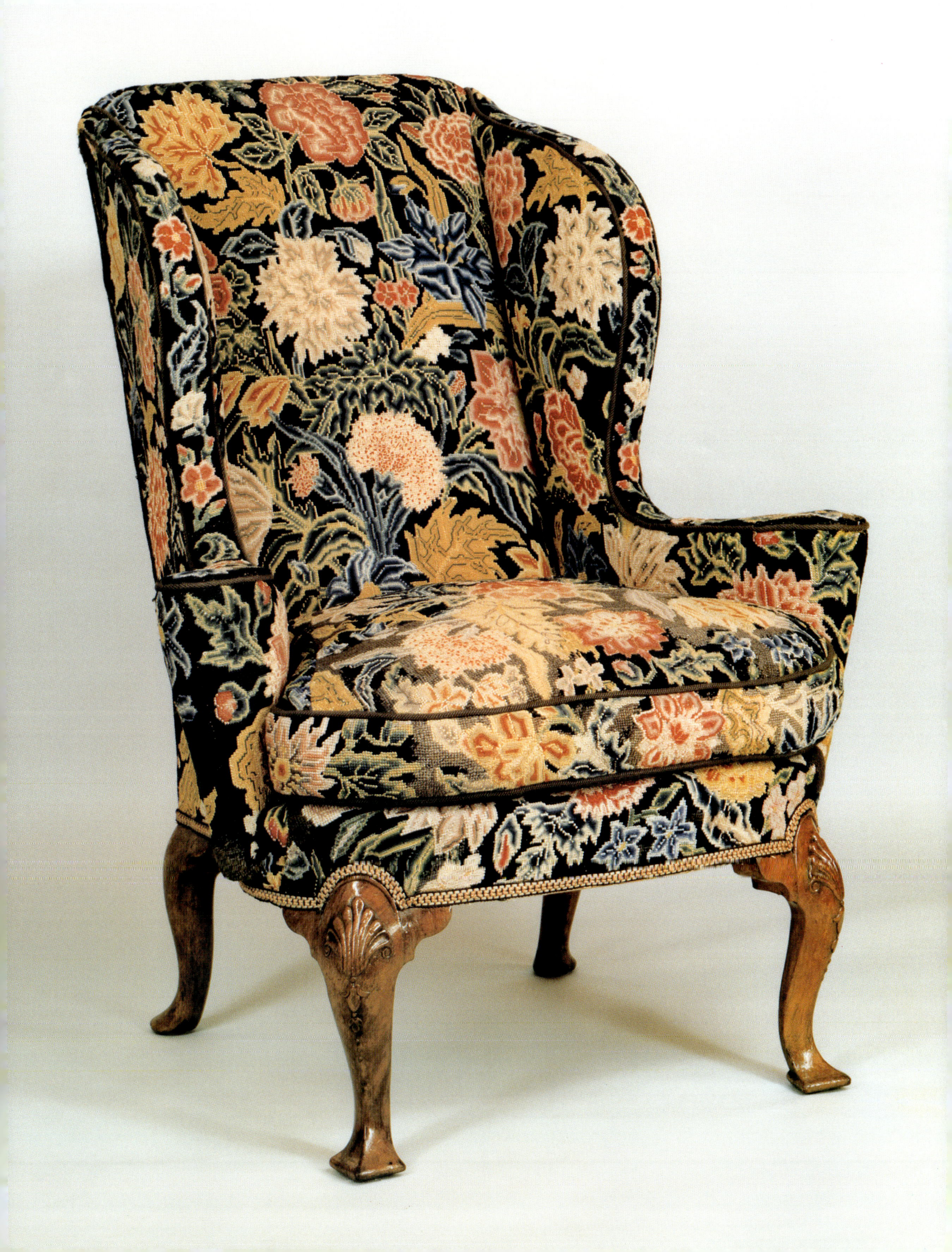

5. A pair of stools, c.1735. The upholstery on these stools shows the vibrant colours achieved by vegetable dyes in the period. The needlework was probably worked by one of the ladies of the household.

OPPOSITE
6. A carved gilt wood chair, c.1740. The needlework for this chair was certainly professionally worked.

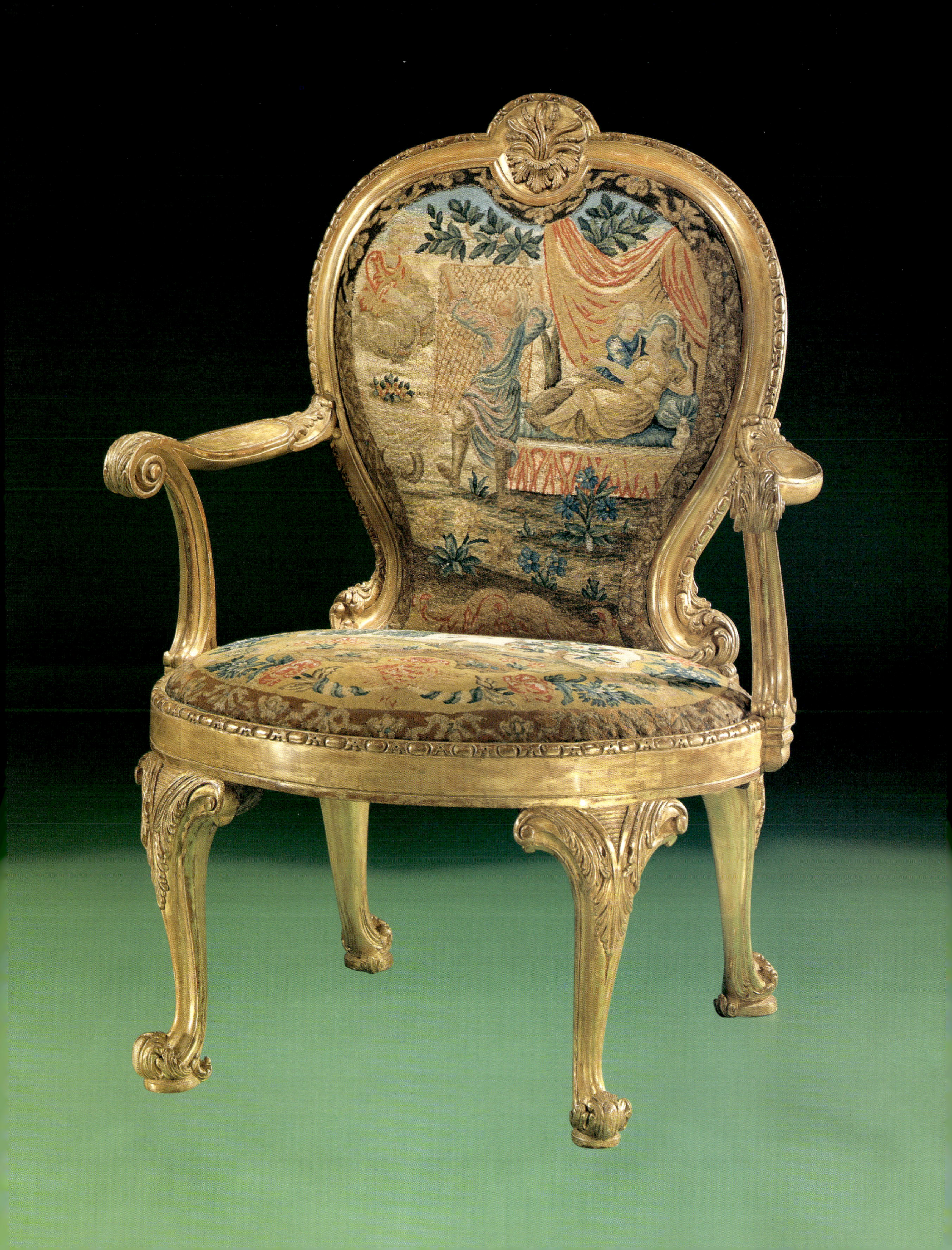

OPPOSITE
7. One of a pair of mahogany and parcel gilt chairs with their original needlework seats, c.1760.

10. Beard, *op. cit.*, p. 184, fig. 180.
11. Sotheby's New York, *The Collection of Mr and Mrs Saul P. Steinberg*, sale catalogue, 26 May 2000, lots 189, 190, pp. 135–41.

SEAT FURNITURE

set at Stoneleigh Abbey[10] depicts scenes from Ovid's *Metamorphoses* within similar conforming borders, the backs being shaped at the sides to accommodate arms. On the side chairs these have been worked-in, indicating that they were purchased ready-made. The frames of the Stoneleigh chairs, which are undocumented, are in burr walnut and with the monogram and arms of the third Lord Leigh worked in gilt gesso. They are supported on legs that are very similar to those on the wing chair illustrated on page 131 (Fig. 4) and are attributed to Thomas Roberts.

The seats on the pair of mid-eighteenth-century mahogany and parcel gilt chairs from Grimsthorpe Castle (Fig. 7) also have their original needlework seats somewhat naively worked with a profusion of summer flowers. The inventive form of their whimsical frames is one of the most magical creations to have survived from the mid-eighteenth century, combining rococo motifs with visions of Cathay (China). The crest rail, which is surmounted by a finial in the form of a temple roof, is clearly derived from the 'Temples' and 'Garden Seats' illustrated in William and John Halfpenny's *Rural Architecture in the Chinese Taste*, whereas the interlaced strap-work of the backs is found in a number of pattern books, including those published by William de la Cour in 1741, Mathias Darly in 1751, and Robert Manwaring in 1766. The profile of the legs closely relates to a manuscript drawing of about 1730 by Nicolas Pineau (1684–1754), now in the collection of the *Musée des Arts Décoratifs*, Paris.[11] This drawing appears not to have been engraved, but the creator of these chairs was presumably cognisant of a French chair derived from it. These chairs date from the time of Peregrine, third Duke of Ancaster (1714–78). The first record of these chairs is in 1924 when they were in the Tapestry Bedroom at Grimsthorpe Castle, the seat of the Willoughby de Eresby family. Although a number of sets of chairs are recorded in the 1813 inventory, none of those recorded appears to refer to the present examples. It is also possible that they were part of the furnishings of Normanton Park in Rutland, the eighteenth-century seat of Sir Gilbert Heathcote, Bart., many of which were removed to Grimsthorpe in the 1920s. Sir Gilbert was a patron of several leading London cabinet-makers, including

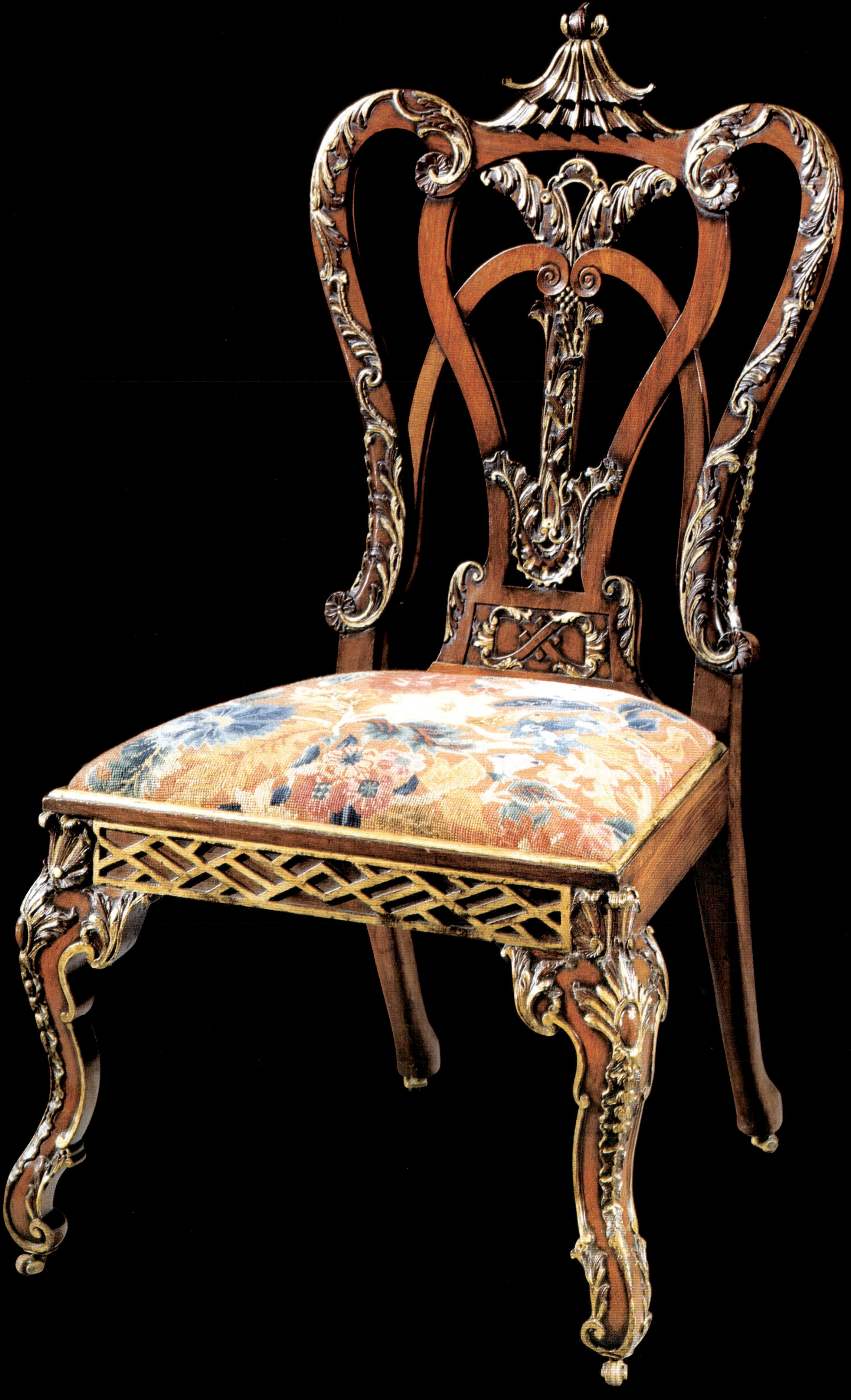

ABOVE
8. A design by Thomas Chippendale for the 'ribband' back chair, plate XVI in the first edition of *The Gentlemen and Cabinet-Makers' Director* of 1754.

OPPOSITE
Detail of one of a pair of 'ribband' back chairs, c.1755, based on the Chippendale's design in the *Director* of 1754.

12. Lees-Milne, *Caves of Ice, Diaries: 1946 & '47*, pp. 127–8.
13. Dunning, *Some Somerset Country Houses*, pp. 37–42.

Thomas Chippendale, Vile and Cobb, and France and Bradburn, all of whom could be considered as the makers of the chairs.

These chairs illustrate the growing influence of pattern books that allowed even provincial cabinet-makers to closely follow current taste in London, which in turn was heavily influenced by designs from France. Pre-eminent among the cabinet-makers who published their own designs was Thomas Chippendale (1718–79). First published in 1754, *The Gentlemen and Cabinet-Makers' Director* contained some 161 engraved plates depicting a wide range of fashionable household furniture. The design of the pair of rococo chairs (Fig. 8) with 'ribband' backs is almost identical to plate XVI from the first edition of this work, Chippendale declaring that the 'Ribband Back chairs … which, if I may speak without vanity, are the best I have ever seen (or perhaps have ever been made).' Conceived in exceptional mahogany with a tight grain, these chairs certainly reflect the supreme virtuosity of Chippendale as a designer in the rococo idiom, but also the mastery of a carver whose skill has translated a flat design to a form that is sculptural in its quality. Originally part of a set of eight, these chairs were formerly at Dillington House in Ilminster, Somerset, a sixteenth-century house considerably altered in the 1830s by Sir James Pennethorne. They were then loaned to the National Trust property Montacute House, James Lees-Milne noting in his diary on 20 January 1948: 'at 2.30 reached Dillington Park, a delightful Tudor House, almost entirely rebuilt in 1810 in imitation of Barrington Court by Pennethorne … The present owner a young Mrs Cameron … They offer us practically anything we like for Montacute … and I selected straight away a number of things, including a fine set of ribbon-back eighteenth-century dining-room chairs.'[12] Dillington House[13] was the seat of the Speke family from 1599 until the 1760s when it became one of the seats of Frederick, Lord North and second Earl of Guilford, Member of Parliament for Banbury, and Chancellor of the Exchequer, who married Ann Speke. In 1795 the house was sold to John Hanning of Barrington Court, his son John taking the name of Lee after the death of his uncle, Major John Lee of Orleigh

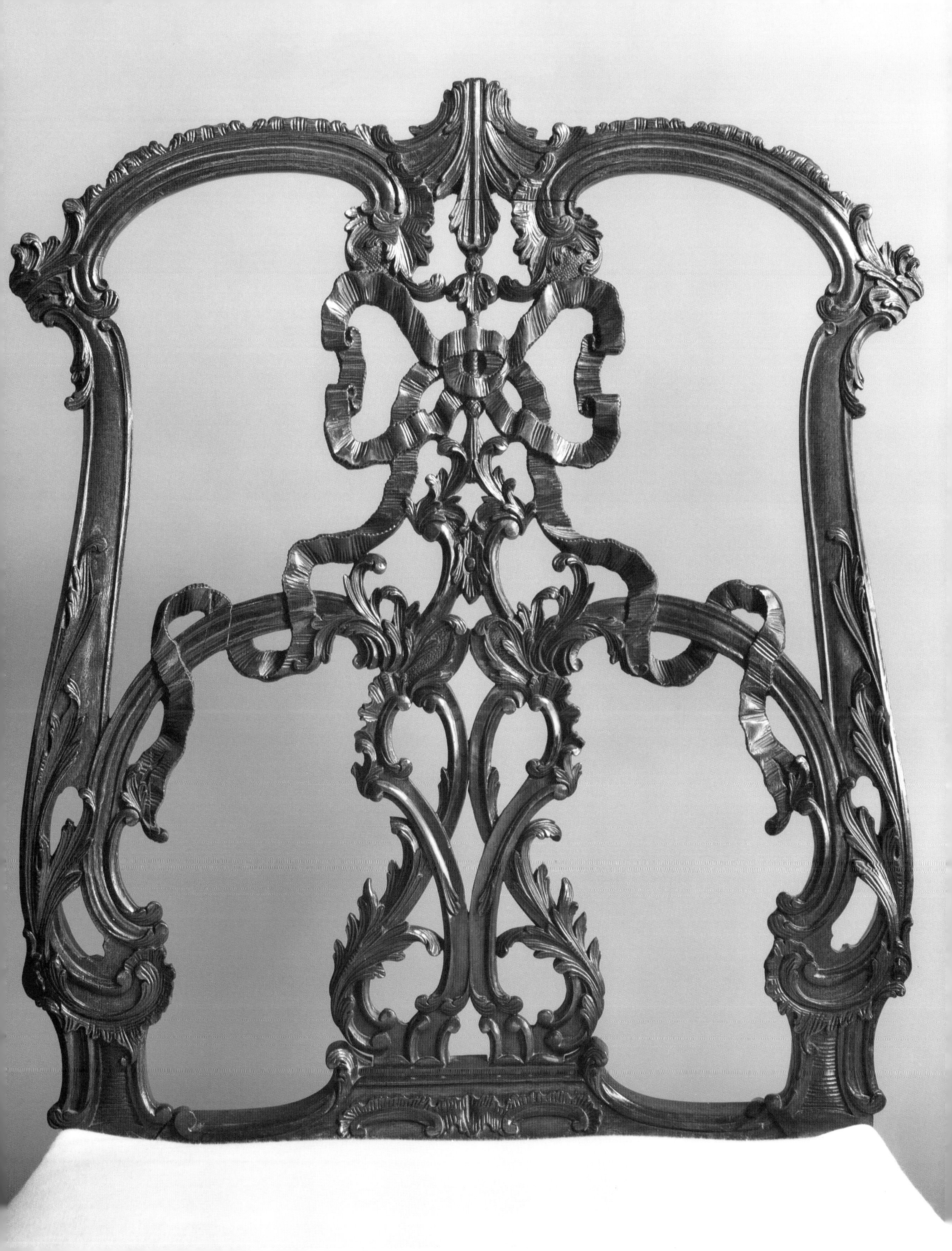

N.º XXII
French Chairs.

Pub: according to Act of Parliam.t 1759.
I. Taylor sculp.

ABOVE
9. A design by Thomas Chippendale for a 'French' chair, plate XXII in the third edition of *The Gentlemen and Cabinet-Makers' Director* of 1763, the plate itself is dated 1759.
OPPOSITE
A 'French' chair, c.1760, one of a pair based on plate XXII in Chippendale's *Director* of 1763.

14. Dell, *Furniture in the Frick Collection*, Vol. VI, pp. 212–31.

Court. The house remained in the possession of his descendants until it became a college in 1950. Unfortunately, it is not known when the chairs first entered the house, the interiors of which, even in the eighteenth century, were not sympathetic to the design of the chairs. They are possibly the finest examples of a design by Chippendale and their quality indicates that they are from his workshop.

Chippendale's *Director* also includes designs for 'French' chairs (Fig. 9), showing one of a pair in mahogany which are based on plate XXII of the third edition of 1763, the plate itself being dated 1759. Conceived in the full rococo style, they include all the elements associated with that design, including flowing acanthus scrolls, ruffles and cabochons adorning a richly moulded and curved frame. The design of the larger gilt wood example (Fig. 10) is also closely related to *Director* designs. One of a pair, they were originally acquired as part of a larger suite by the sixth Duke of Devonshire from Lady Canterbury. Her husband was speaker of the House of Commons from 1817 to 1834, and it is believed that they formed part of the furnishings of the Speaker's residence in the old Palace of Westminster, destroyed by fire in 1834. Upholstered *à chassis*, they were originally covered with Gobelins tapestry which was removed by Henry Clay Frick when he purchased the suite in 1914. Having sold the English frames, the tapestries were placed on modern copies of eighteenth-century French chairs.[14]

The work of Lord Burlington and his circle had been ornamented with rococo designs since the late 1740s. In the early 1760s the fashion for the rococo form remained just as strong, as shown by the third edition of the *Director* published in 1763. However, aristocratic travellers on the Grand Tour, accompanied by young architects such as Robert Adam and James Athenian Stuart, revived the interest in the classical world and Palladianism.

The documented work undertaken by the architect Robert Adam and various firms of cabinet-makers, including Thomas Chippendale, Vile and Cobb, William France and Samuel Norman, for Sir Lawrence Dundas in the 1760s, neatly illustrates the manner in which neoclassicism became assimilated with, and finally superseded, the rococo. Probably

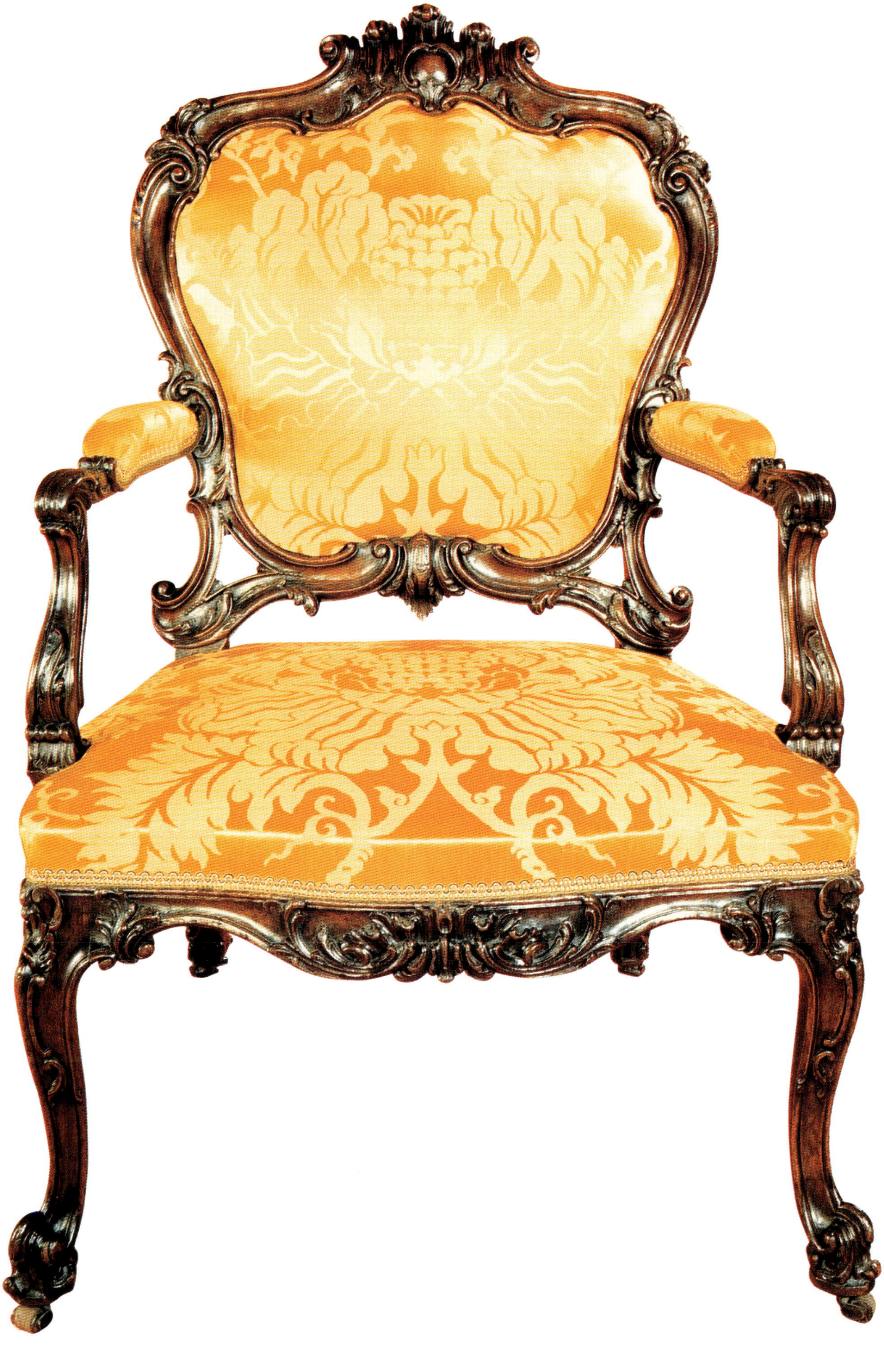

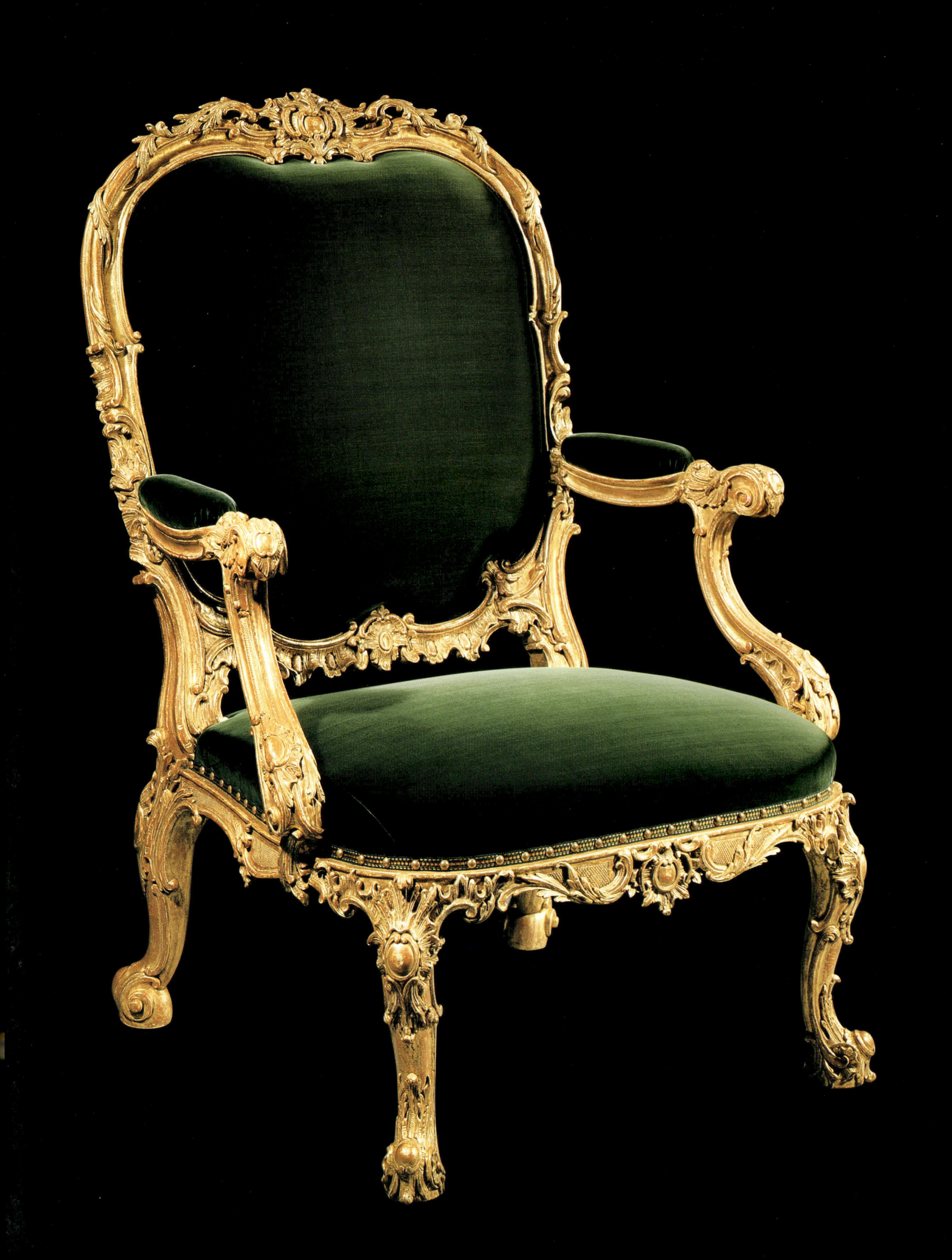

OPPOSITE
10. A gilt wood example of a 'French' chair, c.1765, that relates closely to designs in Thomas Chippendale's *The Gentlemen and Cabinet-Makers' Director* of 1763. The chair may have formed part of a suite that furnished the Speaker's residence in the old Palace of Westminster, which was destroyed by fire in 1834.

11. A pair of gilt wood chairs in the French style that relate to engravings in Thomas Chippendale's *The Gentlemen and Cabinet-Makers' Director* of 1763. This pair of chairs was probably supplied to Sir Lawrence Dundas in the 1760s for Moor Park.

supplied for his Hertfordshire seat, Moor Park, in around 1763, the pair of gilt wood chairs (Fig. 11) are clearly in the French style, their curvilinear frames being accentuated by the strongly scrolled arms and toes, ornamented with acanthus; again related to engravings in the 1763 *Director*. Dundas was a wealthy Scottish entrepreneur who had amassed a fortune during the Jacobite Revolution, the Seven Years' War, and speculation in Government stock and the East India Company. He acquired Moor Park in 1763, a mansion dating from the 1720s and designed by Leoni in high Italianate baroque with decoration by Amigoni and Thornhill. He commissioned Robert Adam to redesign the interior, including the Tapestry Gallery, for which Adam designed the ceiling and commissioned a set of Gobelins tapestries in 1767 from Jacques Neilson, which were delivered in 1769. After Sir Lawrence's death in 1781, Moor Park was sold in 1784 and the tapestries were removed to his London house in Arlington Street. Although the house passed through several hands before it became the property of Lord Ebury in the early twentieth century, it is clear that some of Dundas's original furniture remained *in situ*, including a suite of seat furniture supplied by James Lawson for the Banqueting Hall. Designed in the neoclassical manner, these were sold in 1919 and are now at Kenwood House. The present pair is shown in a photograph of the White Drawing-Room at Moor Park,[15] but the date of their removal is not known, although the present chairs, together with four others and a sofa, are presumably those in the collection of Sir Everard Radcliffe, Bart., of Rudding Park in Yorkshire, in the 1960s.[16] Unfortunately, although a number of the accounts for furnishing his London house at 19 Arlington Street are preserved in the Dundas archives, those for the Moor Park suite have not been traced. Two other suites of seat furniture that are recorded in these accounts were supplied by Thomas Chippendale. The first of these, supplied for the Long Drawing-Room in 1766, is again in the French style, but is somewhat lighter in profile and has a show wood back. The second, which was supplied for the Salon in 1765, is designed in the nascent neoclassical style, its upright back with a reeded frame bound with acanthus leaves

15. Stratton, *The English Interior*, Plate LXXXII.
16. *The Antique Collector*, August 1972, p. 180.

surmounted by an anthemion, the seat frame carved with sphinx and on paw feet.[17] The original drawing by Robert Adam for the sofa still exists; it is the only existing design by him that was with certainty executed by Chippendale.

Also dating from the early 1760s is the pair of carved gilt wood chairs from Spencer House in London (Fig. 12). Again showing the curvilinear form of 'French' chairs, they are, however, far more angular, the frames having 'sharper' edges. They are decorated with fluting, strings of husks, and fan-shaped petal ornament. Commissioned by John, first Earl Spencer (1734–83) for his new mansion in St James's, they were part of a suite of some thirty armchairs, four sofas and sixteen side chairs. The first architect employed by Lord Spencer was John Vardy 'whose designs for the exterior … and ground floor mark the evolution from Palladianism towards a Neo-Classicism inspired by the architecture of ancient Rome', and 'James "Athenian" Stuart, who pioneered the use of Greek architectural ornament in the decoration of the first floor rooms'.[18] The design for the present chairs has been traditionally ascribed to Stuart, although there are no extant drawings by any designer which relate to them. There are also two other almost identical suites of chairs, which are now at the Spencer's family seat at Althorp. One of these is of mahogany, the other white japanned and parcel gilt. Simon, first Earl Harcourt, commissioned another almost identical suite for Nuneham Park in Oxford; Stuart was recorded as working there for Lord Harcourt in the 1750s and 60s.[19] It has been suggested that John Gordon (1748–96),[20] who was later in partnership with John and Richard Taitt, possibly supplied all of the suites. Gordon supplied other chairs to the Duke of Atholl in the 1750s and 60s that have a similar profile to the present examples, all having a shared 'cupid's bow' seat rail. A number of accounts dated 1767 survive, rendered to Lord Spencer for work undertaken by Gordon and Taitt at his various houses, although it appears that his widow burned many of the earlier papers after his death.

Another cabinet-maker used by Stuart was John Adair (fl. 1749–69) of St Anne's Court in Covent Garden, who, under Stuart's supervision, worked as

17. Gilbert, *The Life and Work of Thomas Chippendale*, Vol. II, figs 176, 177.
18. Friedman, *Spencer House: Chronicle of a Great London Mansion*.
19. Sotheby's London, 3 July 2003, sale catalogue, lots 104, 105, 106, 107.
20. Beard and Gilbert, *op. cit.*, pp. 355–7.

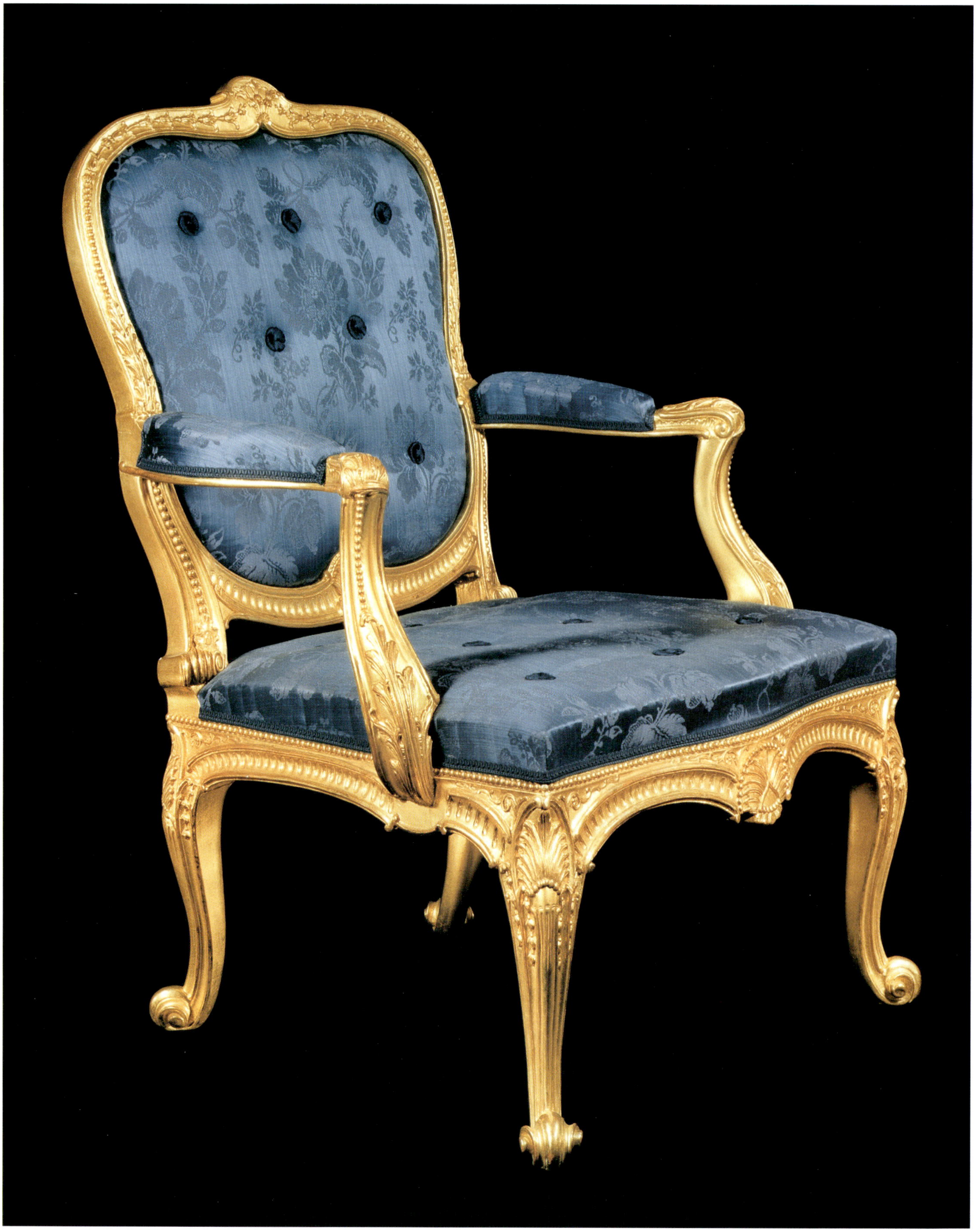

OPPOSITE

12. One of a pair of carved gilt wood chairs dating from the early 1760s that originally formed part of a suite comprising thirty armchairs, four sofas and sixteen side chairs commissioned by John, first Earl Spencer, for Spencer House in St James's, London.

a carver and gilder at Shugborough.[21] A recently discovered account dated 4 August 1764 for '2 Rich Oval Burnish Gold Glass Frames' and for '2 Bracket Tables' delivered to Nuneham in 1763 and 1764 for Earl Harcourt, is annotated 'by Mr. Stuart'.[22] The pair of tables, now in a private collection, is of *demi-lune* form, the fluted friezes with suspended garlands of fruit and flowers. This decoration is closely related to a pair of rectangular pier tables formerly at Spencer House, indicating a common designer and cabinet-maker.

The final pair of chairs (Fig. 13) is again designed in the French taste, with their oval backs, curiously curved arms and cabriole legs. In conception and profile they are much smaller and, if one can use the expression, much daintier than the previous examples. Their carved decoration of husks and leaves is smaller and more detailed, illustrating the attention of the designer who wished to achieve harmony within a neoclassical interior.

The chairs are part of a suite including a confidante sofa, five window seats and eight armchairs, some of these pieces being in the Metropolitan Museum of Art in New York. They were commissioned by John Morant (c.1720–91), who was a wealthy Jamaican estate owner, for either his London house at 17 Park Lane or for Brockenhurst Park in Hampshire, where they are shown in the Music Room in 1956, prior to the demolition of the mansion. Acquired in 1760, the house was extensively remodelled in the 1770s by the architect George Richardson, a close associate of Robert and James Adam. Cabinet-makers mentioned in Morant's accounts and notebooks include Thomas Chippendale, Gordon and Taitt, Alexander Murray and Francis Richardson, indicating payments rather than specific commissions. Although he is not mentioned in these manuscripts, a possible attribution to John Linnell (1729–96)[23] can be made, as the design of these chairs is closely related to a drawing dated around 1775–80 by this maker.[24]

John Linnell, the son of William Linnell, had 'by 1765 certainly mastered Neo-Classical form and ornament'.[25] He had a number of important patrons, some of whom were closely connected with Robert Adam. These included William Drake of Shardeloes,

21. Beard and Gilbert, *op. cit.*, p. 2.
22. Sotheby's London, 3 July 2003, sale catalogue, pp. 162–3.
23. Beard and Gilbert, *op. cit.*, pp. 543–6.
24. Hayward and Kirkham, *William and John Linnell: Eighteenth Century London Furniture Makers*, Vol. II, p. 47, fig. 94.

Lord Scarsdale of Kedleston Hall, and Francis Child of Osterley House. His surviving designs chronicle in a fascinating way the progress of design and taste during the middle years of the eighteenth century through to the rococo period, which encompassed chinoiserie and gothic to neoclassicism.

Although the chairs illustrated above comprise a fraction of those that have passed through Hotspur's hands during the last eighty years, they clearly illustrate the firm's dedication to design and quality, and their commitment to preserving the skill and heritage of the English chair-maker.

SR

OPPOSITE

13. A pair of chairs in the French taste, c.1775, with oval backs, curved arms and cabriole legs. They formed part of a suite comprising a confidante sofa, five window seats and eight armchairs and were commissioned by the wealthy Jamaican estate owner, John Morant.

25. Beard and Gilbert, *op. cit.*, p. 544.

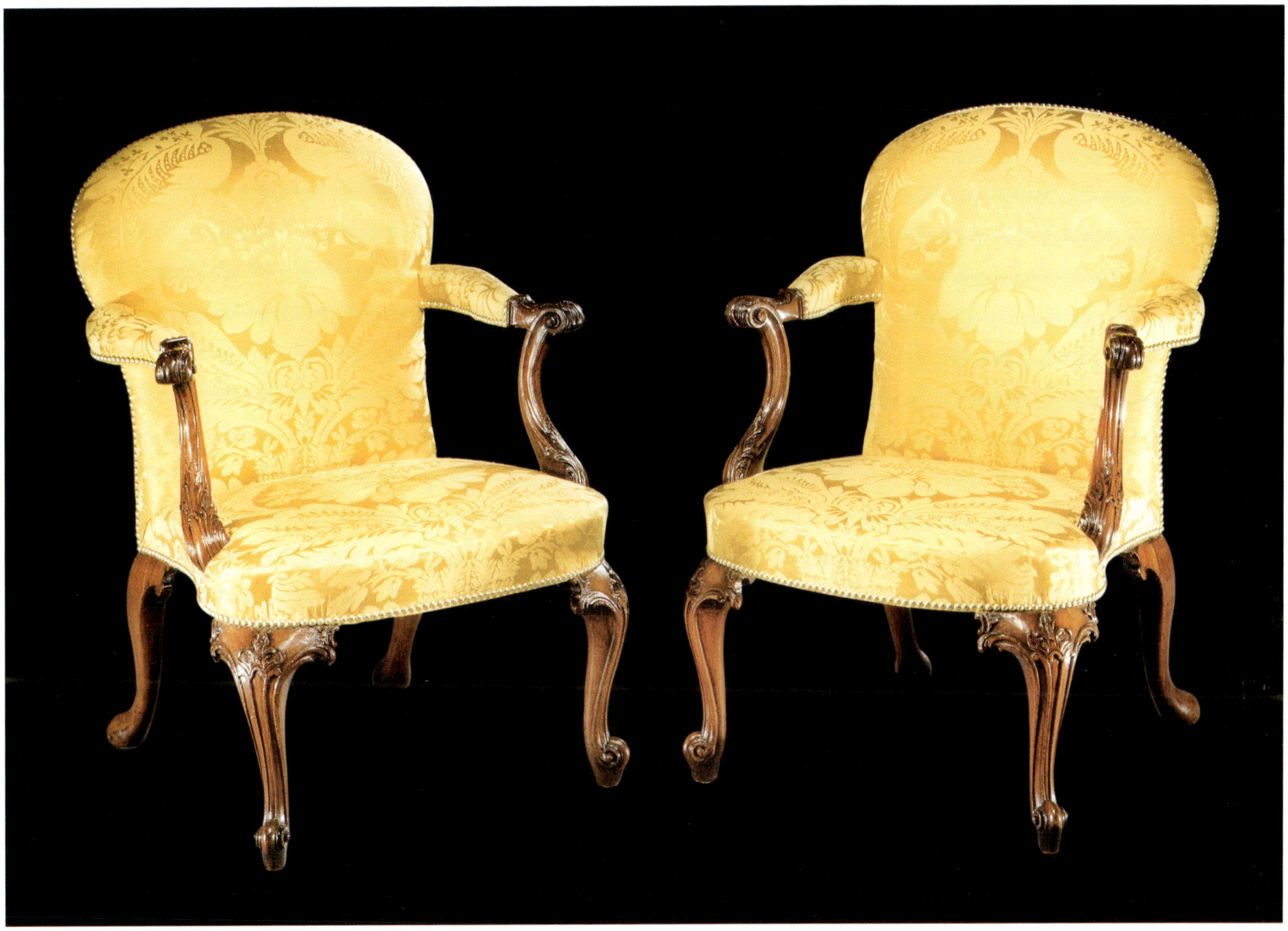

CATALOGUE 1
A walnut chair-back settee, c.1725.
H: 41¾" (106 cm); W: 59" (150 cm);
D: 22½" (57 cm).
In the style of Giles Grendey.

The two linked chair backs with vase-shaped splats are veneered in fine burr walnut and are surmounted by a double shaped head rail, each of which is carved with shells and foliage. The well shaped open arms have carved eagle head terminals, and the shaped drop-in seat is covered in fine contemporary floral needlework of brilliant colouring. The walnut veneered seat frame is supported on three cabriole front legs, carved with a shell motif hipped up into the seat frame and flanked by 'C'-scrolls that terminate in boldly carved claw and ball feet.

LITERATURE
Edwards, *The Dictionary of English Furniture*, revised edition, Vol. III, Plate V. A similar settee is in the Percival Griffiths Collection.

PROVENANCE
Private collection, England.

CATALOGUE 2
A gilt gesso stool, c.1725.
H: 18" (46 cm); W: 25½" (65 cm);
D: 18½" (47 cm).

There is an element of sophistication and great skill of design in this gilt gesso stool with fine cabriole legs, decorated with acanthus on the knees and terminating in bold claw and ball feet of an almost Irish form. The cabriole legs are united by carved and shaped stretchers, a feature found on more important seat furniture; notice also how the drop-in seat is contained in a shaped frame that is carved in gesso with flowers and strap-work.

LITERATURE
Lennox-Boyd, *Masterpieces of English Furniture: The Gerstenfeld Collection*, p. 220, fig. 55.
Christie's Review, 1983, p. 201.

PROVENANCE
Christie's sold an identical pair of stools in their sale at Godmersham Park, the home of Mrs Robert Tritton, 6–9 June 1983, lot 22.

CATALOGUE 3
A walnut wing chair, c.1733.
H: 45" (114 cm); W: 33" (84 cm);
D: 24" (61 cm).

Collectors of eighteenth-century furniture highly prize original seat coverings of needlework, crewelwork, damask or leather, but, needless to say, few examples of chairs, stools or settees retain their original covers. This wing chair is one of the lucky survivors, with its original crewelwork covers of richly coloured floral decoration on a white ground. It is additionally interesting and rare because the chair's crewel-work cover is signed and dated: 'S.C. 1733', thus making this chair one of great importance to the serious collector.

PROVENANCE
Private collection, Canada.

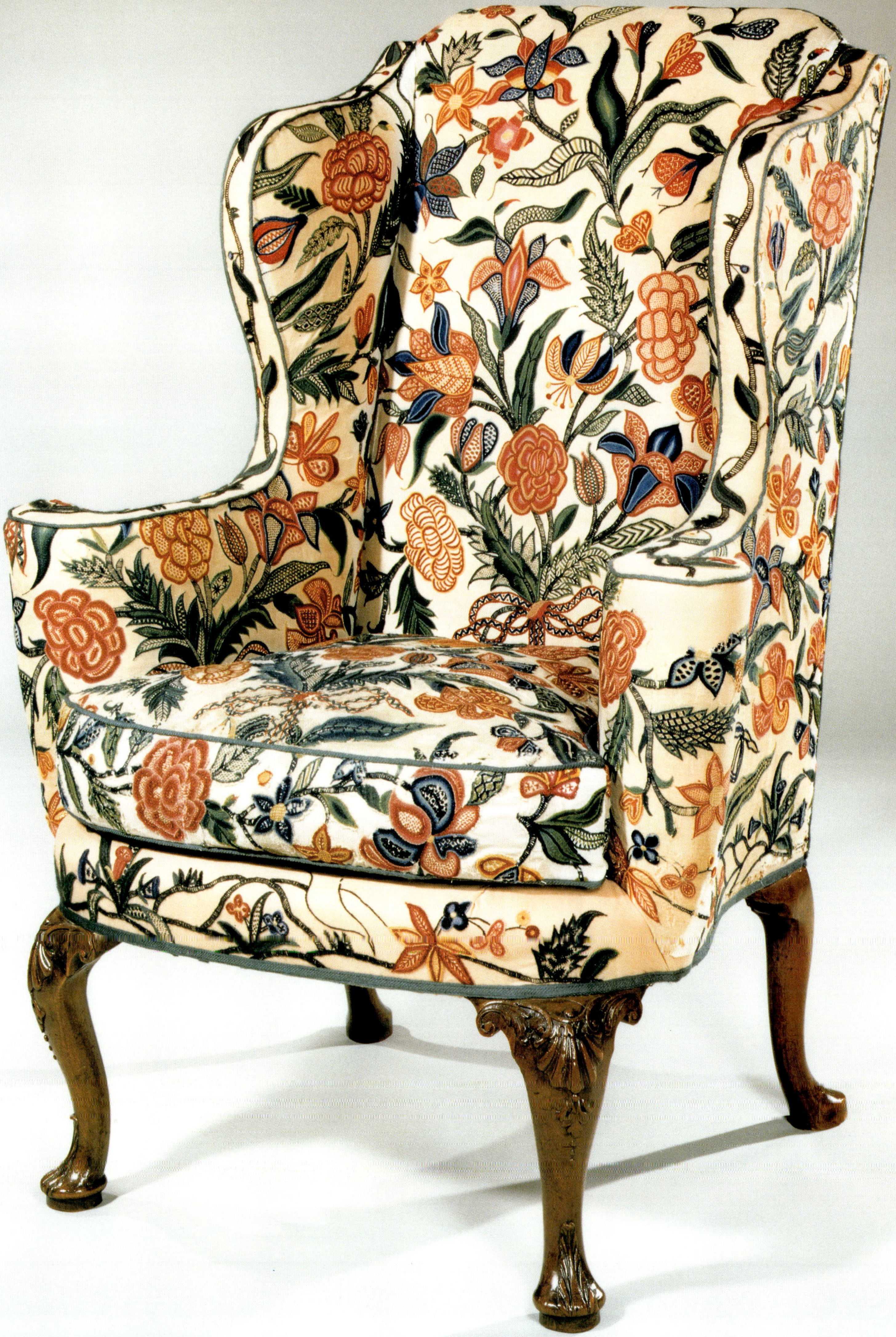

CATALOGUE 4
A walnut, parcel gilt stool
(one of a pair), c.1745.
H: 17¼" (44 cm); W: 21½" (55 cm);
D: 17½" (44.5 cm).

This is a very complicated design for a pair of walnut stools of this period, which are enhanced cleverly by parcel gilt to the carved decoration. This decorative feature is quite common for seat furniture and tables and highlights splendidly the enrichments to the frame. Here we have the usual shell motifs, parcel gilded and hipped up into the frame, which effectively extend the leg, making it more elegant; the carved ears are treated in much the same way with parcel gilding, as indeed are the foliate clasps and the unusual ruffled ankles that overlap the shell-form feet.

CATALOGUE 5
A mahogany hall chair, c.1760.
H: 36″ (91.5 cm); W: 23½″ (60 cm);
D: 15″ (38 cm).

Surely one of the most exuberantly carved rococo hall chairs extant, this remarkable example is carved wood but resembles bronze or marble sculpture. Hall chairs are usually simple and plain and very practical – they suffer a great deal of wear and tear – and I must admit that I have never seen this superior model before, belonging to the Chippendale period of full rococo seat furniture.

PROVENANCE
Private collection, Switzerland.

CATALOGUE 6
A mahogany armchair (one of a pair), in the manner of Mayhew and Ince, c.1760.
H: 39½" (100 cm); W: 25" (63.5 cm); D: 19½" (49.5 cm).

This elegant pair of chairs incorporates an extraordinary mixture of designs that are obviously influenced by Plate X in *The Universal System of Household Furniture* of 1762 by Ince and Mayhew.[1] The cartouche-shaped backs are elaborately carved in the rococo taste with flared and pierced central splats, each flanked by carved roundels. The open arms are well shaped with down-swept supports that are carved with cabouchons, to meet a compass-shaped seat; note how elaborate the carved decoration is on the cabriole front legs, with cabouchons, acanthus decoration and complicated scroll toes. I find the design particularly pleasing and sophisticated and most uncommon.

1. Ince and Mayhew/Mayhew and Ince were not themselves consistent when referring to the Company. *The Universal System of Household Furniture* is by Ince and Mayhew, so it does seem appropriate to refer as such with reference to the book. Recent research (Charles Cator and Hugh Roberts, forthcoming) suggests, however, that Mayhew was the commercial strength behind the business, while Ince was the draughtsman, so in this volume we prefer to refer to Mayhew and Ince, in line with current research.

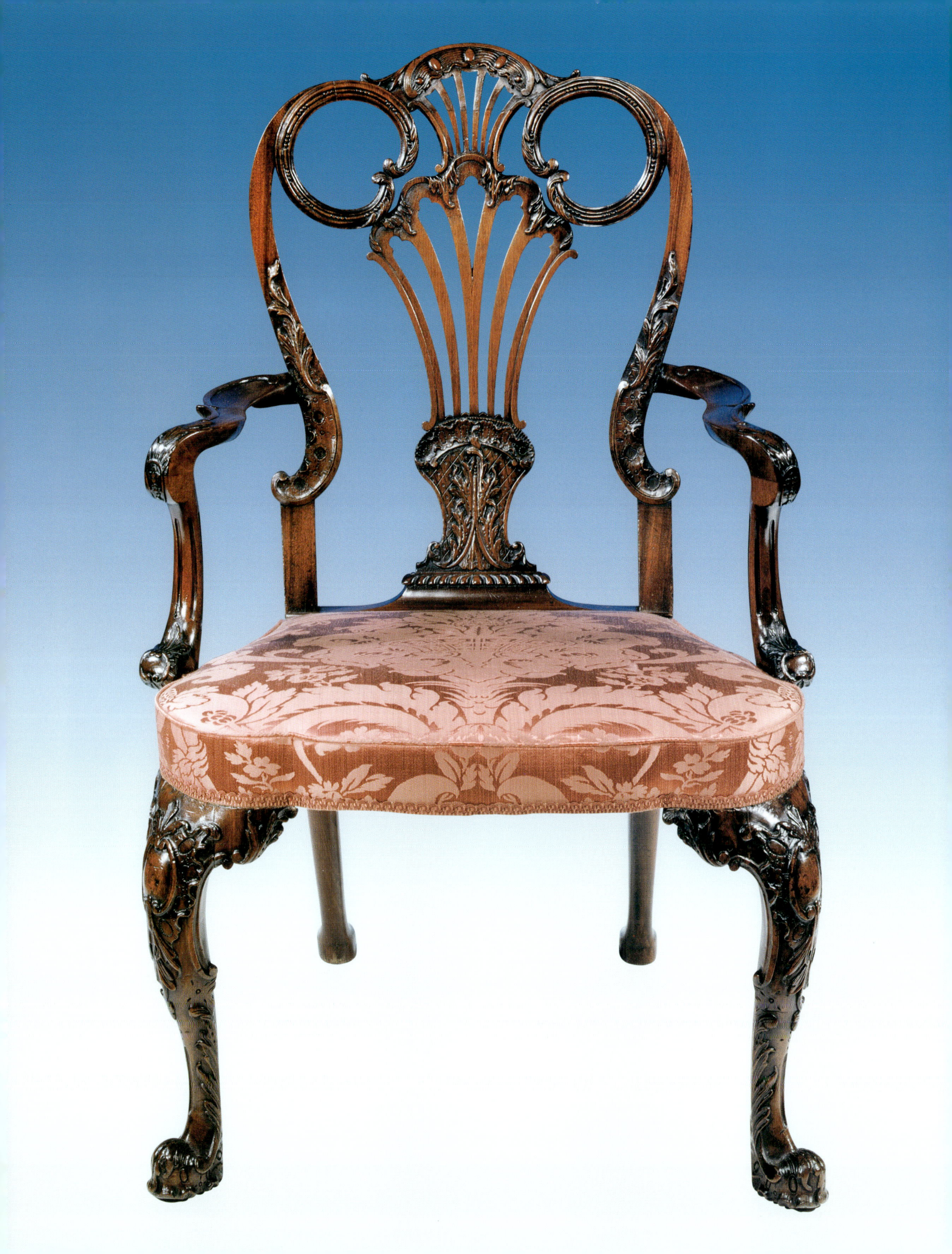

CATALOGUE 7
A gilt wood *bergère* chair, c.1775.
H: 44" (112 cm); W: 28" (71 cm);
D: 21" (53.5 cm).

This chair is an example of elegance and beauty that is difficult to match in the neoclassical period. The oval upholstered back has a show wood gilt frame carved with husks, with foliate cresting at the top. The undulating, arched top wings, all with show wood gilt framing, are carved with chains of husks with upholstered arm pads, and fitted with a loose cushion. The seat rails are carved with continuous honeysuckle motifs, all raised on elegant square tapered legs with carved flowers and square *paterae* below. The design of this armchair has very strong affinities to the workshops of John Linnell.

LITERATURE
C.I.N.O.A. *International Art Treasures Exhibition*, Victoria and Albert Museum, 1962, no. 103, Plate 73.

PROVENANCE
Private collection.

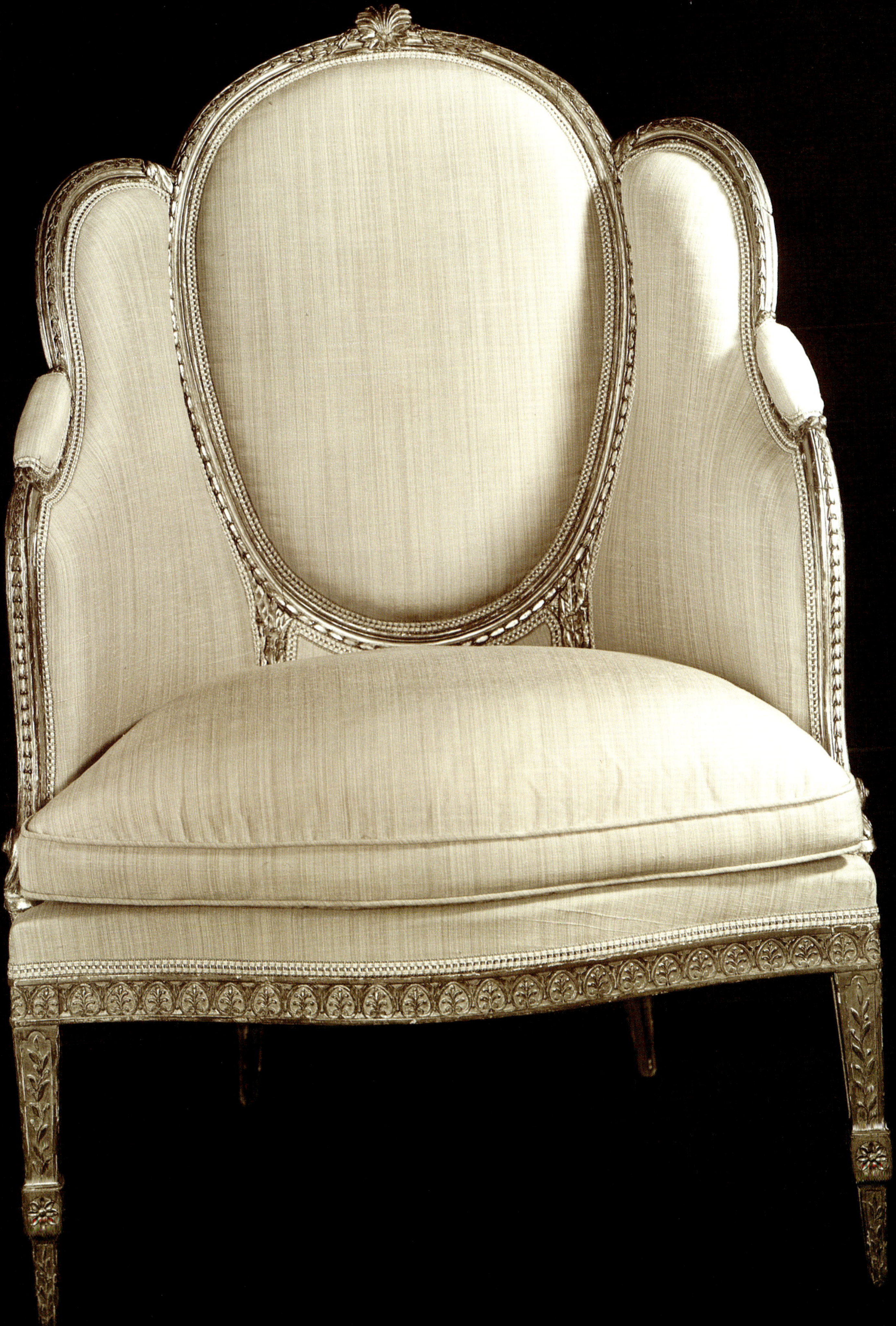

Glass objects and chandeliers

MARTIN MORTIMER

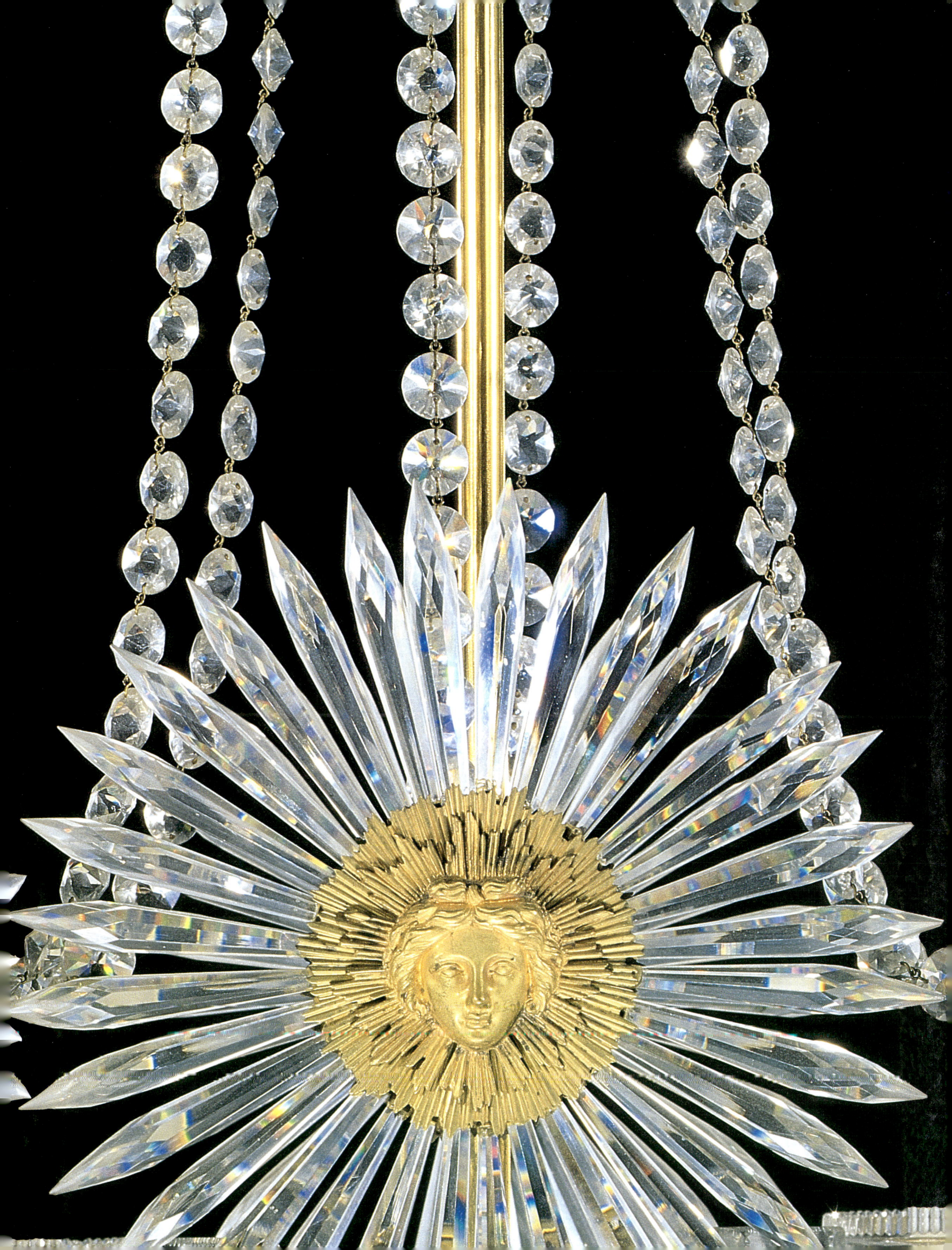

PREVIOUS PAGE
(Detail from p. 182, cat. no. 12)
A 'sunburst' from the chandelier
for six lights, c.1815.

GLASS OBJECTS AND CHANDELIERS

HOTSPUR, FOUNDER EXHIBITORS since 1934, returned to the Antique Dealers' Fair at Grosvenor House after a temporary absence in 1960 and took the stand opposite ours. I had met Rob Kern before, he was an exceptionally kindly man, generous with his knowledge, gained from a lifetime trading in the finest English furniture and specialising, at that time, in early mahogany. He was the second generation in the enterprise and had recently moved the company back to London from Richmond.

That year, or soon after, there bounced onto the scene an immaculate young man apparently little more than fifteen years of age, despite his assurance that he had just completed his national service in the army. I was bemused by his fresh complexion and youthful enthusiasm. He drew me onto the stand to point out constructional details of some piece of furniture, holding forth just like his father, but without his father's voice, a homely buzz. I gradually let my reservations about this upstart ease and let him dance about me like a summer bluebottle.

Very soon we started a long association buying and selling the finest period-glass light fittings. Although from time to time we were able to offer fittings in our possession to Hotspur on a half-share basis, it has to be said that more often the impetus came from Robin. He needed our specialist input, we needed his contacts.

An early occasion took us to Dublin: 'Ronnie Macdonnell has a pair of Irish mirror wall lights, old fella. Let's go and have a look at them.' We did; they were good and we bought them. As an unheard-of bonus, Ronnie also tentatively offered us a single. This, too, was genuine (they frequently are not). A glance at the backboard of the mirror showed writing. I hardly dared look. It was signed 'John D Aykbowm', a celebrated name in Irish glass. We trudged back through Heathrow in triumph, bits in a box, the mirrors under our arms. The signed bracket, having been to New York, is now in the Cecil Higgins Museum in Bedford.

Over the years we have handled several more of these: the epitome of Irish glass. Another trip found us in Copenhagen buying a fine Parker chandelier. After restoration it went to Tel Aviv, thence to South Africa, finally (at present) to Chester

GLASS OBJECTS AND CHANDELIERS

Square in London. When things were quiet Robin was restless. 'What about looking round Thomas Goode's, they've lots of chandeliers.' We bought a huge Hancock chandelier. It had hung there for years, subject only to spray cleaning. It was sticky, and its nozzles filled to the brim with cleaning liquid. It soon went to a wealthy client in Eaton Square. There was no hook, no access to the floor above, and a major dinner party was pending. The newly decorated ceiling was taken down, a steel joist inserted and all was put back, redecorated, and the chandelier installed in time.

In 1976 Robin negotiated the sale of another particularly fine mid-eighteenth-century chandelier with the City of Philadelphia for the Independence Hall, to celebrate the bicentenary of the Signing of the Declaration of Independence (see p. 164, cat. no. 2).

In 1963, Robin's brother Brian, an engineer, left de Havilland's and joined Hotspur. It was a good partnership, the brothers working closely together for many years. During that time, Brian organised an exhibition of Matthew Boulton's ormolu for Hotspur's Golden Jubilee Exhibition in 1974.[1] After thirty-six years, Brian retired to enjoy a more varied life, and Christopher Payne now works alongside Robin.

Robin remains active. Little of that boyish enthusiasm has ebbed. He is still in the office by eight in the morning and on the telephone thereafter, keeping contact with friends and searching for business. He remains a loyal friend, always ready for a half-share purchase. He retains the famous Kern charm. After forty years association with him there are no regrets save his (now overcome) sinister predilection for black candles, and the Hotspur telephone system which plays tunes on hold – a terrible penalty for the pleasure of hearing the silvery voice of Simone. I say no more!

To an extent the small selection of light fittings I have chosen traces the development of the English glass chandelier from its first appearance in the early eighteenth century prior to the advent of mass manufacture in the second half of the nineteenth century. It is no coincidence that given even this small sample, English light fittings take precedence, for as I note in

1. *Hotspur: Golden Jubilee 1924–1974*, June 1974, catalogue with contributions by Nicholas Goodison.

my book, *The English Glass Chandelier*[2] 'as technical potential developed, [chandeliers] were made in increasing numbers throughout Europe wherever demand and money combined to produce a market. Pre-eminent were those made in England, at least during the eighteenth century, for two reasons: one is a matter of taste, the other a matter of fact. Firstly, the chandeliers produced at the end of the eighteenth century by the best manufacturers surely surpass all before in terms of style, quality and fitness for purpose, and it is generally conceded that they surpass all continental parallels. Secondly, English chandeliers, almost from their first beginnings, were made with a degree of precision and mechanical accuracy not matched elsewhere.'

Some of England's most important manufacturers are represented here: William Parker, Parker and Perry, Hancock and Blades, Jerome Johnson and Moses Lafount, along with others who are less easy to identify. I have included an exquisite Irish mirror chandelier notable for its inventiveness as much as for its rarity. Another extraordinary survival is the cut-glass ewer and basin, so rarely found together as a pair, this one probably the work of Thomas Betts.

In the main the objects have come via my firm Delomosne and thus to Hotspur and hold interest for both their quality and design. In each case, Robin and I have shared the pleasure of finding these glorious chandeliers, candelabra and other glass objects and of restoring them on their way to a satisfied client. This enjoyable task of recollection brings back memories, for, like life itself, the objects hold for us numerous anecdotes and experiences.

MM

2. Mortimer, *The English Glass Chandelier*, Woodbridge, 2000.

CATALOGUE 1
A twelve-light chandelier of moulded glass, c.1735. English.
H: 44" (112 cm); W: 44" (112 cm).

The squat proportions of this chandelier should not detract from its historical interest. A set of three of this precise form hangs in the Long Gallery at Doddington Hall near Lincoln. There is a persistent tradition that they were acquired from the Lincoln Assembly Rooms. The late R. J. Charleston examined the Doddington chandeliers many years ago and, typically, took the opportunity to check the numbers stamped or engraved on the arm plates. Though slightly erratic, these clearly indicated there was once an extensive set, perhaps as many as nine.

The present example, now in the City Art Museum in St Louis, Missouri, fits a gap in the numerical order of the arms in the Doddington chandeliers, reasonably confirming that it was part of the original set. It is worth noting that the annular-moulded drip pans are of the pattern seen on the chandelier in the chapel of Emmanuel College, Cambridge. This chandelier was presented to the college in 1732. The short proportions perhaps indicate that the Assembly Rooms were low. They must also have been hot, the company energetically dancing beneath one hundred lit candles.

The famous York Assembly Rooms, designed by Lord Burlington and opened in 1732, were magnificent. Chandeliers were ordered for these rooms too, a gift from Lord Burlington to the city, and it is interesting to note that all, save the central fitting, were, like the Lincoln set, made of reticulated or diamond-moulded glass: the charming contemporary term being 'crinkled'. Two chandeliers from this series, cobbled up from incompatible parts but with a good number of stem pieces of crinkled glass, survive from the series in the Treasurer's House, a National Trust property in York.

CATALOGUE 2
A chandelier for twelve lights, c.1750.
English.
H: 57" (145 cm).

In 1976 Hotspur was approached by the City of Philadelphia. They were seeking a suitable chandelier for the Assembly Room of Independence Hall. It was here that the Declaration of Independence was signed in 1776, and the Hall was receiving a comprehensive restoration as part of the bicentenary celebrations of this historical event. The so-called Lafayette chandelier, previously hanging in the room, was considered unsuitable in terms of style and condition. It was an English neo-classical chandelier dating from about 1780, but had had a hard life and much alteration.

Hotspur approached Delomosne, and I was able to tell Robin about a fine mid-eighteenth-century chandelier we had recently acquired, and which was nearing the end of a programme of restoration. Robin was shown the components and urgently requested a photograph. Since this was not possible at that stage, I suggested an initial drawing with dimensions. Since Philadelphia was in an even greater hurry than Robin, my offer was accepted. I made a scale drawing, halved and sectioned, and, to everyone's surprise, the City bought the chandelier on sight of the drawing.

The chandelier dates from a period when few such fittings were being made. Indeed, one of the principal makers of lustres at this date advertised in 1761: 'Jerome Johnson has now made upwards of twenty.'

The proportions are excellent and there are no ornamental pendants; these arrived a few years later and were prolific by 1765. The pattern of the surface cutting, large diamonds of shallow profile with cross cuts, is comparatively flat, but the same soft cutting is consistent on all components: an indication of a comfortingly original state. This is an extremely rare chandelier for this date.

165

CATALOGUE 3
A cut-glass ewer and basin, c.1765.
English.

The rarity of this piece lies more in the basin than in the ewer. There are several examples of similar massive ewers of this date: one, for example, in the Victoria and Albert Museum, others in the Museum of London and in the Holburne Museum of Art in Bath. A further pair, now well known, surfaced when the remaining contents of Gunton Park in Norfolk were sold in 1980. They were blue.

   The probate valuation of the stock of Thomas Betts, the prominent London manufacturer and retailer lists: 'two large blue Ewers unfinished'. He died in 1765. None of the ewers listed above has a matching basin. In the days when these were made, one could have purchased whatever one liked, and many ewers might have been acquired without basins. It is thus the combination of the two pieces that is the rare feature here.

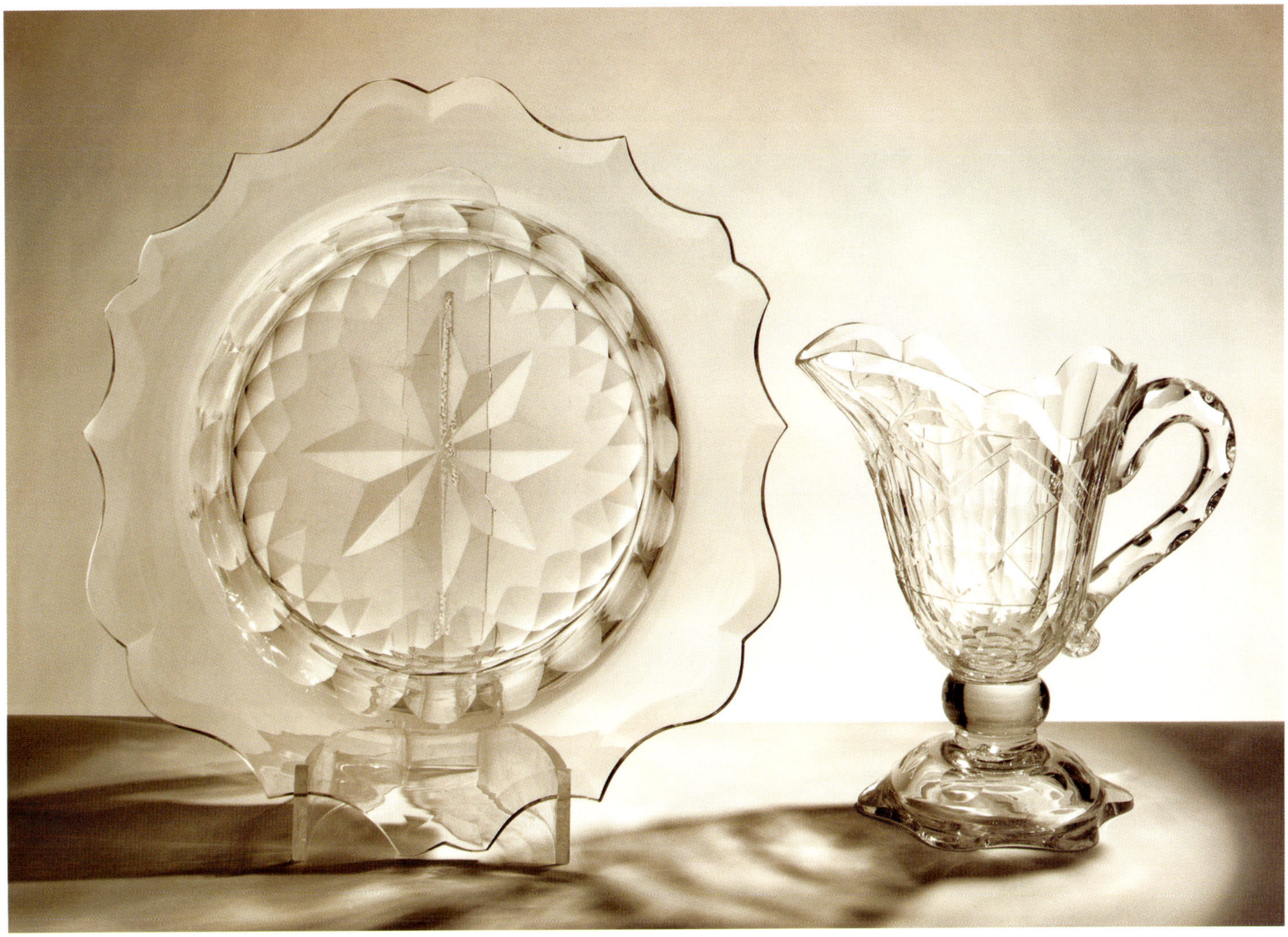

CATALOGUE 4
A mirror chandelier, c.1785, Irish.

The Irish were nothing if not inventive. They had the idea of hanging a small chandelier in front of a looking glass, the idea being to double the light source. Here, all the central stem pieces are cut in half and attached to the vertical frame member. Thus the five-arm fitting becomes a small ten-light chandelier. The looking glass is made in three parts, with the horizontal jewel-covered section supporting the plate for the five arms. No other Irish mirror chandelier of this type is recorded.
It appears that the Waterford Glass Works had a warehouse in Dublin. The name of John Kennedy appears in the directories as proprietor between 1789 and 1811. In 1804, he advertised in the *Belfast News Letter* that he had for sale at Bank House, Castle Street in Belfast: 'rich cut lustres and reflectors' amongst many other things.

169

CATALOGUE 5
Sweetmeat stand, c.1790.
English, probably London.
H: 28" (71 cm).

The base of this centrepiece is of a type normally seen as the support to a series of table candelabra popular at the end of the eighteenth century. These were made in various workshops but the best were those made at that time by William Parker and his son. Indeed, at present those are the only candelabra that can be closely attributed by comparison with documented examples. Here, the component parts of the sweetmeat stand fit with those of candelabra known to have been supplied by this maker. The jasper drums were frequently bought in from Wedgwood, but also from Turner and Adams. The use of yellow drops was a fashion popular for only a few years around the time this piece was made. Its survival is a miracle, as the Vandyke-bordered dishes are removable. In use it would have been at the centre of a busy dinner table, laden with sweetmeats for the dessert, the dishes passed around and replaced on the delicate glass arms by inexperienced and casual hands. It is in exceptionally fine condition, the dressings bright with few chips, indicating a relatively quiet life. Perhaps such an elaborate centrepiece was found to be impractical and it was packed away, reserved for use only on a special occasion.

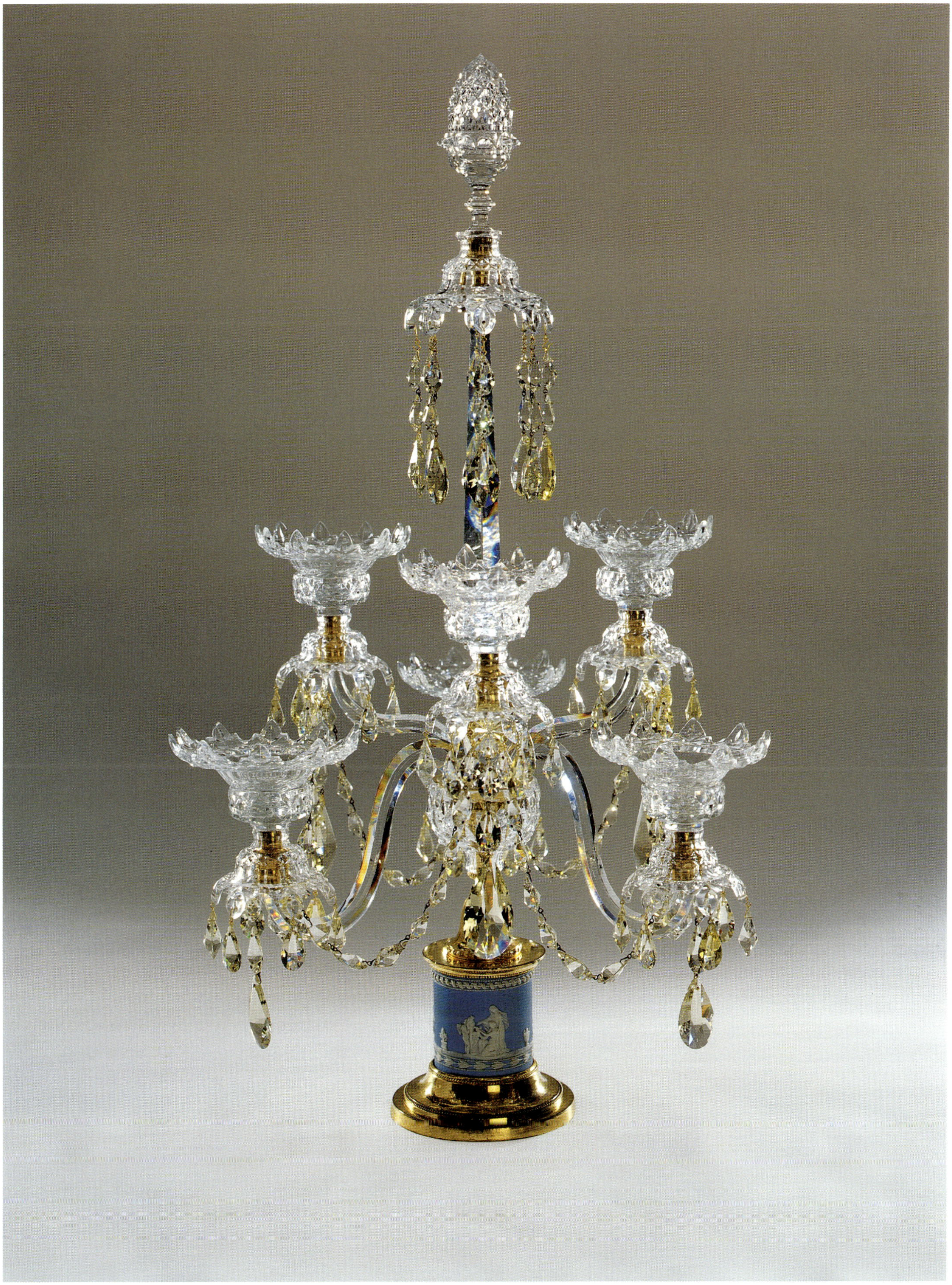

CATALOGUE 6
A pair of candelabra for two lights with bases of two-colour jasper mounted in ormolu, c.1795. Attributed to William Parker, 69 Fleet Street, London.
H: 38½" (98 cm); W: 19½" (49.5 cm); D: 13" (33 cm).

The layout of these magnificent candelabra, together with the patterns of the components, permits firm attribution to the workshop of William Parker. By the time these were made at the end of the eighteenth century, this celebrated concern was under the direction of William's son, Samuel. The design shows the workshop's inventiveness. Further examples with degrees of elaboration on a standard theme are to be seen at Chatsworth in candelabra supplied to the Duke of Devonshire by Parker as early as 1782. More similar is an outline drawing of instruction for assembly of a candelabrum in the collection at the Metropolitan Museum of Art in New York. Both of these examples, however, predate the present candelabra. Plain six-sided arms came into favour at the end of the century.

The upper structure of these rare fittings is excellent in terms of design and condition, but it is the quality of the bases that is the remarkable feature. Parker rarely asked his foundry to produce ormolu as elaborate as this, though there are other examples. The form of the ormolu mouldings is classic for Parker, but the depth of the castings and chasing of the decoration is quite exceptional. The two-colour jasper drums add further rarity; above all, the candelabra are of a huge size.

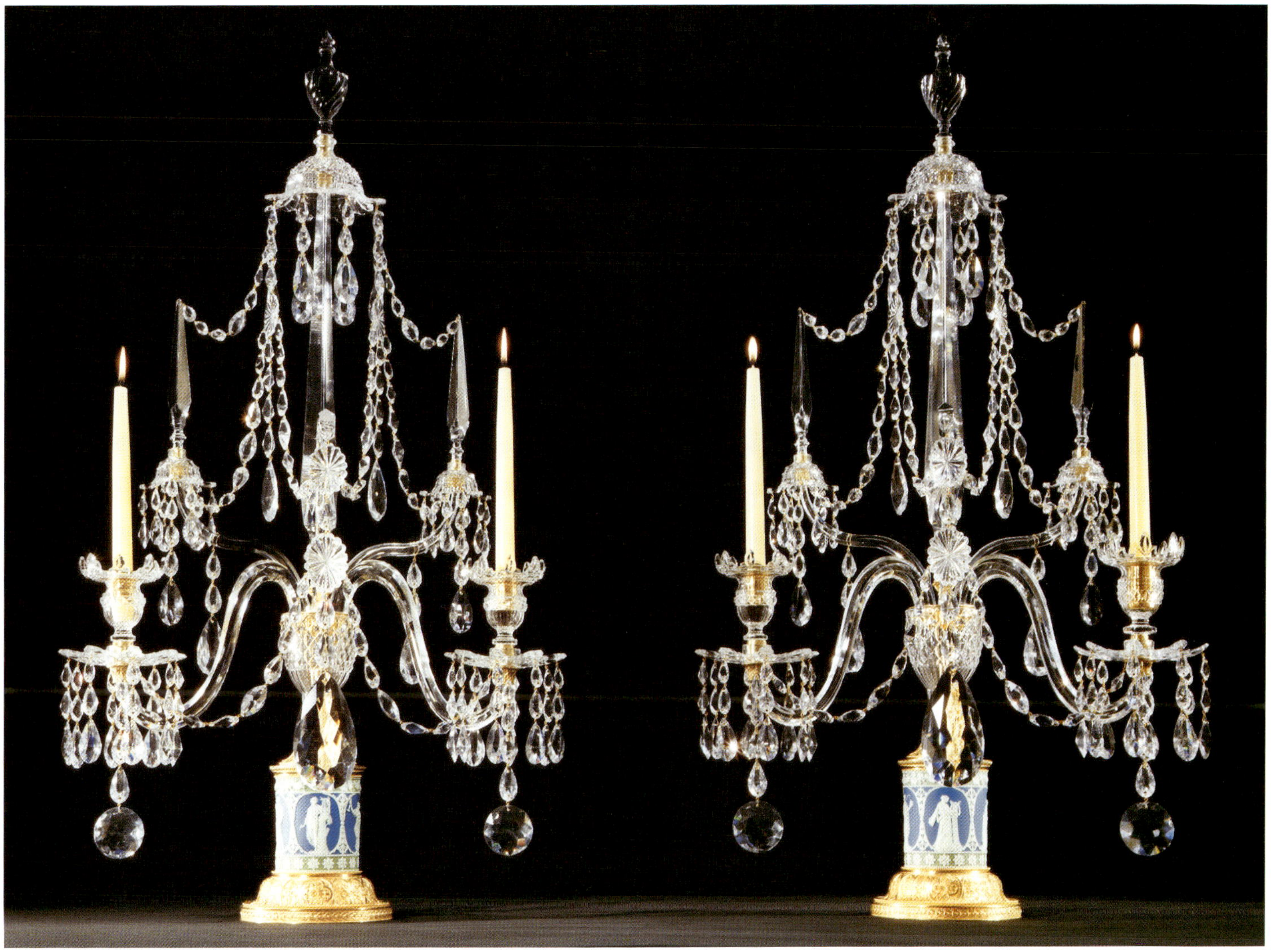

CATALOGUE 7
A chandelier for eight lights with
ormolu mounts, c.1795–1800.
English, probably Parker and Perry,
London.
H: 72" (183 cm); W: 45" (114 cm).

This chandelier illustrates the height that this formal neoclassical design reached at the end of the eighteenth century. Already makers were exploring other patterns and the first frame chandeliers were being installed with matching dense chains of drops hanging from ormolu frames, which supported candles held in short arms.

This chandelier is arranged in classic form with a vase centre, canopies above and below, and arms in two tiers. The upper tier bears spires or prisms, the lower, candle sconces and drip pans. The most costly of these chandeliers had chased ormolu furnishings, like this one. That the neoclassical chandelier was still being made after the close of the eighteenth century is confirmed by the known date, 1804, of the Saloon chandelier at Arbury Hall in Nuneaton.

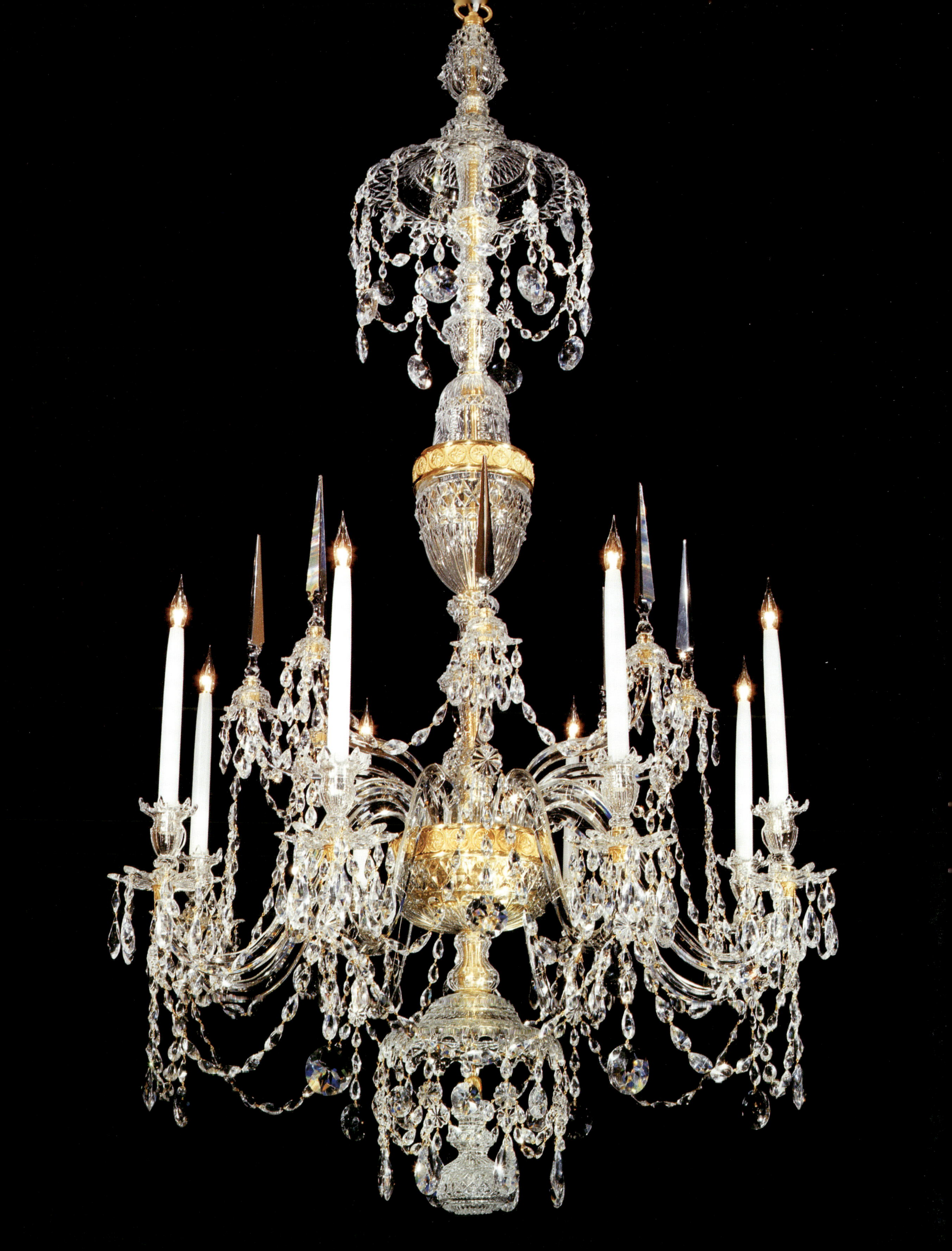

CATALOGUE 8
An eight-light chandelier and a pair
of similar wall brackets, c.1795–1805.
English, probably London.
Chandelier, H: 53" (135 cm);
candelabra, H: 28" (71 cm).

It is obvious that this chandelier and the following pair of wall brackets are designed on the same principle. Moses Lafount entered into agreement with the Cox brothers of the Falcon Glass House in December 1796. The agreement provides for the Cox's concern to supply the glass components for chandeliers and allied fittings made to the designs of Lafount.

The design for the upper crooks and lower arms allows the two components to appear as one, sweeping in an uninterrupted curve of glass through the central console. The design of Lafount fittings varies between examples, from simple moulded components to those of similar form competently cut. In the present case, the chandelier is fully cut; the wall brackets are fitted with drawn-moulded arms, a detail of manufacture frequently seen in this family.

Perhaps the Cox brothers provided for the simple finish only, while Lafount went elsewhere for richer detail. Most of the chandeliers so far seen have had cut components, yet in the Athenaeum in Bury St Edmunds there is a suite of seven chandeliers designed on the Lafount principle, all of which have drawn-moulded arms. They may date from 1804, the year in which the rooms were refurbished. The mounts of the present chandelier, as well as the pair of wall brackets, carry the stamp of Lafount as patentee, though it is possible more than one maker was used.

Articles of agreement between Moses Lafount, Alexander Thomas and James Cox for the exploitation of Lafount's invention are dated 19 December 1796 and read:

Moses Lafount of … county Middx. 'Lustre mounter'. The Coxes, 'both of the Falcon Glass House in the Parish of Christ Church in the county of Surrey, Glass manufacturers'. WHEREAS the said Moses Lafount after the great study industry and application hath invented a certain Plate & Hoop or Band of a circular or other form either attached to or detached from each other to be made use of in the Mounting of Glass Chandeliers Gerandoles or other Lustres which in consequence thereof are much more Elegant in form than any which have been heretofore used As by means of such Invention the Upper and Lower Branches have the Appearance of being one Branch only …[1]

The glass was, therefore, to be supplied by the Coxes at a mutually agreed price. The chandeliers were to be exposed at the Falcon Glass House, but also elsewhere as agreed between the parties, as well as sold to private customers. Lafount's name was to be used for the finished product.

1. Manuscript in the Guildford Museum.

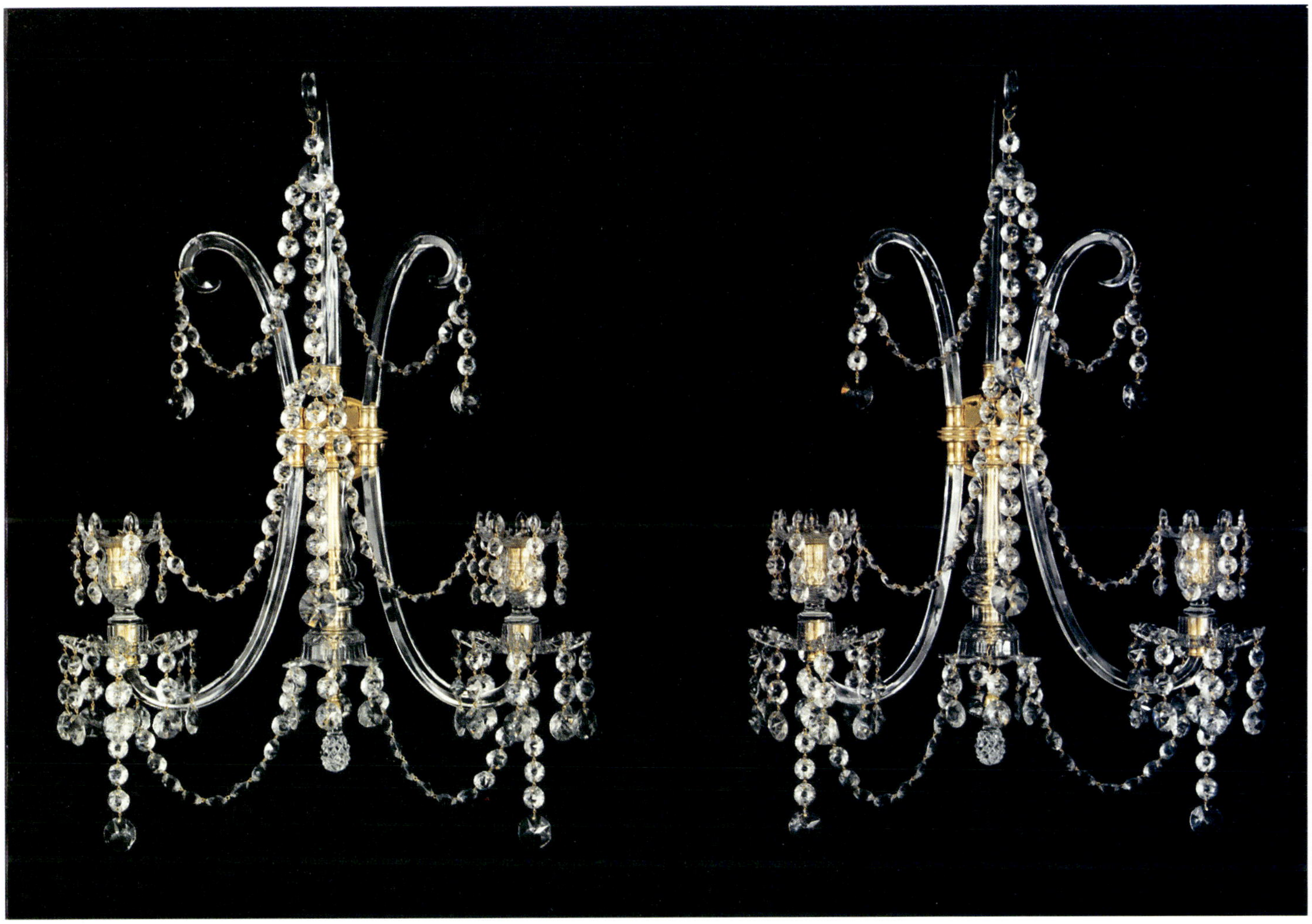

GLASS OBJECTS AND CHANDELIERS

CATALOGUE 9
A small chandelier of neoclassical form with glass branches for six lights, c.1805. English.
H: 48" (122 cm).

This chandelier illustrates the last of the elegant neoclassical style that dominated the final years of the eighteenth century. It still has glass stem pieces, but the urn centrepiece has evolved into an ovoid. The shallow profile of the arms, with a tight top bend and wide lower curve, allow this attribution to Parker and Perry.

178

CATALOGUE 10
A six-light chandelier with ormolu frame, fitted with storm shades with engraved borders, c.1800–10.
English.
H: 48" (122 cm).

This delightful chandelier illustrates very well the difficulties of attribution. The frame and layout conform to a type normally attributable to John Blades. The cutting of the pans supports this, being of a pattern known as pillar-and-diamond. Yet it is fitted with shades whose engraved border of palmettes matches those on the splendid pair of wall brackets at the Winterthur Museum in the United States. Furthermore, the Winterthur brackets have arms, the profiles of which are inescapably Parker and Perry. Of course, there was plenty of copying and there is the strong possibility that a maker independent of either contender supplied the shades. Perhaps the most prominent, though much larger, chandelier of this family is that of Boodle's Club in St James's. Note also that chains of drops, which provide the outline of the design, have superseded the principal stem pieces.

CATALOGUE 11
A chandelier of rare form, c.1815.
Possibly Hancock and John Blades,
London.
H: 54″ (137 cm); W: 29″ (74 cm).

This elaborate chandelier has candle nozzles of a pattern used by Hancock, yet it is suspended on chains, which, with their glass inserts, are unmistakably the signature of a creation by John Blades. The splendid ormolu frame contains a shallow dish cut with radial mitre flutes within a band of elongated diamonds. Although clearly not lit by oil, it falls into the category of chandelier known in the early nineteenth century as a Grecian lamp. The apparent anomaly in the varied components is readily explained: Hancock and Blades were both London retailers. The nozzles could have been made to a pattern preferred by either, perhaps made to order by a third maker. The probable sharing in the making of component parts makes accurate attribution difficult.

181

CATALOGUE 12
A chandelier for six lights, c.1810.
Probably Irish.
H: 54" (137 cm).

This extraordinary conceit appears to be unique in chandelier form. The 'sunbursts' appear not infrequently in candelabra, but not until now on chandeliers. When it was acquired it had no meaningful provenance, and it was the study of the quality of its ormolu and, more importantly, of its cut-glass elements that led to the tentative assumption of a probable Irish manufacture. The sunbursts were a nightmare to restore: each 'icicle' is plastered into a tiny cylindrical brass mount with a minute threaded stud so that the whole can screw into the ring, which lies behind the mask in splendour.

    When Robin announced its sale to the National Gallery of Victoria in Melbourne, Australia, my horrified comment was, 'You must be mad. It will never get there.' It did.

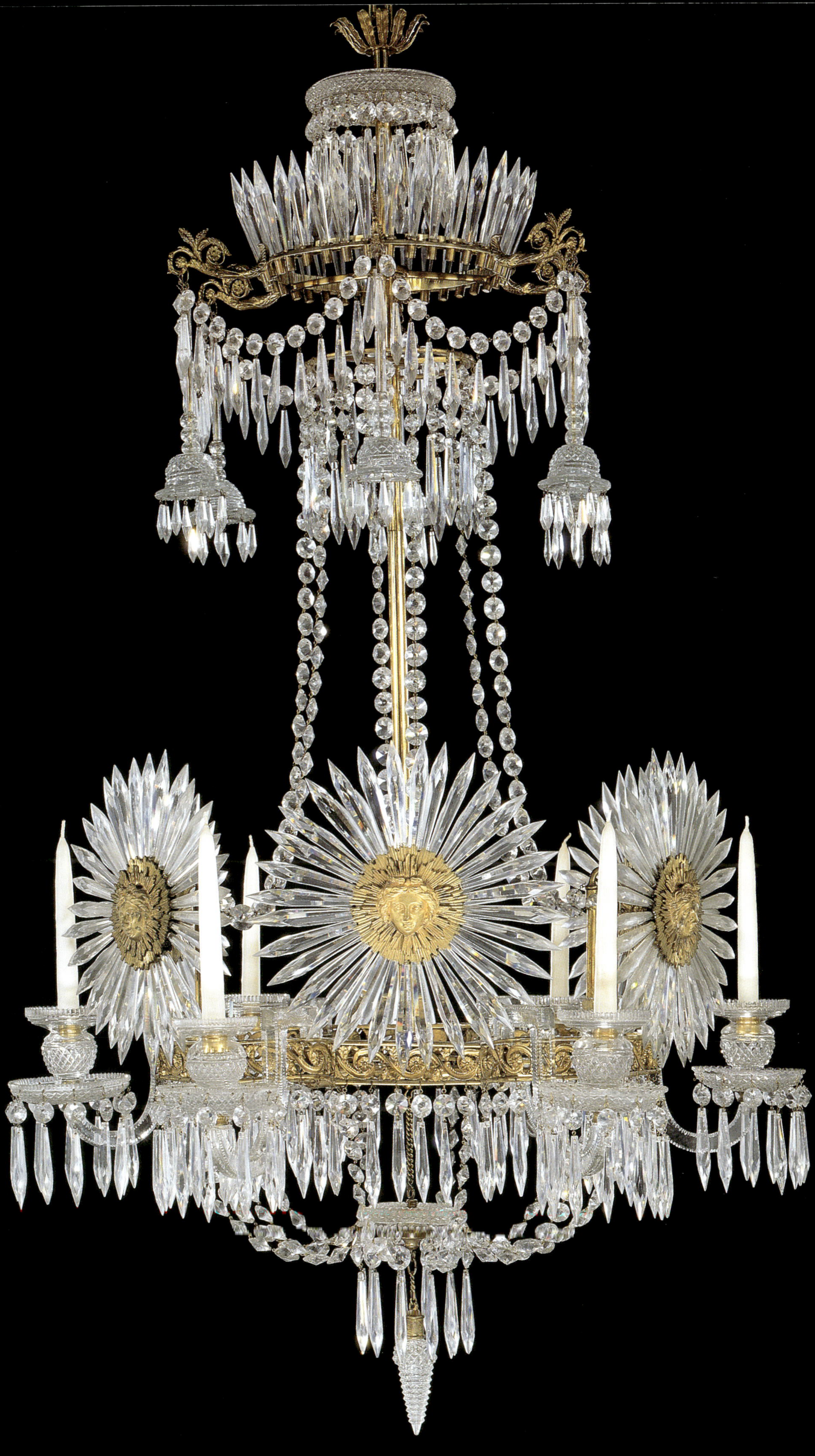

Case furniture and carvers' work

ANTHONY COLERIDGE

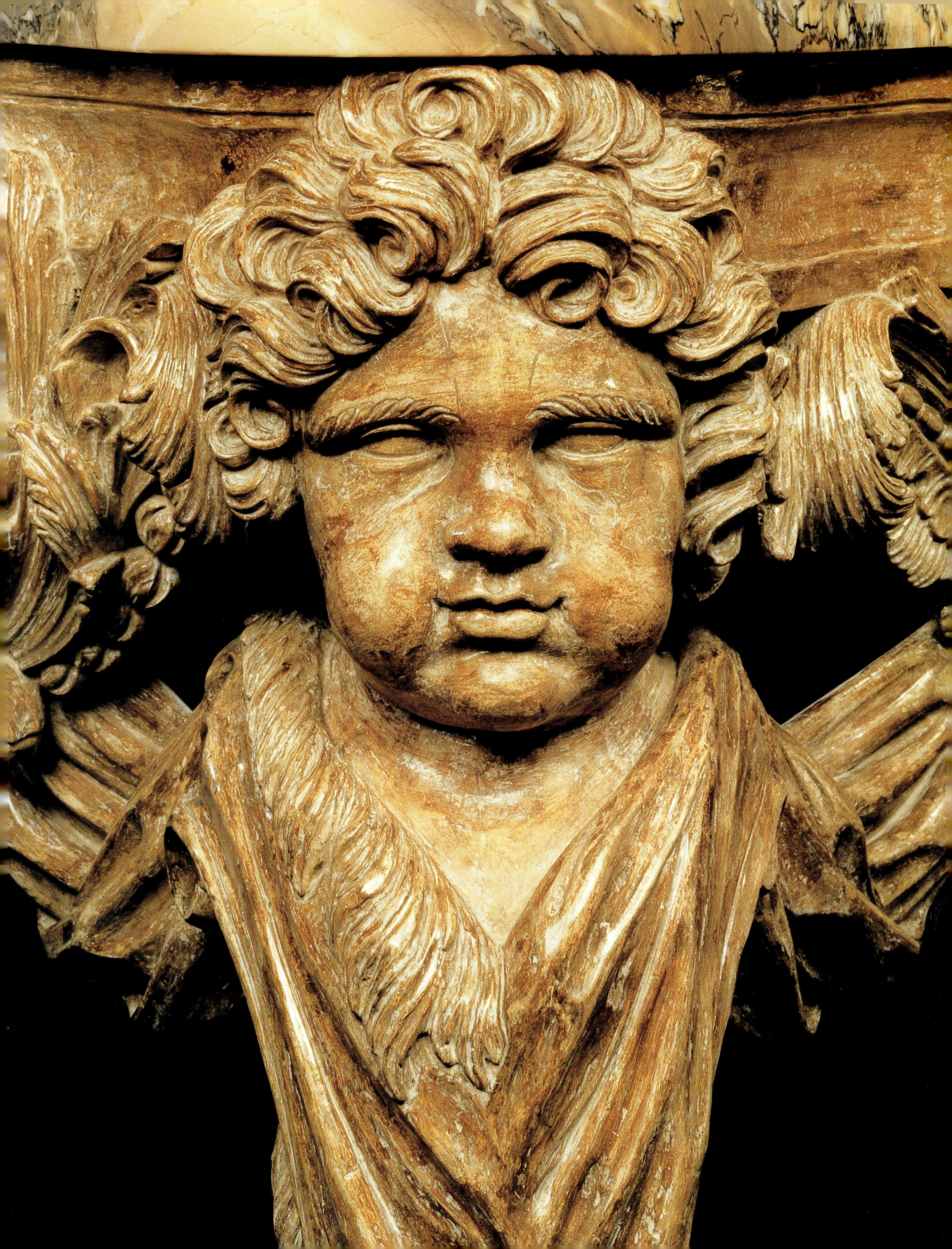

PREVIOUS PAGE
(Detail from p. 199, cat. no. 5)
One of the *putti* from the gilt wood console table, *c*.1740.

I HAVE BEEN fortunate in enjoying a friendship with the Kern family for many years. It all started in the mid-1950s when, after I had come out of the army, I joined the furniture department in Knight Frank and Rutley's auction rooms. It quickly became quite obvious to me that the more one looked, the more one learnt. I spent as much time as I could at museums, collections and houses open to the public, attended views and sales at Christie's, Sotheby's and other auction houses, and, above all, bored kind friends in the furniture trade almost to death as I studied their stocks and the prices of their pieces.

The kindest and most long-suffering of them all was Rob Kern of Hotspur. He was a very busy man but was always welcoming and let me wander round the splendid premises in Lowndes Street, Belgravia, to which he had moved from Streatham Lodge, Richmond in 1951. This unspoilt house, built during the second quarter of the nineteenth century in the Lowndes development, was, and of course still is, an ideal setting for the finest of English furniture and objects in which the Kern family has always specialised. Rob Kern's father, who had also dealt in furniture, had arranged for his son to work with a firm of restorers when he was a young man and he became fascinated by the dexterity of the carvers' hand. He often said that he could never understand how a carver 'could see what was inside the piece of timber, just trying to get out'. He must at the same time have learnt to appreciate the importance of proportion, line, construction and, above all, colour and patination and, furthermore, why the selection and choice of woods were such vital ingredients to the success of a piece of furniture.

The great breadth of knowledge, experience, taste and scholarship, which he gained over the following years, together with his unerring eye for quality, was then, and still is, the hallmark of all that the Kern family stands for.

Rob Kern was immensely generous with his knowledge and experience and his enthusiasm was infectious. He shared these qualities with all those with whom he came in contact but, above all, with his two sons, Robin and Brian, who joined him in 1956 and 1963 respectively. They had, of course, grown up with their grandfather's and father's knowledge and enthusiasm as part of their daily life but, in addition to all of this, one must be born with an 'eye'. If you are lucky enough to have an eye, a great piece of furniture can talk to you across a room as you walk into it and can stand out in the crowd, like a Derby winner in the paddock or a beautiful girl at a party. One can study the history of English furniture ad nauseam and examine endless pieces of it until the cows come home, but unless you are blessed with the eye, you will labour under a considerable handicap. Robin and Brian inherited their father's eye for the best, and with their father and grandfather as their mentors, they enjoyed the best possible grounding – apprenticeship, if you like – that any of us interested in the subject could wish for in our wildest dreams.

During this time Ralph Edwards and Robert Symonds, two of the greatest pioneers of English furniture scholarship, were frequent visitors to Lowndes Street. Ralph Edwards, with Percy Macquoid, jointly wrote and compiled *The Dictionary of English Furniture*, published between 1924 and 1927.[1] Apart from this *magnum opus*, essential to the study of English furniture, he wrote, in collaboration with Margaret Jourdain in 1946, *Georgian Cabinet-Makers*. This was the first serious attempt to bring together the *oeuvres* of individual English cabinet-makers practising between the Restoration and the Regency. Robert Symonds, who advised on the formation of important collections of English furniture for a select group of aficionados, also wrote extensively on the subject. He was particularly interested in the patination, colour and choice of woods, the construction and quality of carving and inlay of English furniture, and much of his published work, both books[2] and articles, was directed to these all-important aspects of the subject. These two unusual characters, inevitably, must have had a great deal in common with the Kerns. Their aims and interests were shared. Ralph Edwards pioneered research into the lives and work of English cabinet-makers and Robert Symonds stressed the importance of the execution and condition of English furniture – both subjects of equal concern and import to Rob Kern and his two sons.

Apart from growing up in this environment of

---

1. Edwards and Macquoid, *DEF*, 3 vols; Edwards, *DEF*, revised edition, 3 vols, 1954.
2. Symonds's four major books on furniture were: *The Present State of Old English Furniture* (London, 1926); *English Furniture from Charles II to George II* (London, 1929); *Masterpieces of English Furniture and Clocks* (London, 1940); and *Furniture Making in Seventeenth and Eighteenth Century England* (London, 1955). For a complete biography of his publications, see *Furniture History*, XI, 1975, pp. 88–107. See also Lennox-Boyd, *Masterpieces of English Furniture: The Gerstenfeld Collection*, in the 'Introduction: Collecting in the Symonds' Tradition', pp. 14–31.

all that is best and most stimulating in the English furniture trade, the two brothers also took their homework seriously. The 1960s was a time when the study of English furniture history came into its own. It was Macaulay who wrote: 'Knowledge advances by steps but not by leaps'[3] – by now it was indeed advancing by steps, but they were giant ones. Faber and Faber, for example, were publishing their series of monographs on furniture and these were but a few of the serious titles, which, full of new research, were being published. Encouraged by all of this, those most interested in the subject banded together in 1964 to found the Furniture History Society, and it has been a fount of knowledge and a mainspring of initiative ever since. Apart from lectures, seminars, a newsletter and study visits, both nationally and internationally, its most important role has been the publication of the annual journal dedicated to original research in its field. The Society will, additionally, always be remembered for another most important publication in 1986, *The Dictionary of English Furniture Makers, 1660–1840*,[4] which vastly expanded the scope of Ralph Edwards's and Margaret Jourdain's *Georgian Cabinet-Makers*.

The Kerns were in the vanguard of this new thirst for knowledge and research and it now became all-important to study cabinet-maker's accounts, account books detailing purchases of furniture, eighteenth- and nineteenth-century inventories and many other archival sources. If one could relate pieces of furniture in a house to documentary evidence of purchase, the value of the pieces were greatly enhanced, of course, depending on the stature of the cabinet-maker involved. It was an exciting time and this was when I really got to know Robin and Brian.

I had joined the furniture department at Christie's in 1962 and became, like the Kern brothers, passionately interested in furniture research. We all wrote articles based on research in country house muniment rooms, along with other subjects, and shared a love of fine English furniture. (I later used many of those that I had written in my book.[5]) The furniture catalogues produced by the auction houses, likewise, became much more erudite, as did those of the furniture trade. Buyers became

3. Babington Macaulay, 'Essays and Biographies', *History*, (n.d.)
4. Beard and Gilbert, *DEFM*.
5. Coleridge, *Chippendale Furniture: The Work of Thomas Chippendale and his Contemporaries in the Rococo Style*.

interested in the provenance of pieces and attached great importance to this, particularly when from a primary source, and, of course, they were equally if not more interested in who made and supplied the pieces.

The Kerns quickly realised the importance and potential of this renewed interest in research, and, as scholarship progressed, fascination in the subject increased. The formation of a collection or indeed the purchase of a single piece was a serious business, more than understandable bearing in mind the rapid spiral in prices that was under way.

These new avenues of research into furniture history have helped the family, over many years, to build up a close connection with many of the major museums in this country, the United States, Europe and Australia, to name a few, and with collectors on both sides of the Atlantic and much further afield too. They have acted for English Heritage on behalf of the nation over negotiated sales, which is a compelling indication of the high esteem in which the firm is held. Following in their father's footsteps, they have always been free with their knowledge to anyone interested in the subject. Brian retired in 1999 to pursue his many different interests but keeps in regular touch. Christopher Payne has ably filled this gap and now forms the team with Robin, while Simone Barnard compliments them both beautifully with her administration. It certainly all augurs well for the future.

The historic relationship between the fine art trade and the auction houses is inextricably entwined and our fortunes wax and wane together. Friendships from both sides of the rostrum, built up on a shared interest of whatever one's specialisation may be, are most rewarding; long may they flourish. When I conducted the furniture sales at Christie's, I had the pleasure of knocking down many lots to the House of Hotspur. Over the years, I quickly realised what an unerring eye was possessed collectively by all its members.

When Robin and I initially discussed the format for this book I mentioned an article[1] that I had recently written about my career at Christie's to mark my retirement after forty years. Robin was particularly amused by one incident I relate in it that illustrates the hazards encoutered by a short-sighted

1. Christie's, *Bulletin for Professional Advisers*, summer 2003, Vol. 8 no.1, pp. 28-44

auctioneer such as I am:

The story concerns the sale of the property of the late Cecil Beaton, taking place in a long marquee on Monday 9 June, 1980.

… Lot 20 [was] a small table of low value. It was a cloudy day and I was finding it difficult clearly to see the back of the marquee. A lady in the second row below me was bidding against 'someone' standing in the gloom at the very back of the tent who appeared to be raising her arm aloft, I imagined in the hope, that if she left it there, she might see off any opposition. When the bidding reached 5,200 guineas and I was beginning to think it all a bit strange, one of my colleagues, a close friend, came up behind me and whispered "You are taking bids from a carved wooden statue at the back of the tent". Indeed I was – *Lot 14, a South German Baroque statue of a partially draped female figure with raised left arm 70" high.*

It was time to restart the bidding. I once asked Robin what was the most expensive lot that he had purchased in our rooms. It was two sofas, which, in my opinion, are from the grandest and most important extant set of seat furniture made in this country. Thomas Chippendale supplied the sofas to Sir Lawrence Dundas for his house at 19 Arlington Street, St James's, in 1765. Robert Adam's design for one of the sofas is dated 1764. It affords the proof that Thomas Chippendale did on occasion work from a design provided by Robert Adam (see also p. 143). Chippendale charged £376 for the eight armchairs and four sofas in 1764, and in 1997 Robin paid £1,541,500 for the two sofas. You would find it difficult to beat the product or the price: game, set and match!

When I discuss below some of the finest pieces of case furniture and mirrors that have passed through those splendid rooms in Lowndes Street, I will try, where appropriate, to describe the pleasure, challenge and fun that we had together whilst trying to research into their history. To facilitate the discussion of the examples that have been selected, I have tried to arrange them in some sort of chronological order.

AC

CATALOGUE I
A mirror with bevelled plate in a carved and pierced gilt wood and silvered wood frame, c.1685.
H: 54″ (137 cm); W: 30″ (76 cm).

This rare survival from the late seventeenth century in many ways epitomises the flamboyance and exuberance of the Restoration of Charles II.

The elaborately carved and pierced gilt wood frame retains its original gilding and it is designed with entwined garlands of leaves and flower heads, which are interspersed with silvered boisterous *amorini*. Similar playful figures flank and support the blank escutcheon to the centre of the cresting. The ground behind the pierced frame still retains its original red wash.

Its conception and design must owe much to that of silver and silver-gilt mirrors in contemporary toilet services.

CATALOGUE 2
A walnut and marquetry cabinet on a stand, the doors of which enclose an elaborately fitted interior, c.1700. Possibly made in the workshop of Thomas Pistor.
H: 75" (190.5 cm); W: 64" (163 cm); D: 23" (58.5 cm).

This walnut cabinet on a stand, dating from either side of 1700, is inlaid with panels of floral marquetry of outstanding delicacy and intricacy. The design of the marquetry inlay is of a particularly complex nature formed of urns, bouquets and sprays of flowers.

Whoever was responsible for this work owed a great debt to France and the Netherlands. Pierre Golle, who had left the Netherlands to settle in Paris, specialised in floral marquetry, as did Philippus van Santwijk in the Hague and Jan van Mekeren in Amsterdam, all of whom flourished at the end of the century.

There was a deep interest in naturalistic ornament on both sides of the channel and following the Restoration there was an influx of craftsmen of continental origin to England, given a second wind by the accession of William and Mary. The most successful of whom, specialising in marquetry was Gerreit Jensen, apparently of Dutch or Flemish origin.

However, Jensen had a serious rival. Recent research by Adriana Turpin[1] has brought to the fore a family of cabinet-makers who supplied furniture decorated with floral marquetry of the highest quality – Thomas Pistor, father and son. She discusses the furniture that they supplied to James Grahme, Keeper of James II's Privy Purse, between 1684 and 1687. Amongst their extant accounts at Levens Hall in Cumbria is an entry for 'a Large wall flower'd Looking glass and Tables and stands flowered … [£] 09 10s. 0d.'

Future research will, hopefully, further enhance the reputations of Thomas Pistor, senior and junior, patently major players in their field.

PROVENANCE
Oglander Family, Nunwell House, Isle of Wight.

1. Turpin, 'Thomas Pistor, Father and Son, and Levens Hall', *FHSJ*, Vol. XXXVI, 2000, pp. 43–58.

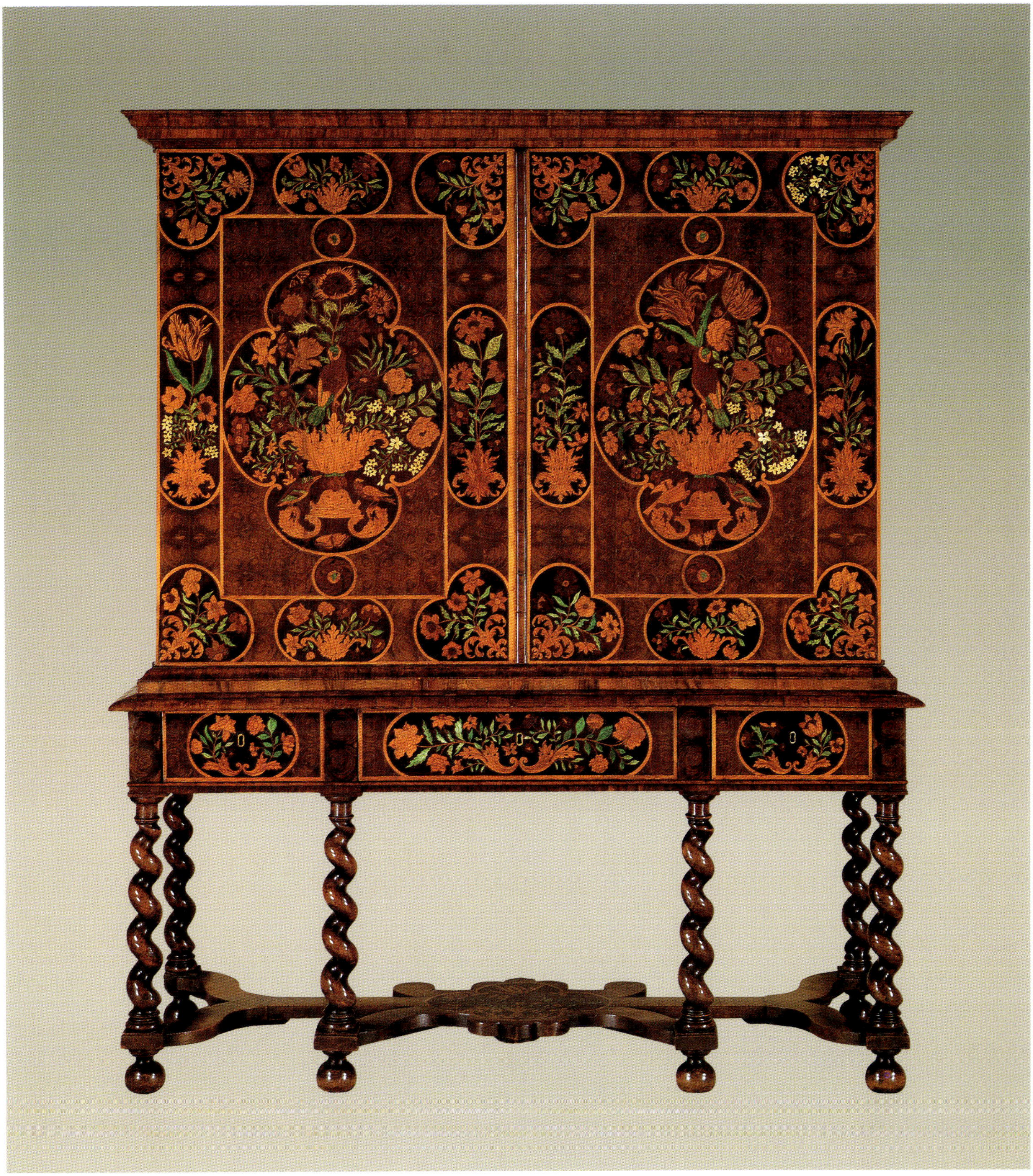

CATALOGUE 3
A gilt gesso centre table, c.1710–15.
Attributed to James Moore.
H: 30½″ (77.5 cm); W: 45½″ (115 cm);
D: 22½″ (57 cm).

It is not known for whom or where this gilt gesso centre table was supplied. It can be dated to the early years of the eighteenth century and was almost certainly made in the workshops of the celebrated cabinet-maker James Moore the Elder, who supplied furniture, particularly in gesso, to the Crown, the Duchess of Marlborough and other noble patrons.

Primed with data from Robin Kern and Ian Caldwell, who has researched Moore's *oeuvre*,[1] I wrote an article on the table in *Antique and New Art*.[2] Free-standing centre tables with decoration on all four sides were rare creations in gesso, but examples can be seen at Windsor Castle and in great houses such as Blenheim Palace, Boughton House, Chatsworth and Ham House: the Hotspur table makes a welcome addition to this select band.

Many of its decorative and structural details are echoed in documented and other pieces in Moore's *oeuvre*. For example, the grotesque masks on the richly carved aprons on either side of the table are similar to those on the Bateman marriage chest in the Victoria and Albert Museum which, on stylistic grounds, is attributed to Moore.[3] The stretchers, with a foliated urn resting on the central platform, can be compared with those on a pair of stands for contemporary Japanese lacquered cabinets at Windsor Castle.[4] Ian Caldwell has demonstrated that this pair of cabinet stands may have been supplied by Moore to Queen Anne for Kensington Palace in 1707 at a cost of £27.

Actually, in the final analysis it does not really matter if the table was made by James Moore the Elder[5] or by one of his rivals, such as Jean Pelletier or John Belchier, who were also specialising in gesso work during this period: what does count is that the table is, patently, a rare and exceptional example of its kind.

1. Caldwell, 'John Gumley, James Moore and King George I', *Antique Collector*, April 1987; and 'James Moore and the Bateman Chest', *Antique Collector*, February 1988.
2. Coleridge, 'Gilt and Attribution', *Antique and New Art*, Vol. 8, no. 19, May 1992.
3. Caldwell, op. cit., note 1.
4. Edwards and Jourdain, *Georgian Cabinet-Makers*, Plate 39, where attributed to Benjamin Goodison.
5. His son, James Moore the Younger, continued to run the family business after his death. See Murdoch, 'The King's Cabinet-Maker: The Giltwood Furniture of James Moore the Elder', *Burlington Magazine*, CXLV, June 2003, p. 420. This recently published article discusses Moore's clients and *oeuvre* in great depth.

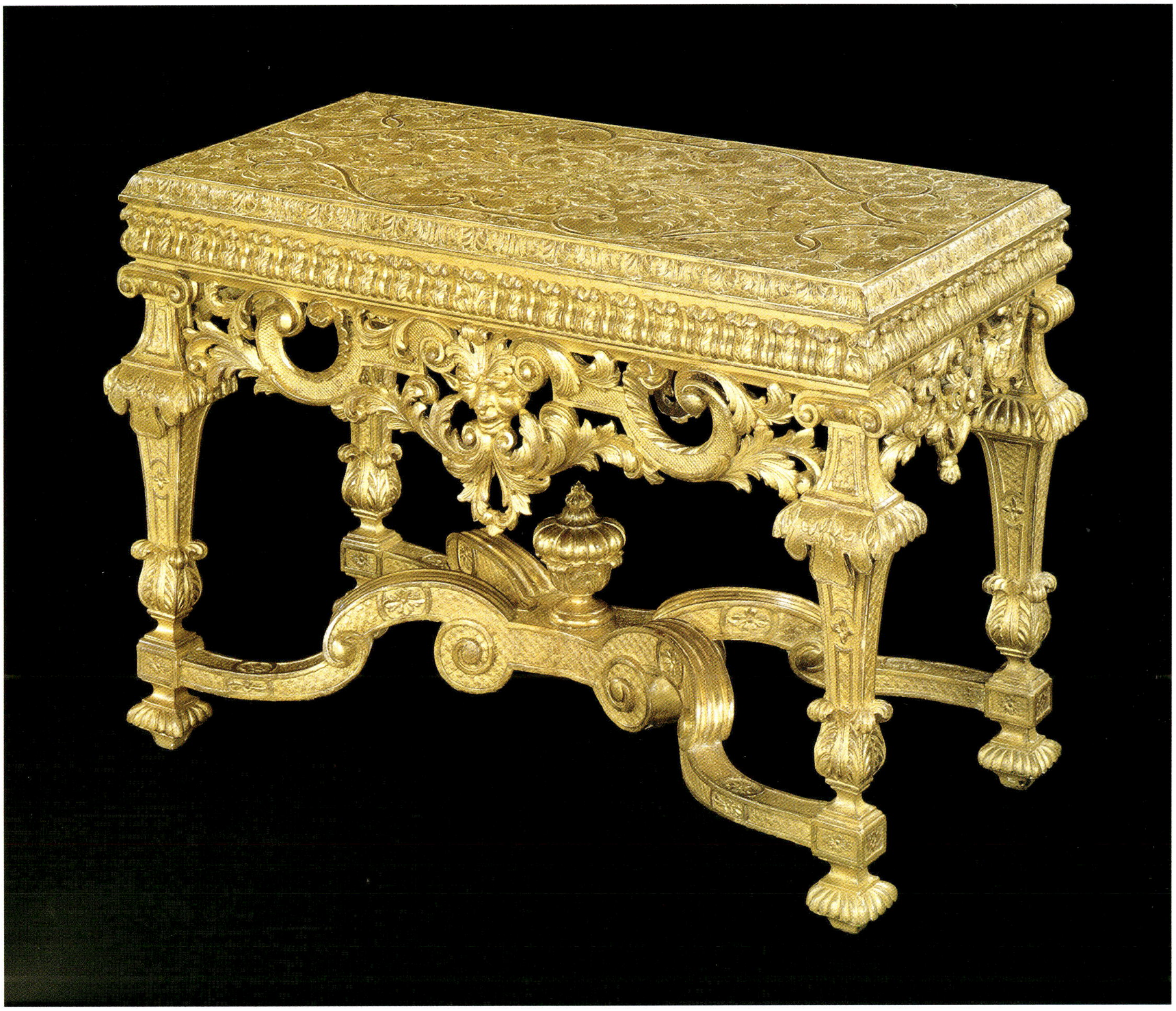

CATALOGUE 4
A gilt gesso pier-glass (one of a pair), surmounted by an earl's coronet, c.1735. Possibly by John Boson.
One, H: 69" (175.5 cm); W: 36" (91.5 cm).
The other, H: 65½" (166.5 cm); W: 34½" (87.5 cm).

This pair of pier-glasses would have been commissioned by Anthony Ashley-Cooper, fourth Earl of Shaftesbury, who on his coming-of-age in 1732 set about the aggrandisement of St Giles's House in Dorset, which had been built by the first Earl of Shaftesbury, Lord Chancellor to Charles II.

Christie's, in their catalogue of 6 July 2000,[1] suggest that, on account of the fine quality carving, these pier-glasses surmounted by an earl's coronet may have been executed by John Boson, a specialist carver of note employed, amongst others, by Frederick Prince of Wales and Richard Boyle, third Earl of Burlington.

Furthermore, Christie's note that in the fourth Earl's account books there are two payments to a Mr Swan for glass, dated 1734 and 1735, for £18 1s. 6d and then another for £18 18s. 6d respectively, and for additional payments. It is more likely that these payments were for windows than mirror plates, but it is possible that they refer to the latter. Also in the account books, a payment of the considerable sum of £295 in 1735 is recorded to a Mr Gibson. This entry may refer to the upholsterer, Christopher Gibson of St Paul's Churchyard in London, who could have been involved in supplying the pier-glasses.

PROVENANCE
Supplied to Anthony Ashley-Cooper, fourth Earl of Shaftesbury (d. 1771) for St Giles's House, Dorset, and by descent at St Giles's.

1. Christie's London, 6 July 2000, lot 26.

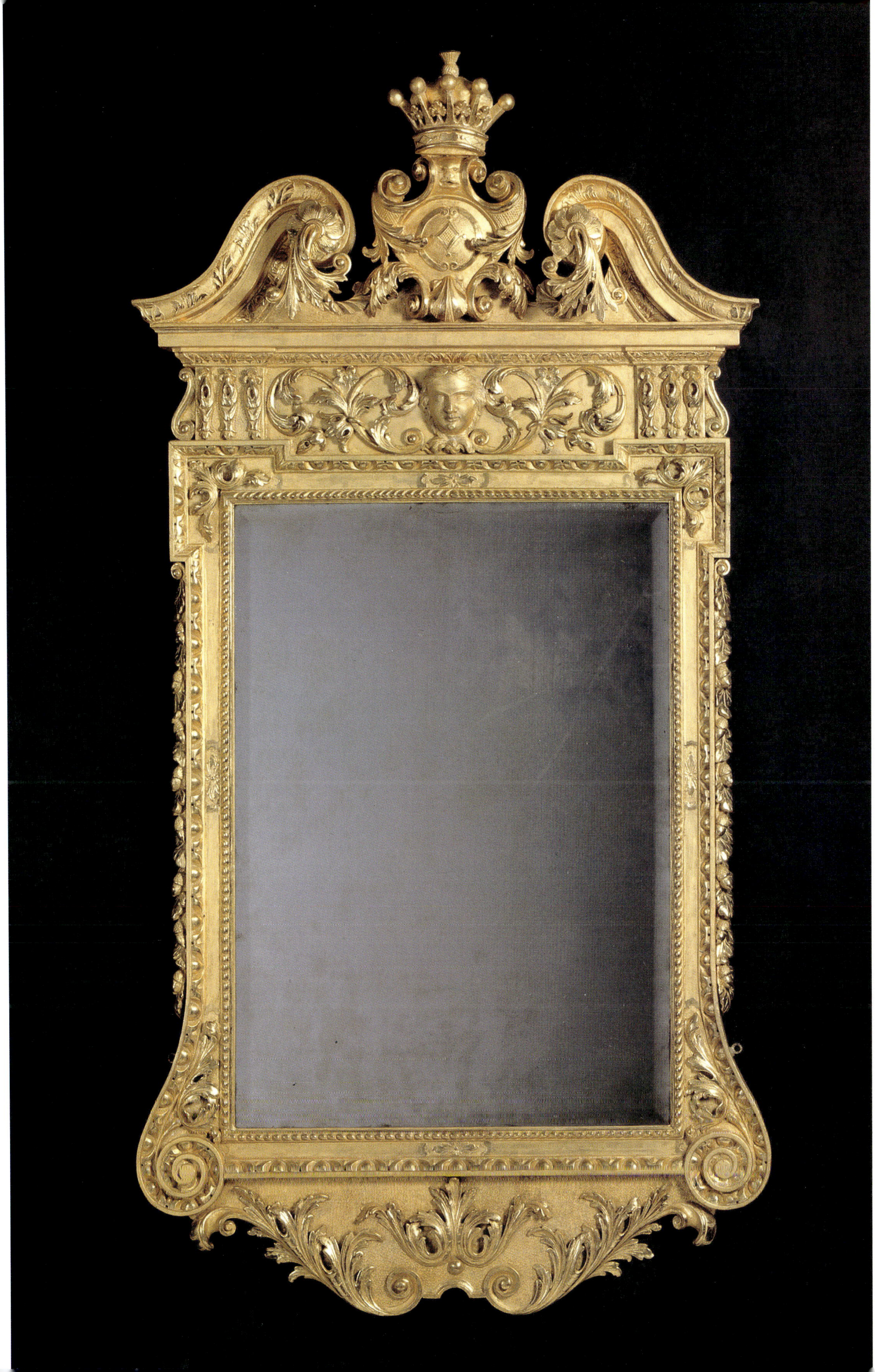

CATALOGUE 5
A gilt wood console table, c.1740.
Attributed to Matthias Lock.
H: 35½" (90 cm); W: 50½" (128 cm);
D: 27½" (70 cm).

This gilt wood console table, which is carved with great dexterity, is perhaps by the hand of the carver and gilder Matthias Lock and is influenced by his designs. In two trade cards, dated 1764, he is referred to as a 'carver' and 'designer' with an address in Nottingham Court, Castle Street, near Long Acre.

Little is known of his life apart from his published book of ornaments and designs between 1740 and 1769; his designs for plates in the first (1754) and third (1762) editions of Chippendale's *Director*; and his designs for 'carver's work', which are in the Victoria and Albert Museum.

The Hotspur table should be compared to two drawings by Lock of side tables,[1] particularly the bearded and moustachioed satyr masks carved on the central aprons shown in both designs and the *putti* masks to the angles of the console table. The latter drawing is for a rococo console table bought by Earl Poulett in around 1745 for Hinton House in Somerset.[2] It is annotated with the number of days worked by Lock and each of his assistants, and also the price charged – eighty-nine days work at a cost of £22 5s. 0d, excluding the cost of the gilding. The table under discussion could well have cost much the same.

Although we know little about Matthias Lock's life apart from his published and unpublished designs, I was lucky enough to find a fitting epitaph to him in 1964 whilst working in the Muniment Room at Hopetoun House in West Lothian. On a scrap of paper was written: 'The enclosed drawings are valuable being designed and drawn by the famous Mr. Matt Lock recently deceased who was reputed the best draftsman in that way that had ever been in England.'[3] It says it all.

1. Coleridge, *Chippendale Furniture: The Work of Thomas Chippendale and his Contemporaries in the Rococo Style*, Plate 90 (the Hinton House console table), Plate 95.
2. Hayward, 'Furniture designed and carved by Matthias Lock for Hinton House, Somerset', *Connoisseur*, December 1960, pp. 284–6.
3. Coleridge, *op. cit.*, p. 54.

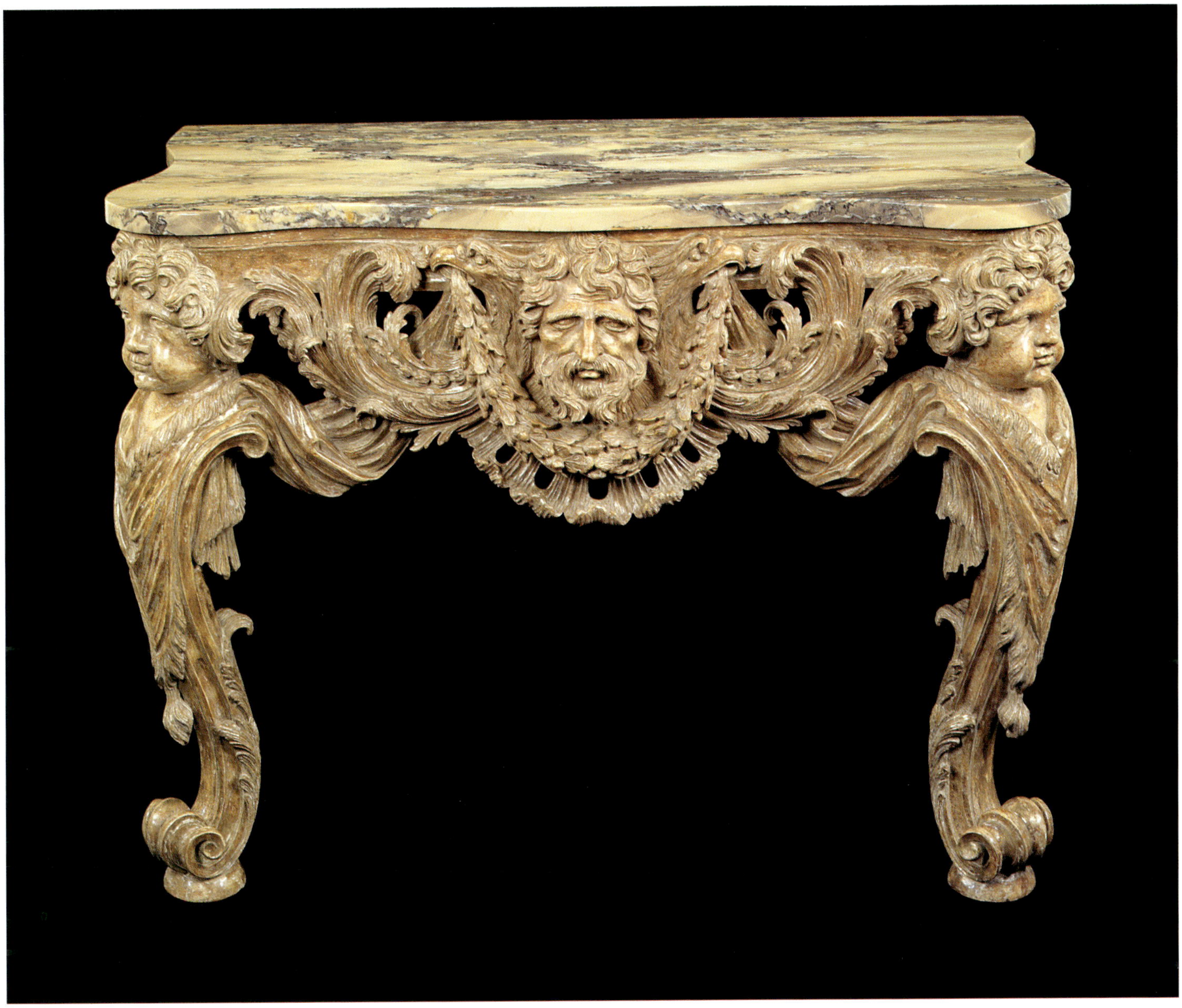

CATALOGUE 6
A carved mahogany commode, c.1745.
Attributed to William Hallett senior.
H: 35½" (90 cm); W: 54" (137 cm);
D: 26½" (67 cm).

This commode, which was in the collection of Francis Garvan, a distinguished American collector of the 1920s,[1] in earlier years would probably have been attributed to William Vile.

In 1954 Ralph Edwards, in his article 'Attributions to William Vile',[2] wrote: 'The practice of assigning furniture to this maker on inadequate evidence has increased, is increasing and ought to be diminished – to adapt a famous parliamentary pronouncement made in his [Vile's] lifetime ... Vile published no designs, nor are any original drawings by him known, and these important facts should be born in mind by those who light-heartedly invoke his name.' This was a timely warning indeed and I, for one, was guilty of paying insufficient heed to these wise words. I coupled William Vile's name with various examples of case furniture illustrated in my book[3] without sufficient supporting documentary evidence. Geoffrey Beard,[4] who has done much research on this subject, has suggested that the large body of furniture of the period 1740 to 1750 which is attributed to Vile should probably be given to his master William Hallett senior, or perhaps to John Boson or Benjamin Goodison.

William Hallett senior, who was joined by his son bearing the same name in the early 1750s, had probably for many years been producing pieces of case furniture that were similar to those I illustrated in his workshops in Great Newport Street, Long Acre.

Writing in 1965,[5] I gave a number of reasons for suspecting that there was a close business relationship between the Halletts and Vile and Cobb. In 1753 the Halletts left Long Acre and purchased premises next to Vile and Cobb in St Martin's Lane. The two partnerships shared important clients over the years. More cogently Hallett senior swore an affidavit to prove Cobb's will and was appointed a trustee by Vile, who had the highest opinion of his 'honour, ability and integrity'. There are a number of payments from Cobb to Hallett in the former's bank account and there is a notice in *The Gentleman's Magazine*, of 6 September 1783, in which Cobb is said to have been 'formerly partner with the late Mr. Hallett of Cannons'. However, Geoffrey Beard clinches the closeness of their relationship when he refers[6] to a letter of August 1749 from William Vile to George Selwyn[7] (who seldom missed witnessing an execution in London), which makes it clear that his 'master' was William Hallett senior. Vile appears to have once been a journeyman in Hallett's employment.

During the early 1750s by which time Hallett senior had probably withdrawn from active participation in the business, leaving his son in charge, Vile and Cobb came to the fore and their output rapidly expanded, culminating in their Royal appointment and subsequent work for the Crown between 1761 and 1765.

The Garvan/Hotspur commode has now been attributed to the Hallett workshop and dated to the mid-1740s. Robert Symonds must have known this commode well and thought highly of it, as he illustrated it in three articles between 1944 and 1958.[8] In his 1958 *Connoisseur* article, 'Changing Taste in Furniture Collecting', the words of his caption were: 'In the 1920s this type of mahogany commode, circa 1740, was looked on as a most desirable collector's piece.' Garvan presumably acquired it during the 1920s and it is as desirable today, and probably more so, as it was then, and indeed as it was when Symonds was writing in 1958. For pieces of this distinction, *rien ça change*.

There is a note in *London Furniture Makers* in which Ambrose Heal writes in 1953,[9] 'I am informed by R.W. Symonds that he has found reason for thinking that there was a business connection between Hallet and his next-door neighbours, the firm of Vile and Cobb.' It is tantalising that, as far as I am aware, Symonds never expressed an opinion as to whether either the Halletts or Vile and Cobb might have been responsible for the construction of this remarkable commode.

PROVENANCE
Francis P. Garvan.
Private collection, USA.

1. A selection from the Francis P. Garvan collection was offered at the American Art Association, New York, 8–10 January 1931.
2. Edwards, 'Attributions to William Vile', *Country Life*, 7 October 1954.
3. Coleridge, *Chippendale Furniture: The Work of Thomas Chippendale and his Contemporaries in the Rococo Style*, Plates 1–11.
4. Beard & Gilbert, *DEFM*, p. 924.
5. Coleridge, 'A Reappraisal of William Hallett', *FHSJ*, 5, Vol. 1, 1965; and Coleridge *op. cit.*, p. 44.
6. Beard & Gilbert, *DEFM*, p. 923.
7. Castle Howard archives.
8. Symonds, 'The Serpentine Line in English Furniture', *Antique Collector*, November/December 1944, p. 187, fig. 4; Symonds, 'Old Mahogany Furniture', *Country Life*, 11 June 1953, p. 1893, fig. 11; Symonds, 'Changing Taste in Furniture Collecting', *Connoisseur*, June 1958, p. 15, fig. 13.
9. Heal, *London Furniture Makers (1660–1940)*, p. 74.

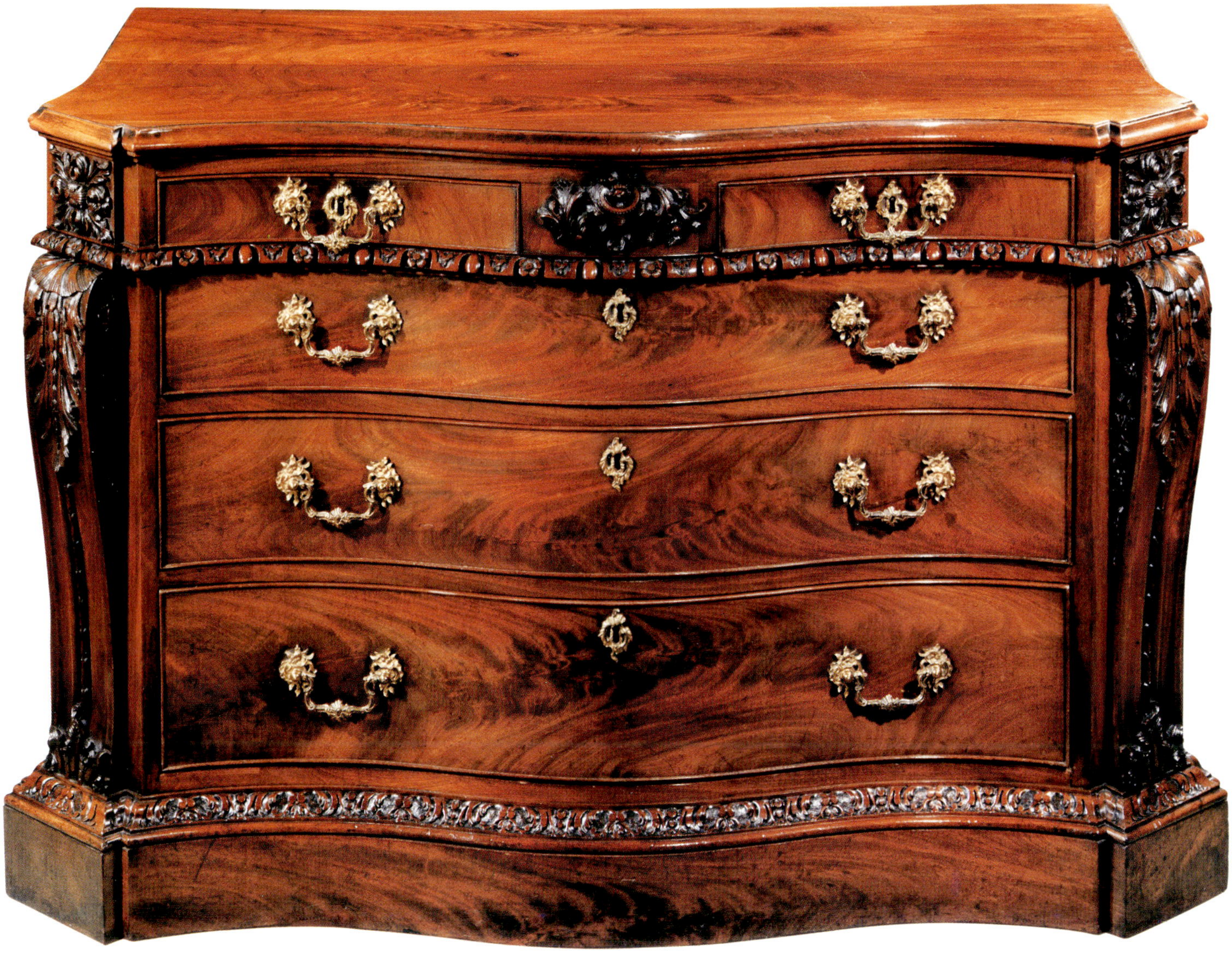

CATALOGUE 7
A mahogany dumb waiter, or two-tier table, with open fret borders and carved tripod support, c.1755.
H. 37" (94 cm); W. 25" (64 cm).

A 1755 inventory of the contents of Chicheley Hall in Buckinghamshire records a mahogany dumb waiter in the Common Parlour, an early use of the term.

Sheraton in his *Cabinet Dictionary* of 1803 defines a dumb waiter as 'a useful piece of furniture, to serve in some respects the place of a waiter, whence it is so named'. Miss Mary Hamilton in her diary of 1784 writes 'we had dumb waiters, so our conversation was not under any restraint by ye servants being in ye room'.[1]

Chippendale does not include designs for dumb waiters in *The Director*.

This distinguished example was exhibited at the Victoria and Albert Museum in 1962[2] and is now in the Noel Terry Collection, Fairfax House in York.[3]

1. Edwards, *DEF* (1954), II, p. 226.
2. C.I.O.N.A., *International Art Treasures Exhibition Catalogue*, Victoria and Albert Museum, 1962, no. 85.
3. Brown (ed.), *The Noel Terry Collection of Furniture and Clocks*, p. 108, Plate 106.

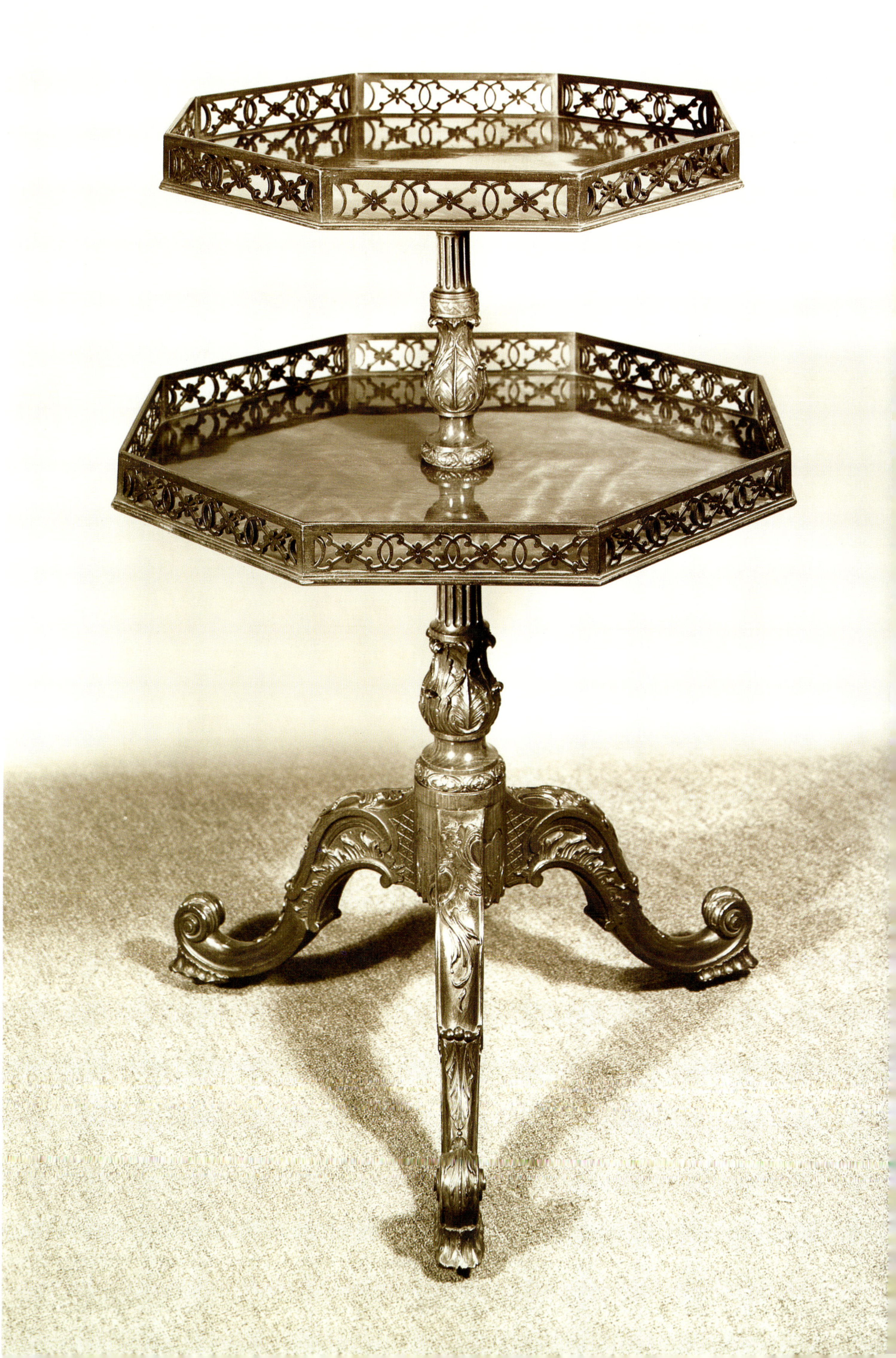

CATALOGUE 8
A mahogany artist's table, c.1755.
H: 28½" (72 cm); W: 25" (63.5 cm);
D: 19" (48.2 cm).

These tables were extremely popular during the middle and later years of the eighteenth century and were held to be 'very healthy for those who stand to read, write or draw',[1] which was a high proportion of the educated population.

With its double rising top and 'X'-shaped side panels, it can be compared to a similar example in the Noel Terry Collection, Fairfax House in York.[2]

1. Brown (ed.), *The Noel Terry Collection of Furniture and Clocks*, p. 103.
2. Ibid., p. 102.

205

CATALOGUE 9
A set of gilt wood and polychrome painted carvings from the Tapestry Room at Ditchley Park House, c.1755. Attributed to William and John Linnell. Comprising: *a canopy*, H: 14" (35.5 cm); w: 39" (99 cm); *winged heads*, H: 26" (66 cm); w: 25" (63.5 cm); *drapery*, H: 20¾" (52.5 cm); *cockerels*, H: 32" (81.2 cm); *eagles*, H: 28" (71 cm); and an *'India' figure*, H: 30" (76 cm).

George Lee, the second Earl of Lichfield, who died in 1743, built Ditchley Park House in Oxfordshire. The third Earl, who was responsible for adding the chinoiserie carvings, died in 1772. Four years later, on the death of the fourth Earl, the estate was inherited by his niece, Lady Charlotte Lee, who married the eleventh Viscount Dillon. It remained in the Dillon family until 1934 when Mr and Mrs Ronald Tree purchased the house and much of its contents, including the chinoiserie carvings in the Tapestry Drawing-Room.[1]

The Tapestry Drawing-Room, with a stuccoed ceiling by Henry Flitcroft, contains a splendid chimneypiece invoiced by John Cheere in 1743. The carvings described in this entry formed a part of the chimneypiece surround and were introduced by the third Earl, who, after hanging the walls with tapestry panels during the late 1740s, commissioned the carvings with *en suite* girandoles.

After the third Earl's death in 1776, an inventory was taken which includes this entry for the Tapestry Room: 'No 35 – A pair of girandoles with two India figures'. The 'India' figure amongst the above carvings was at the other end of the room. The pair of cockerels amidst palm frond wreaths, which are also amongst the carvings, may have been inspired by *Aesop's Fable* of 'The Bird Catcher, the Partridge and the Cockerel', illustrated by Francis Barlow in 1665.

Who supplied these carvings to the third Earl of Lichfield? They have been attributed to the workshops of the London cabinet-makers, William and John Linnell of Long Acre, John joining his father during the late 1740s. William had worked under Flitcroft's direction at Woburn Abbey, Bedfordshire, during the 1740s[2] and thus the architect and the cabinet-maker were acquainted by that date. The fourth Duke of Beaufort later employed the Linnells at Badminton House in Gloucestershire; the firm was commissioned to decorate the 'India' apartment, the details of which are similar in feeling to the Ditchley carvings. The Duke of Beaufort and the Lee family were in contact as they were both involved in the Jacobite cause.[3] Additionally, a Linnell design for a mirror in the Victoria and Albert Museum includes a chinoiserie figure which is related to the Ditchley carved 'India' figure.[4]

Could these carvings have been designed and executed by John Linnell, who was celebrated as 'an excellent carver in wood'? He had been trained in the St Martin's Lane Academy established by William Hogarth and there studied the nuances of French rocaille and chinoiserie, which he subtly interpreted in the English tradition.

PROVENANCE
Supplied to George Henry Lee, third Earl of Lichfield (d. 1762), Ditchley Park House, Oxfordshire.
By descent at Ditchley Park House to the Viscounts Dillon.
Acquired with the house from the eighteenth Viscount Dillon by Ronald and Nancy Tree in 1934.
Mrs Nancy (Tree) Lancaster, then moved to Haseley Court, Oxfordshire, until 1972.
Christie's New York, 18 October 2002, lot 325.

1. The carvings were included in the sale at Christie's New York, held on 18 October 2002, lot 325. I have drawn gratefully on the catalogue description and notes.
2. Cornforth, 'William Linnell at Ditchley', *Country Life*, 15 December 1988, p. 104.
3. Cornforth, 'Ditchley Park, Oxfordshire II', *Country Life*, 24 November 1988, p. 85.
4. Hayward and Kirkham, *William and John Linnell*, Vol. 2, p. 94, Plate 180.

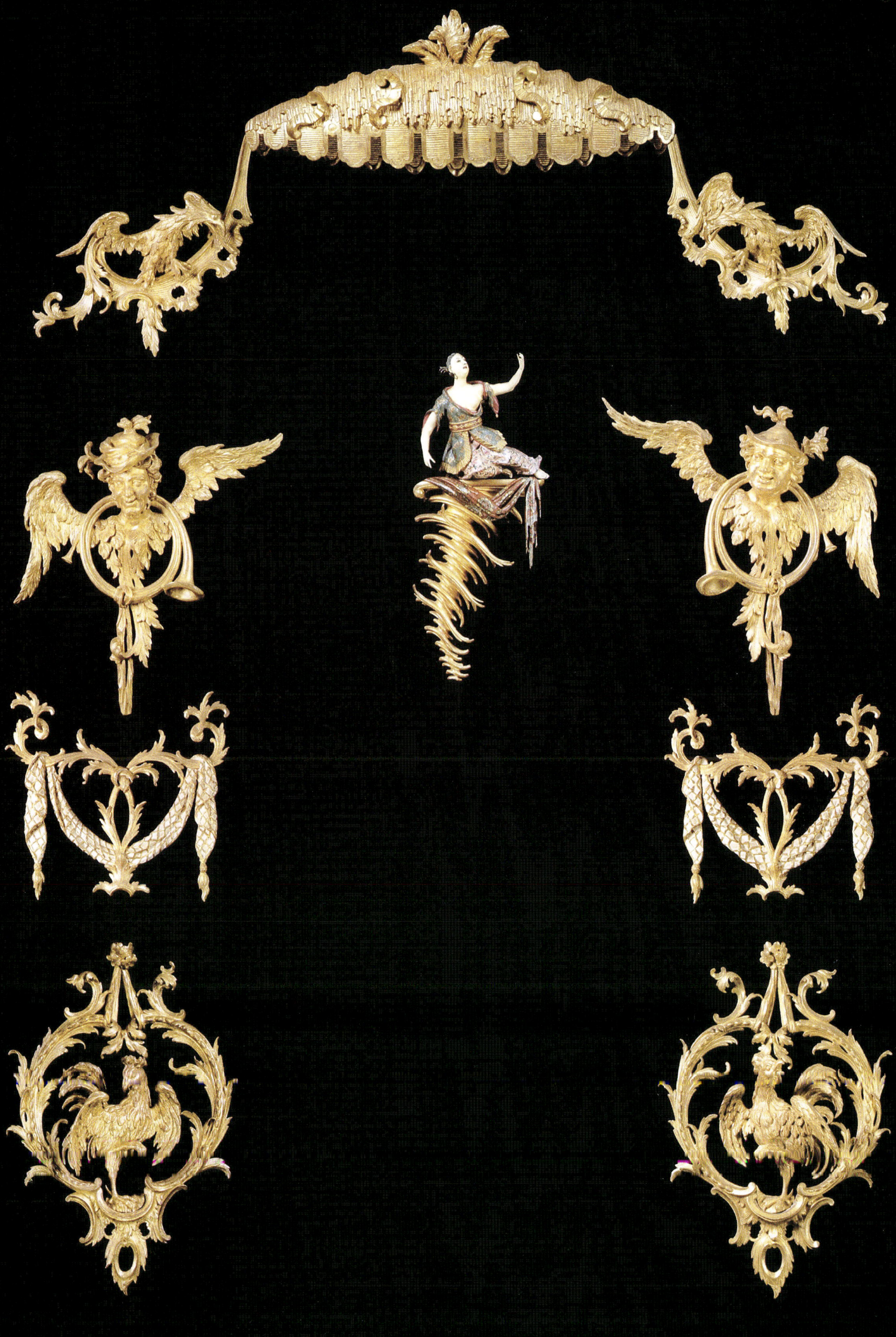

CATALOGUE 10
The Hope-Weir Cabinet: mahogany and figured walnut with carved gilt wood enrichments and inlaid with Florentine *pietre dure* plaques, late 1750s. Probably Scottish (Edinburgh).
H: 95" (241.5 cm); W: 78¼" (198.5 cm); D: 14" (35.5 cm).

After Hotspur had purchased this extraordinary cabinet, Robin and I enjoyed the fun and challenge of trying to unearth its history and I wrote an article on it, which was published in the magazine *Antiques* in New York.[1]

The cabinet was commissioned by Charles Hope-Weir, the second son of the first Earl of Hopetoun, who set out on his Grand Tour of Europe with Robert Adam in 1754. The pediment of the cabinet is centred by his wax miniature which is inscribed 'CHW Roma 1755'.

They reached Florence in January 1755 and soon joined the circle of Sir Horace Mann, the British Minister to the Tuscan Court from 1740 to 1786. It was probably through the introduction of Don Enrico Hugford, a Benedictine monk, that Hope-Weir visited the workshops of the Grand Duke of Tuscany in the *Opificio delle Pietre Dure*. There can be little doubt that it was there that he purchased the *pietre dure* plaques that now adorn his cabinet. These plaques have always been extremely expensive and were greatly prized as spoil from the Grand Tour.

Hope-Weir and Adam arrived in Rome in February 1755 where he sat for his wax miniature portrait. Whilst there, he and Adam may have already been discussing the concept of incorporating the plaques and miniatures into a grand cabinet to be filled with antiquities and curiosities, presumably collected during the Tour, for pride of place in a library that he would build on his return to Craigiehall, his house in West Lothian in Scotland.

I suggested in the article that John Adam, Robert's elder brother, who was running the Scottish end of the partnership, might have designed the cabinet to be placed in the library, which Robert was to design in 1766. If John Adam did design the cabinet, it is possible that Hope-Weir would have discussed with him who should be entrusted with its construction. The cabinet has certain unsophisticated features that lead to the conclusion that it is not of London manufacture. Let us presume that Hope-Weir turned to Edinburgh wrights[2] not only for nationalistic reasons but also, perhaps, so that he could keep an eye on its construction and progress. I suggested that it might have been made by Alexander Peter, a leading wright, and William Mathie, who was apprenticed to Peter and specialised in carving and gilding (both of whom worked for the Earl of Dumfries at Dumfries House), under the supervision of the London cabinet-maker, James Cullen, who moved to Edinburgh in around 1752.

When the library at Craigiehall was demolished, the cabinet descended in the family until its recent sale. It is arguably one of the greatest, and certainly one of the grandest, pieces of furniture made in Scotland during the eighteenth century.

1. Coleridge, 'The Hope-Weir Cabinet', *Antiques*, June 1997, New York. I have gratefully drawn freely from my text.
2. A 'wright' is the Scottish term for all who made their living by working with wood.

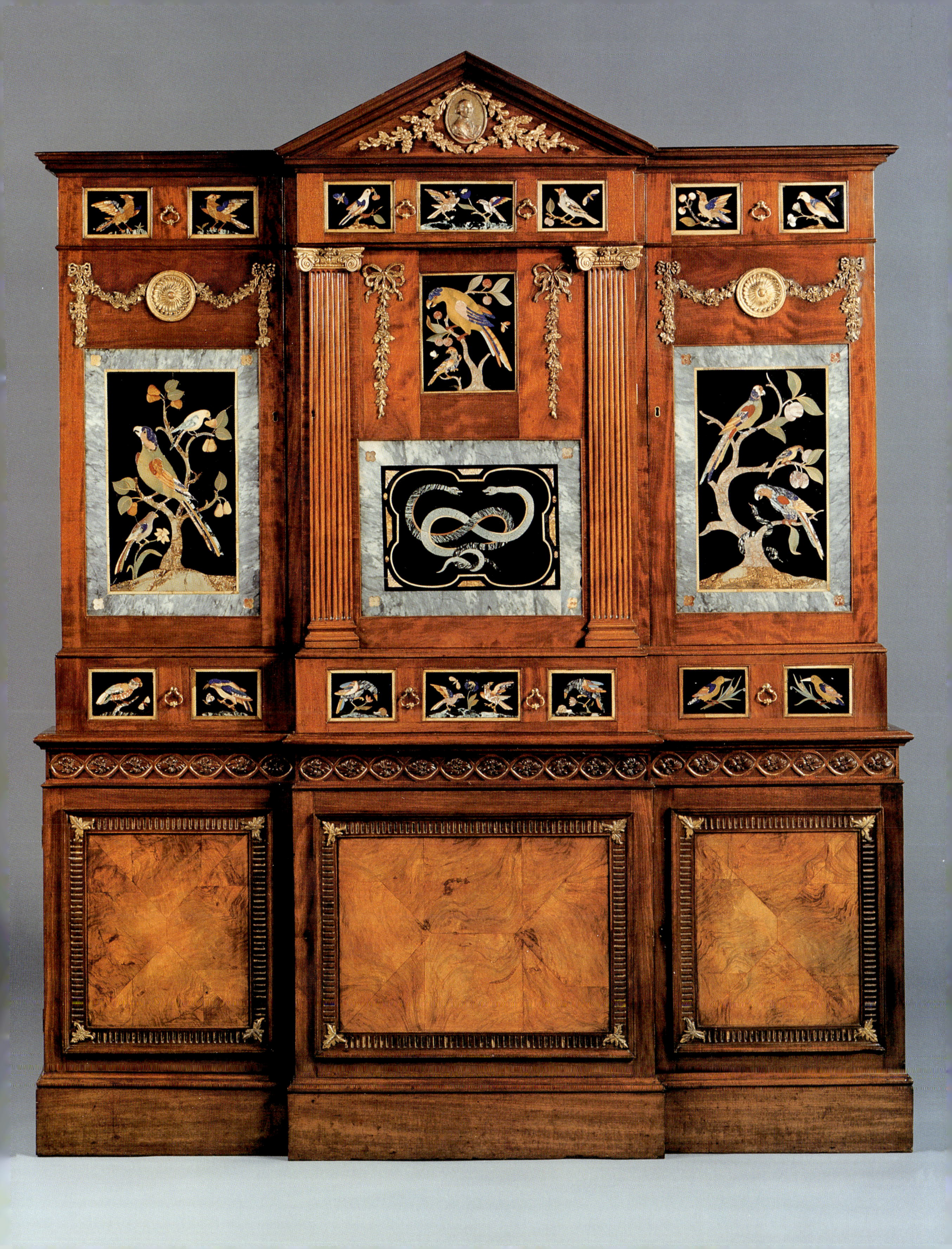

CATALOGUE 11
A mahogany and Chinese soapstone tripod table, *c*.1760. Attributed to Mayhew and Ince.
H: 27½" (70 cm); W: 13½" (34 cm).

This mahogany tripod table that supports a Chinese soapstone octagonal panel, carved in shallow relief with a scene of a pavilion and blossoming peony trees in a hilly landscape, is a rarity.

This most unusual marriage represents 'an English interpretation of the contemporary French fashion for porcelain and hardstone-mounted *tables de cabaret* invariably commissioned by [Parisian] *marchand-merciers*'.[1]

Soapstone (steatite) is a soft stone that lends itself to carving. These Chinese artefacts, exported to Europe during the eighteenth century, were highly prized and were occasionally mounted on pieces of furniture. Another example of the fashion is a mahogany cabinet on a stand in the Chinese taste, the simulated lacquer doors set with carved soapstone panels, which was at Langley Park in Norfolk, where Chippendale is thought to have been employed.[2]

The elegant mahogany table frame, which supports the soapstone panel, is based on designs for 'Tea Kettle Stands' published in Ince and Mayhew's *The Universal System of Household Furniture*, 1762, plate XIV.

This piece is not only an unusual marriage, it is also a most successful and, deservedly, lasting one.

PROVENANCE
Hotspur Ltd, London 1980.
Christie's New York, 24 November 1998, lot 34.

1. Quoted from Christie's New York sale catalogue, 24 November 1998, lot 34.
2. Coleridge, *Chippendale Furniture: The Work of Thomas Chippendale and his Contemporaries in the Rococo Style*, Plate 280.

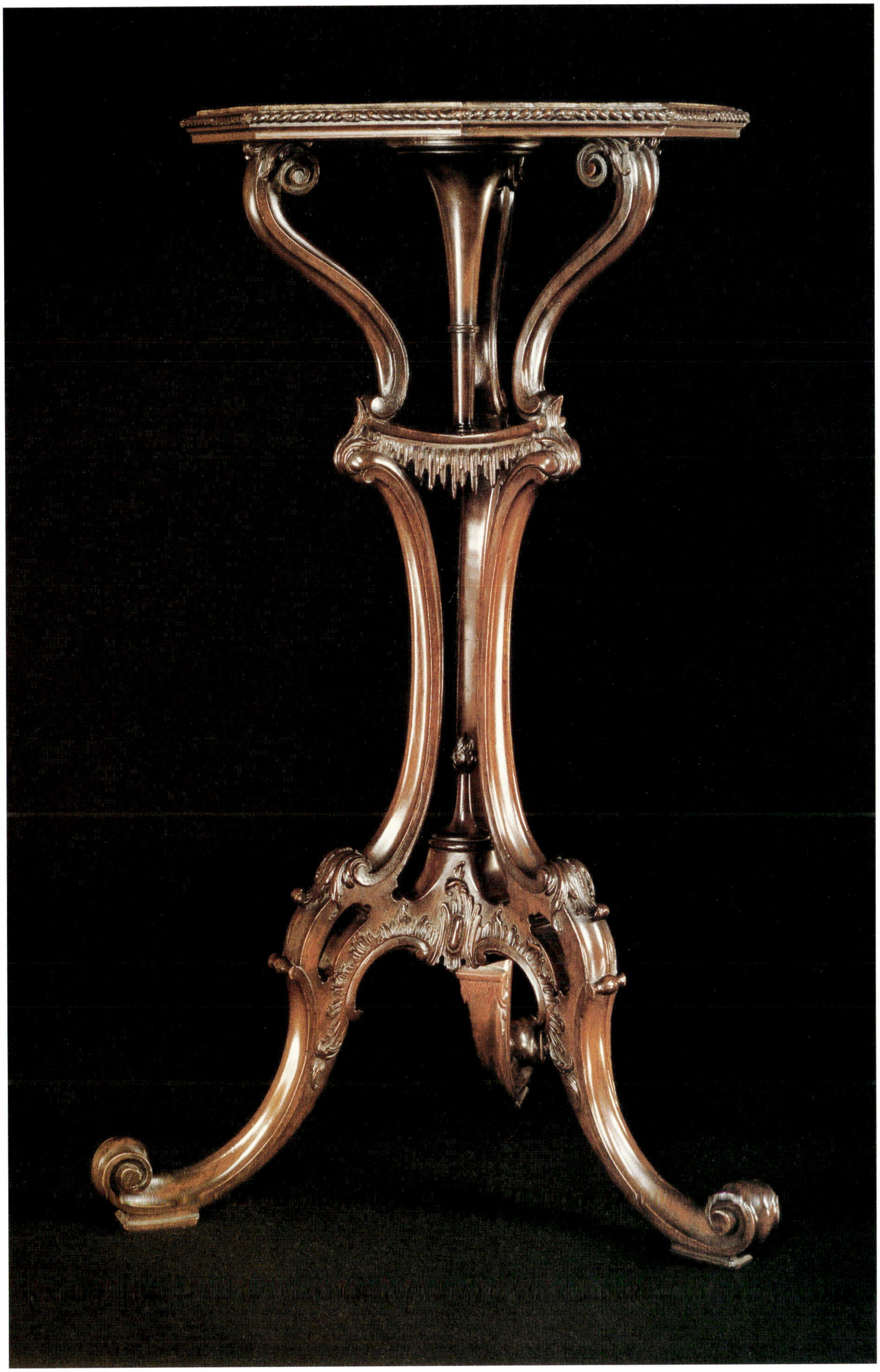

CATALOGUE 12
A mahogany secretaire, c.1760.
Attributed to William Vile.
H: 72½" (183.5 cm); W: 28" (71 cm);
D: 21½" (54.5 cm).

This fine piece of cabinet furniture belonged to Robert d'Arcy, Earl of Holderness, of Hornby Castle in Yorkshire, who was Secretary of State to George III. It was bequeathed by his wife to her granddaughter Augusta Leigh, Lord Byron's half sister, so as with this fascinating lady, it has an interesting past. Lady Holderness obviously much prized this cabinet, as a codicil to her will of July 1801 states: 'I leave to my said Grand daughter Augusta Mary Byron my little cabinet with china within and at Top; it stands in my bedchamber next to the chimney.'

The cabinet[1] was acquired from Hotspur by Arthur Leidersdorf, whose collection was sold at Sotheby's in June 1974.[2] Its pair, two inches narrower, was formerly in the collection of Miss Madeleine Hoffman.[3] A very similar cabinet, but with a panelled back to the upper section, formerly at Dudley House in London, is now in the Noel Terry Collection at Fairfax House in York.[4]

Although there is no documentary evidence relating to who supplied these cabinets, there are features in their decoration that relate to William Vile's Royal commission. The fretted sides and backs to the upper sections can be compared to those which surmount the celebrated mahogany secretaire-cabinet which was supplied by William Vile for Queen Charlotte's apartments at St James's Palace in 1761 at a cost of £71 10s. 0d.[5] It was invoiced as: 'an exceedingly ffine mahogy secretary with drawers and a writing drawer, a sett of shelves at Topp and the sides and back all handsome cuttwork'. The carved foliate panels on the legs and borders beneath the drawers on the cabinet appear on two medal cabinets recorded in the Royal accounts[6] – one now in the Victoria and Albert Museum, London, the other in the Metropolitan Museum of Art, New York.

The Earl of Holderness could perhaps have received this cabinet with its 'sides and back all handsome cuttwork' as a Royal gift. If this were so, could it and its companion have originally been commissioned from William Vile for the use of the King, Queen Charlotte, or another member of the Royal family?

PROVENANCE
Robert d'Arcy, Earl of Holderness, Hornby Castle, Yorkshire.
The Countess of Holderness.
The Hon. Augusta Leigh.
Hotspur Ltd.
Arthur D. Leidersdorf, Sotheby's London, 27 June 1974, lot 23.
Sotheby's London, 18 November 1983, lot 60.

1. As quoted in the Leidersdorf catalogue. Known as the 'Leidersdorf cabinet' because of this sale on 27–8 June 1974. See note 2.
2. Sotheby's London, 27 June 1974, lot 23.
3. Parke-Bernet Galleries, New York, 12 April 1969, lot 120. Illustrated in Edwards, *DEF* (1954), Vol. 1, p. 151, fig. 58.
4. Brown, *The Noel Terry Collection of Furniture and Clocks*, pp. 96–7.
5. Edwards, *DEF, op. cit.*, fig. 54, p. 148; Coleridge, *Chippendale Furniture: The Work of Thomas Chippendale and his Contemporaries in the Rococo Style*, p. 23, Plate 13.
6. Coleridge, *op. cit.*, Plate 21; Shrub, *The Vile Problem*, Victoria and Albert Museum Bulletin, Vol. 1, October 1965, pp. 26–35.

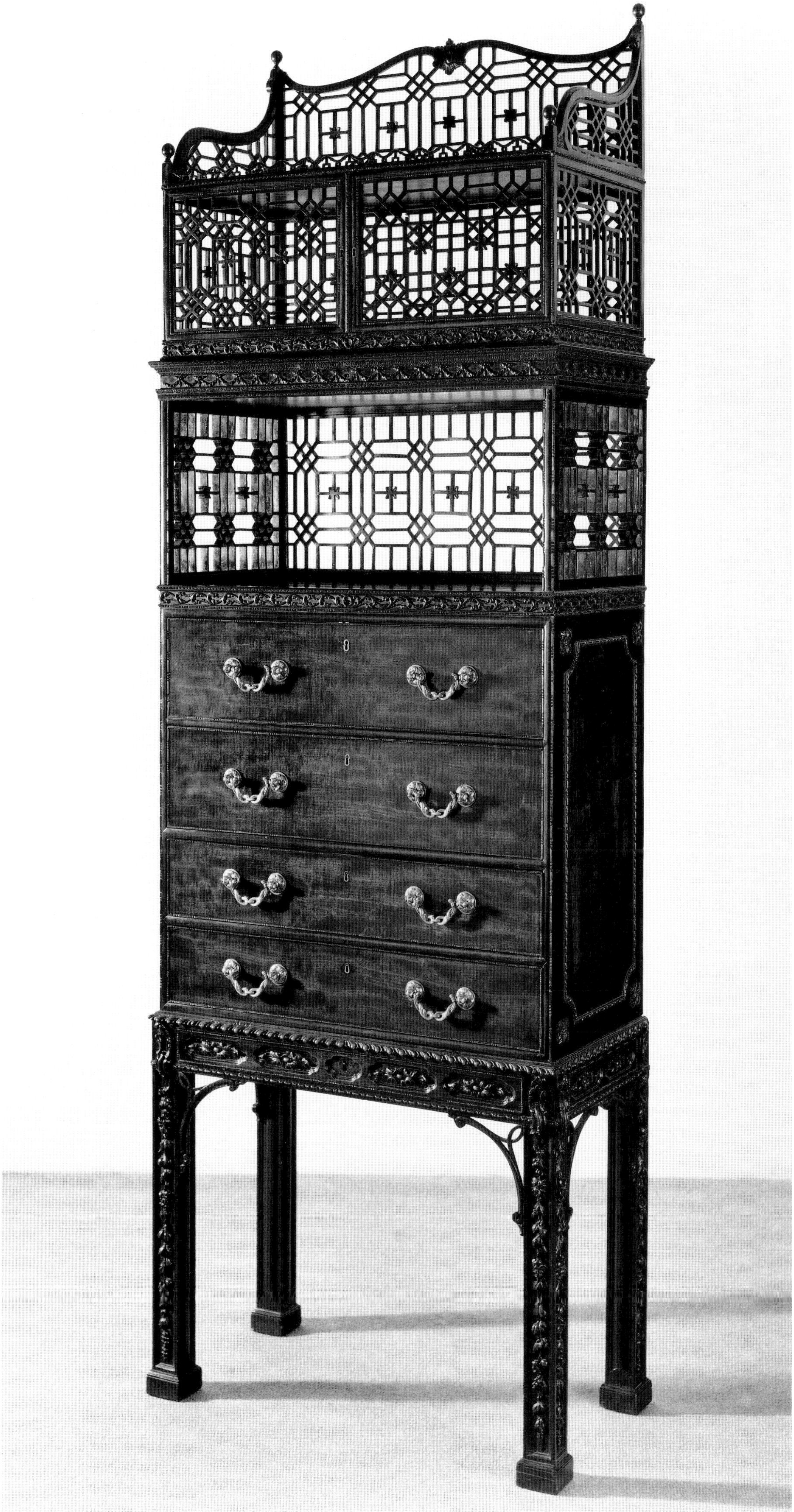

CATALOGUE 13
An oval pier-glass in an elaborately
carved gilt wood frame (one of a pair),
c.1760. Attributed to Thomas Johnson.
H: 51½" (131 cm); w: 32¾" (83 cm).

This pair of pier-glasses is based on a plate[1] in Thomas Johnson's series of designs for 'carver's pieces' issued in monthly parts, which were bound together in one volume in 1758. There was no title but it was dedicated to 'The right Honble Lord Blakeney, Grand President of the Antigallican Association'.[2]

Thomas Chippendale, Matthias Lock, Ince and Mayhew, William Linnell and the other exponents of the rococo style in this country had a serious rival in Thomas Johnson who, in addition to being a designer, was also a carver and gilder. His designs were not directed to the public, as was Chippendale's *Director* to some extent, but towards larger firms of cabinet-makers who might call upon his specialist skills as a designer and carver – so, rival as he was in many ways, he was also keen to collaborate.

Eccentric as his designs may appear, several of them have been faithfully executed in wood, glass and metal, some probably by Johnson himself, others by carvers copying his designs.[3] However, as no account from Johnson has to date been found, one must tread very warily with regard to attribution.

As an illustration of this, George Cole of Golden Square delivered a pier-glass to the Duke of Atholl during 1761 for Dunkeld House in Perthshire. The original instructions to Cole remain in the Muniment Room at Blair Castle, the Duke's seat nearby, and it was to cost about £50. When the pier-glass was delivered, the Duke was obviously delighted with it and ordered three others of similar design with console tables *en suite*.[4] Helena Hayward has demonstrated[5] that the pier-glasses at Blair Castle include many decorative motifs that suggest the hand of Thomas Johnson. Did Cole submit to the Duke for his approval a design specially commissioned from Johnson and, having received this, instructed Johnson to carve the frame from his own design, or did Cole simply use Johnson's design? Of course we do not know the answer, but Johnson's hand appears to be clearly discernible in these pier-glasses, either as their designer, or their carver and gilder, or perhaps both.

There is a further instance of the Cole/Johnson connection. Paul Methuen of Corsham Court in Wiltshire made considerable payments in 1761 to 'Mr. Cole the Upholsterer', and there are examples of carver's work after designs in Thomas Johnson's publications in the house[6] – it appears to be the same story again.

Thomas Johnson, a patriotic Englishman and presumably an Anti-Gallican, played a major role in the promotion of the rococo style in this country, as the Hotspur mirrors aptly demonstrate.

1. Hayward, *Thomas Johnson and English Rococo*, Plate 10 (centre).
2. Blakeney, one of the military heroes of the time, had defended Minorca against the French and had helped to defeat the Highlanders in the 'Forty Five' Rebellion. He was thus an admirable choice as *Grand President of the Laudable Association of Anti-Gallicans* founded in 1745 'to oppose the insidious arts of the French Nation'.
3. Coleridge, *Chippendale Furniture: The Work of Thomas Chippendale and his Contemporaries in the Rococo Style*, pp. 58–61, from which I have quoted freely.
4. Ibid., p. 60, Plates 100–2.
5. All Johnson's known designs are published by Hayward, *op. cit.*, where the possible Johnson/Cole connection is discussed, pp. 37–8.
6. Coleridge, *op. cit.*, pp. 60–1.

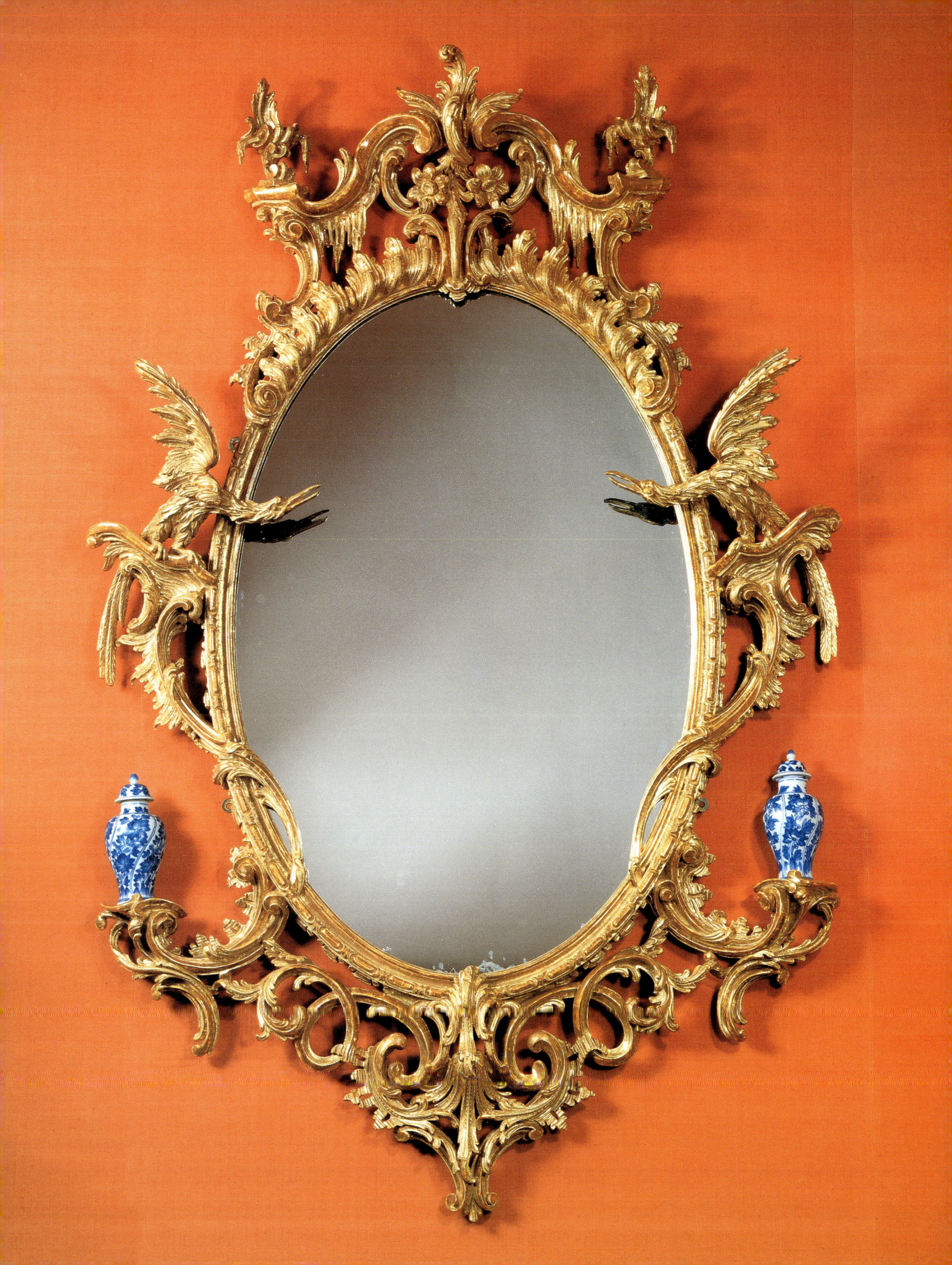

CATALOGUE 14
A pier-glass in an oval carved gilt wood frame, c.1760. Attributed to Vile and Cobb, and based on a *Director* design.
H: 88" (223.5 cm); w: 50" (127 cm).

This oval pier-glass can be attributed to the Royal cabinet-makers William Vile and John Cobb, who in 1750 acquired premises in St Martin's Lane, next to William Hallett and ten doors away from Thomas Chippendale.

Eleven years later, on 6 December 1761, the partners invoiced to the sixth Earl of Coventry, one of their major clients, an account that included the following entry:

For 2 Large Oval Glasses, in Handsome Carv'd and part painted, and part Gilt in Burnish'd Gold frames £173
For 2 Handsome Carv'd Table frames, to Stand under the Oval Glasses, part painted, and Gilt in Burnish'd Gold £33. 12. 0.

These 'glasses' and 'table frames' were commissioned for the piers of the Saloon at Croome Court in Worcestershire. Whilst discussing the set,[1] Christopher Gilbert writes: 'The mirrors relate interestingly to the left-hand design for glass frames (dated 1760) in the third edition of Chippendale's *Director*, plate CLXXII. It is possible Chippendale was specially commissioned to supply the design since he worked at Croome Court and supplied a plate of looking-glass for a frame designed by Adam for the Earl of Coventry's London house.' If this were so, it could prove that Chippendale and Vile and Cobb would collaborate if so instructed.

The carved enrichments of the Hotspur pier-glass are very similar to those on the Croome Court pair, which are painted white and gilt on their 'Handsome Carv'd Table frames', now at Temple Newsam House in Leeds. The detail and finesse of the carving of the frames of these pier-glasses is of exceptional quality, as would be expected of pieces emanating from Vile and Cobb's workshops.

1. Gilbert, *Furniture at Temple Newsam House and Lotherton Hall*, Vol. I, colour frontispiece, pp. 218–19, Vol. II, pp. 361–2.

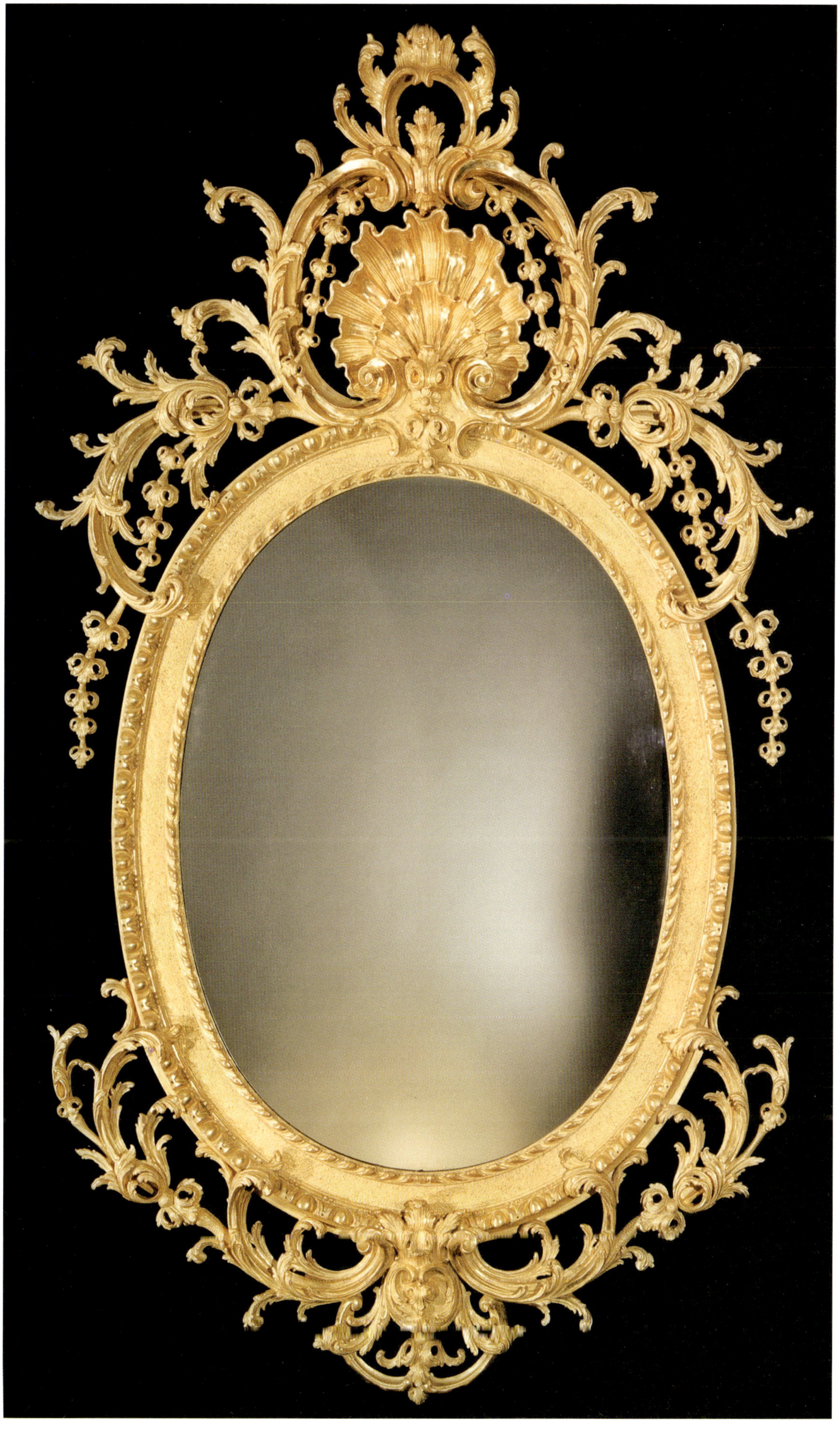

CATALOGUE 13
A small Chinese mirror painting in a
contemporary gilt wood frame, c.1760.
H: 18" (45.8 cm); W: 12" (30.5 cm).

This charming scene of a young girl seated in a garden and reading a book is an excellent example of a Chinese painting on mirror glass. These mirror plates, painted in China and exported to Europe, were much prized by lovers of chinoiserie. They were often framed on arrival in gilded softwood, which afforded the carver an ideal challenge. The frame of this example is carved with restrained rocaille detail by a hand entirely in accord with this short-lived but widely popular taste, imported from France, Germany and the continental mainland.

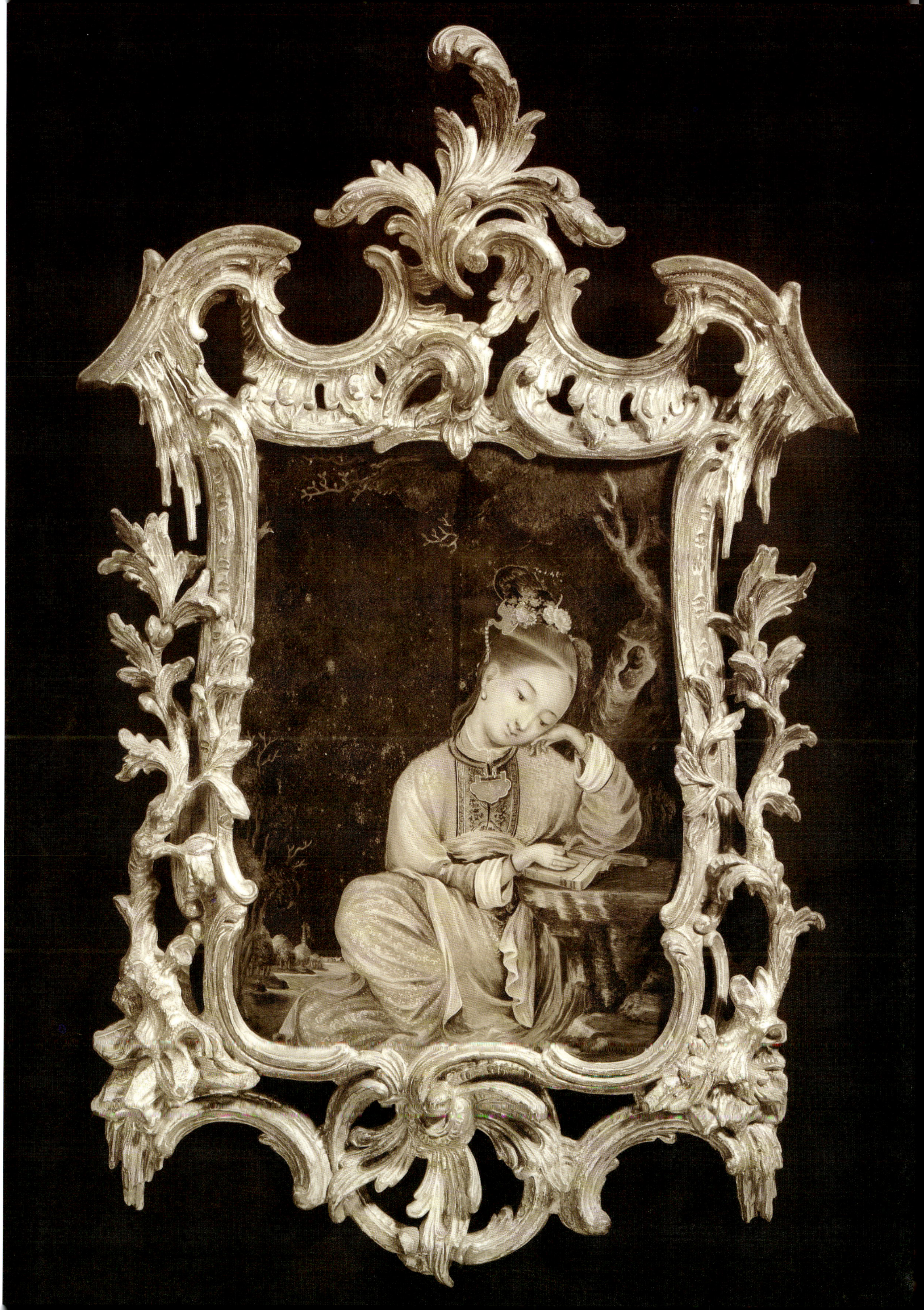

CATALOGUE 16
A mahogany bureau-bookcase, c.1765.
Described as a 'Desk & Bookcase' by
Chippendale, based on a *Director* design
of 1762 H: 98½" (249.5 cm);
W: 47½" (120.5 cm); D: 25" (63.5 cm).

This mahogany bureau-bookcase is nearly a mirror image of plate CVII in the third, 1762 edition of Thomas Chippendale's *Director*. Christopher Gilbert, who illustrates it and its engraved design in his *Life and Work of Thomas Chippendale*, writes thus in the caption:[1] 'Desk and Bookcase corresponding to a *Director* design; it has S-shaped keyholes and the lower stage contains sliding trays lined with marbled paper; the spandrel ornament relates to Chippendale's documented work. One of the few unprovenanced pieces of cabinet furniture which can be attributed with reasonable confidence to Chippendale's workshop.'

He continues:[2] 'As a rule it is fruitless to speculate about such [unprovenanced] furniture, but one item, a desk and bookcase published by R. W. Symonds in 1931, can with confidence be attributed to Chippendale's workshop.'

The Hotspur 'Desk & Bookcase' was exhibited at Grosvenor House in 1996,[3] and in the catalogue Robin Kern writes:

In addition it shows idiosyncrasies that confirm that it is Chippendale's work. These include the S-shaped key escutcheons, the sliding trays behind the cupboard doors lined in marbled paper, and the carved anthemion spandrels flanking the two mirrored doors. The arched-top mirrors are not bevelled, but complement the panels on the cupboard doors below. The carved circular *paterae* on the quarter quadrants are reflected in the backplates of the handles, and the carved spandrels on the doors represent the earliest form of neoclassical decoration, the anthemion, on this remarkable piece.

An almost identical example was offered at Christie's in London on 4 July 2002.

1. Gilbert, *The Life and Work of Thomas Chippendale*, p. 57, Plates 88, 89.
2. Ibid., p. 290.
3. Grosvenor House Fair catalogue, 1996, p. 93.
4. Christie's London, 4 July 2002, lot 50, property of the late Dame Pamela Hunter.

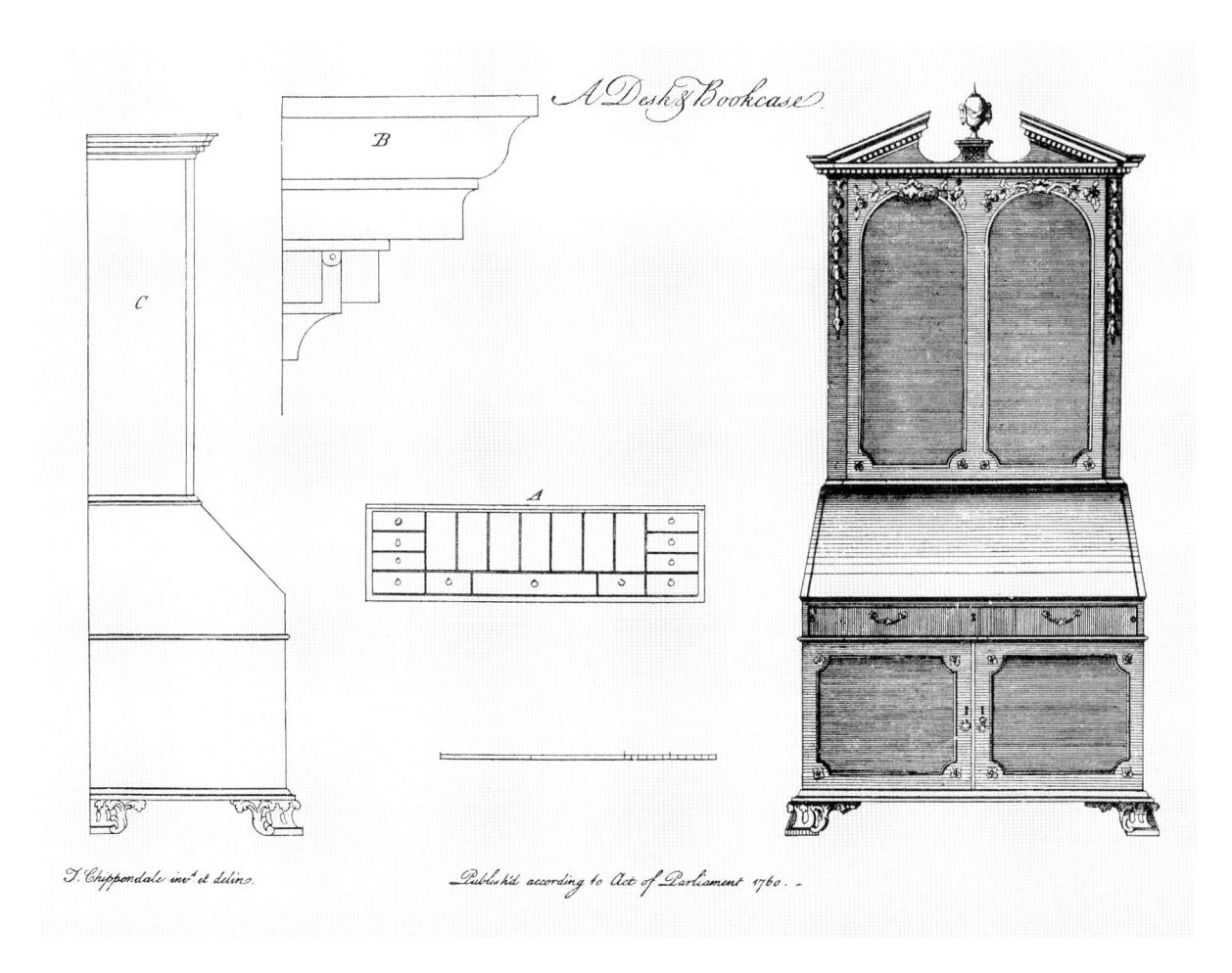

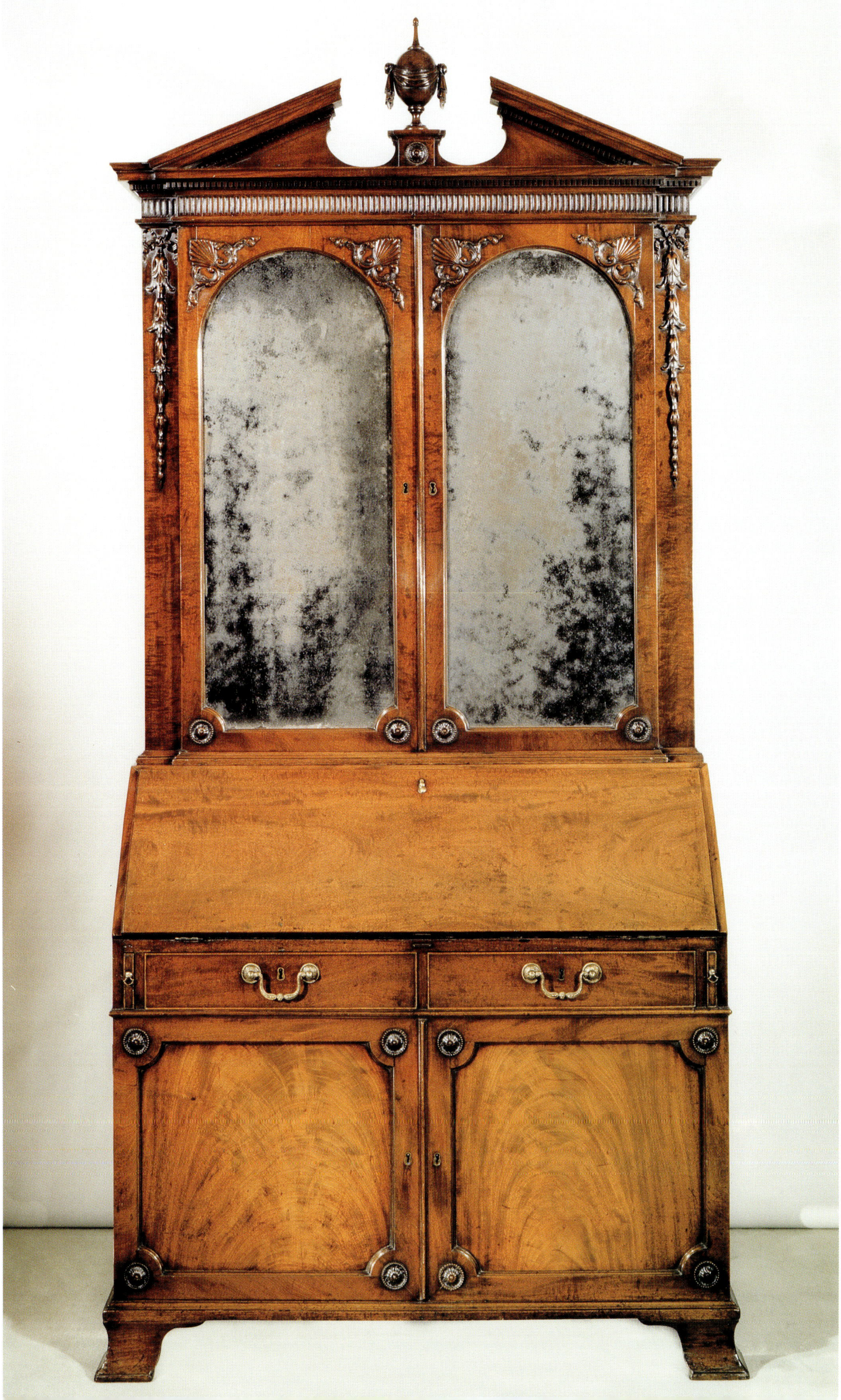

CATALOGUE 17
A mahogany folding centre table carved in deep relief with rococo and neo-classical ornament, c.1765.
H: 29" (74 cm); W: 72½" (184 cm); D: 45½" (115 cm) when opened.

Robin Kern and I also much enjoyed trying to research this extraordinary, superbly carved mahogany folding centre table, which proved to be quite an enigma. Constructed from finely grained, dense Cuban mahogany, it is a *tour de force* of virtuoso carving, created in London during the middle years of the eighteenth century. Rob Kern would have been fascinated by the dexterity of this carver's hand, which it appears could indeed see 'what was inside the piece of timber, just trying to get out'.

The table retains its original and massively thick mahogany top, ideal for the display of something substantial and very heavy such as silver gilt. However, what makes this table possibly unique is the refinement that the top is hinged in the centre and is supported on a concertina-action frame. The steel hooks that lock this hinged mechanism bear the stamp of 'H. Tibats'.[1]

Who designed and supplied this table, and for whom? As there is no documentary evidence relating to it, these questions must remain unanswered. However, several possible candidates have been discussed and, of them, two merit some consideration. The first is William Gomm (b. 1698) who, in partnership with his eldest son Richard, was well established both in Clerkenwell and in Cornhill by 1767. The Gomms boasted a distinguished coterie of clients, and foremost amongst them was the fifth Baron Leigh of Stoneleigh Abbey in Warwickshire. In 1763, the year of his majority, he commissioned William Gomm and Son of Clerkenwell Close with the considerable sum of £819 9s for stock to be delivered over two years. The most expensive individual item in the account, invoiced on 30 June 1764, was, 'An Exceeding handsome Mahogy Communion Table … richly Carv'd – £31 10s'; this swagger rococo altar table, now in the Victoria and Albert Museum, can be favourably compared with the design, form and carved detail of the table under discussion.

The second, and more likely, candidate is the splendidly named Gideon Saint (1729–99), carver and gilder at 'The Golden Head in Princes Street, near Leicester Fields'. He is remembered chiefly for his remarkable scrapbook of carvers' designs now in the Metropolitan Museum of Art in New York. It consists of 290 prints and 162 drawings, which Saint assembled and pasted onto 364 numbered pages of an album in order that his clients could pick and choose from them. On one of these pages there are various designs for side tables with exuberant carved rococo ornament and one table with neoclassical ornament. Elements of these carved details are very close to those on the table under discussion.

Whoever designed and carved the table was the possessor of manifold talents and, hopefully, the discovery of fresh documentary evidence may solve the conundrum as to his identity.

PROVENANCE
Christie's New York, 19 April 2001, lot 200.
Art Institute of Chicago.

1. H. Tibats was the proprietor of a manufactory that specialised in the production of hinges for fine case furniture, probably located in Birmingham or London.

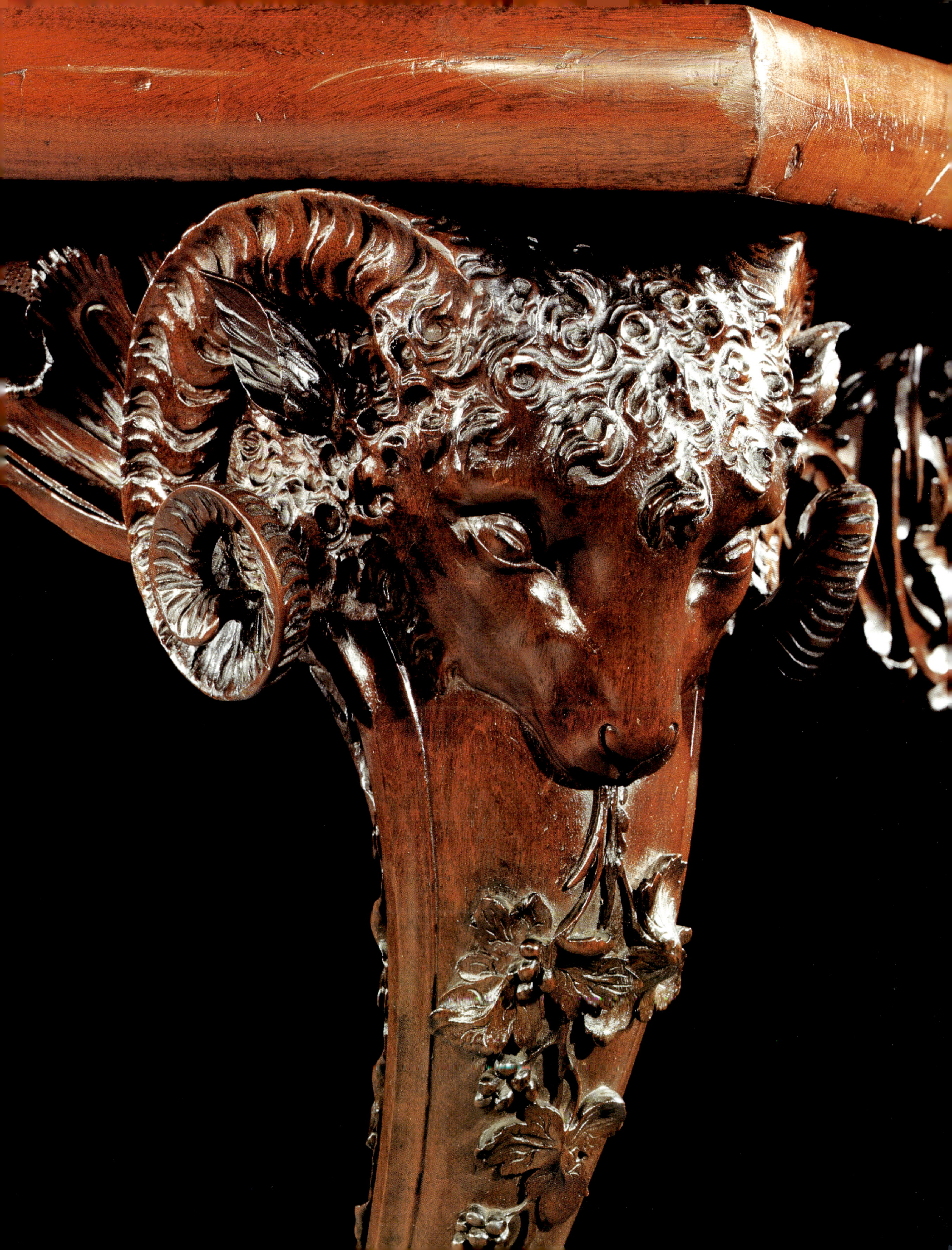

CATALOGUE 18
A yew-wood and marquetry veneered commode with an unusual design of leaves and flowers and with applied carved gilt wood mounts, c.1765.
Attributed to Mayhew and Ince.
H: 32½" (82 cm); W: 59½" (151 cm); D: 23½" (59 cm).

This commode, with applied carved gilt wood mounts to its angles and an ormolu mount to the apron, a rare feature indeed, is one of a small group of rococo yew-wood and marquetry commodes that are attributed to Mayhew and Ince of Broad Street, Carnaby Market in London. These commodes display in various combinations three features found in much of Mayhew and Ince's documented work and now identifiable as characteristic of their style: the idiosyncratic use of yew-wood as a veneer; ebonised borders and mouldings; and marquetry foliate scrolls or clasps, relying on subtle engraving for effect, often combined with floral sprays similar to the end-cut marquetry of B.V.R.B.[1] The Hotspur commode is veneered in yew-wood inlaid with marquetry designs typical of that described above; it is banded in padouk rather than ebony, so it displays two of the three features characteristic of Mayhew and Ince's style, typical of the firm's work of the 1760s.

There are two other commodes in this group that are close to the Hotspur commode. The first was in the collections of Olaf Hambro[2] and Mr and Mrs Charles Mills, the second, identical in practically every respect, was in the collection of Martin Summers.[3]

PROVENANCE
Private collection, USA.

1. Quoted from the catalogue note of lot 77 in Christie's London sale of the collection of Sir Michael Sobell, 23 June 1994.
2. Sold by Olaf Hambro Esq., Linton Park, Maidstone, Kent, at Christie's house sale 2–3 October 1961, lot 110; and subsequently by Mrs Charles Mills, Hilborough Hall, Norfolk, at Christie's house sale 21–3 October 1985. Illustrated in Coleridge, *Chippendale Furniture: The Work of Thomas Chippendale and his Contemporaries in the Rococo Style*, plate 45.
3. Sotheby's London, 18 March 1966, lot 151.

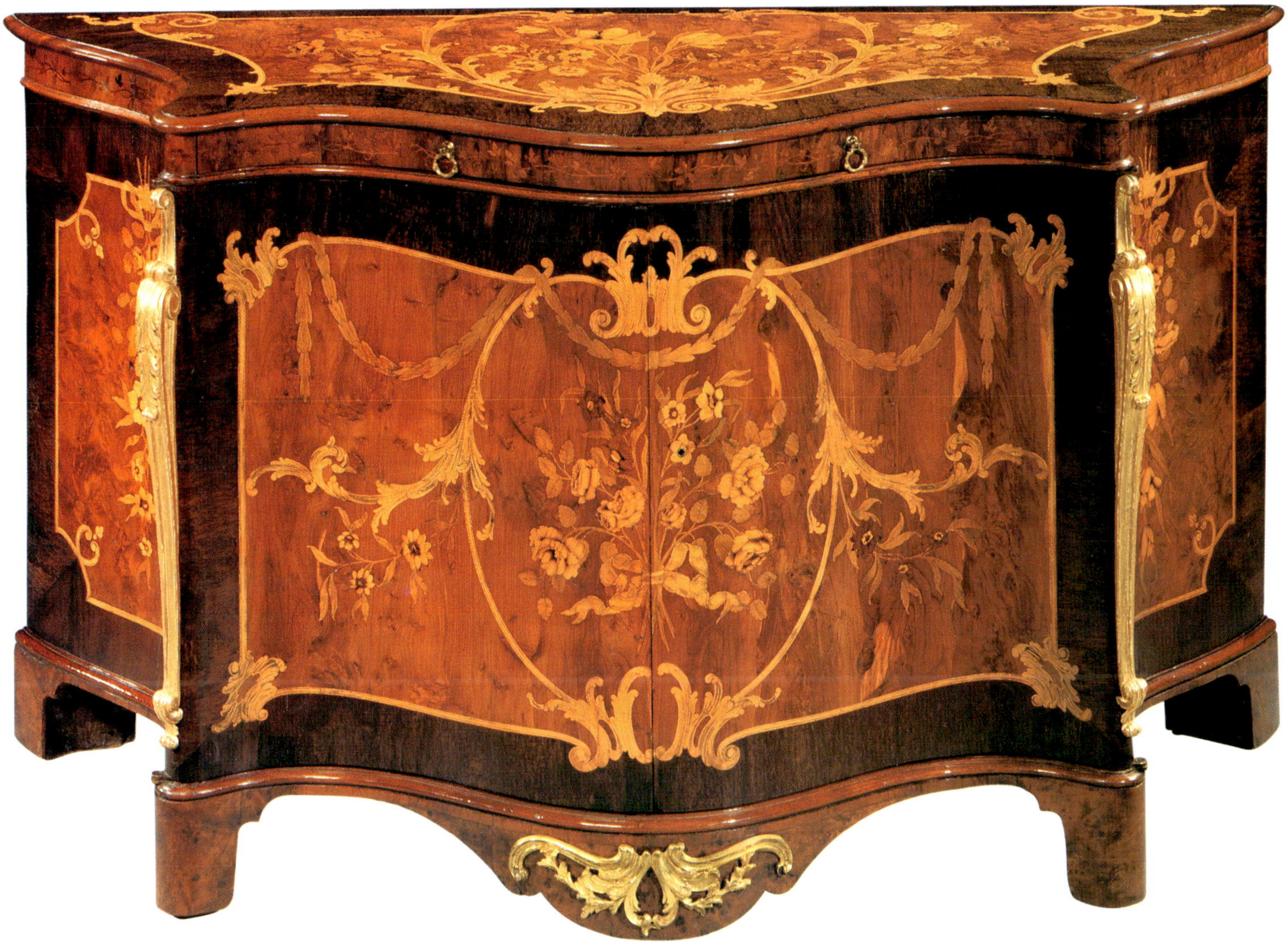

CATALOGUE 19
A stained sycamore and inlaid
mahogany commode with ormolu
enrichments, c.1765–70.
Attributed to John Cobb.
H: 35½" (90 cm); W: 48½" (123 cm);
D: 25" (63.5 cm).

Lucy Wood discusses a group of similar commodes, the doors and sides of which are inlaid with large oval medallions.[1] The most celebrated of this group is the example with pedestals *en suite* which John Cobb supplied to Paul Methuen for Corsham Court, Wiltshire, in 1772.[2] Probably the second most cited commode in the group is the example sold from the collection of the second Baron Tweedsmouth of Guisachan House, Inverness, in 1905.[3] The oval panels that centre the doors of both commodes are intricately inlaid with vases of flowers. They also have similar oval panels to the sides, the Methuen example being inlaid with a coat of arms, the Tweedsmouth example with blank panels.

Wood illustrates the Hotspur commode.[4] The stained sycamore ground to the two doors and side panels is inlaid with large figured mahogany oval panels, whilst the serpentine-shaped top is inlaid with a most unusual quatrefoil-shaped medallion. The ormolu mounts, the borders and carrying handles conform to those on the two commodes discussed above. The attribution of the Hotspur commode to John Cobb, as with the other examples in the group, is based on comparison with the splendid commode supplied by John Cobb to Lord Methuen.

PROVENANCE
Mary, Countess Howe,
35 Curzon Street, London.
Moss Harris.
H. H. Mulliner.
Christie's London, May 1933, lot 95.
Frank Partridge and Sons, 1946.
Hotspur Ltd.

1. Wood, *Catalogue of Commodes*, p. 88, no. 7.
2. Ibid., p. 91, figs 75–7.
3. Ibid., p. 93, figs 81–2.
4. Ibid., p. 97, fig. 93.

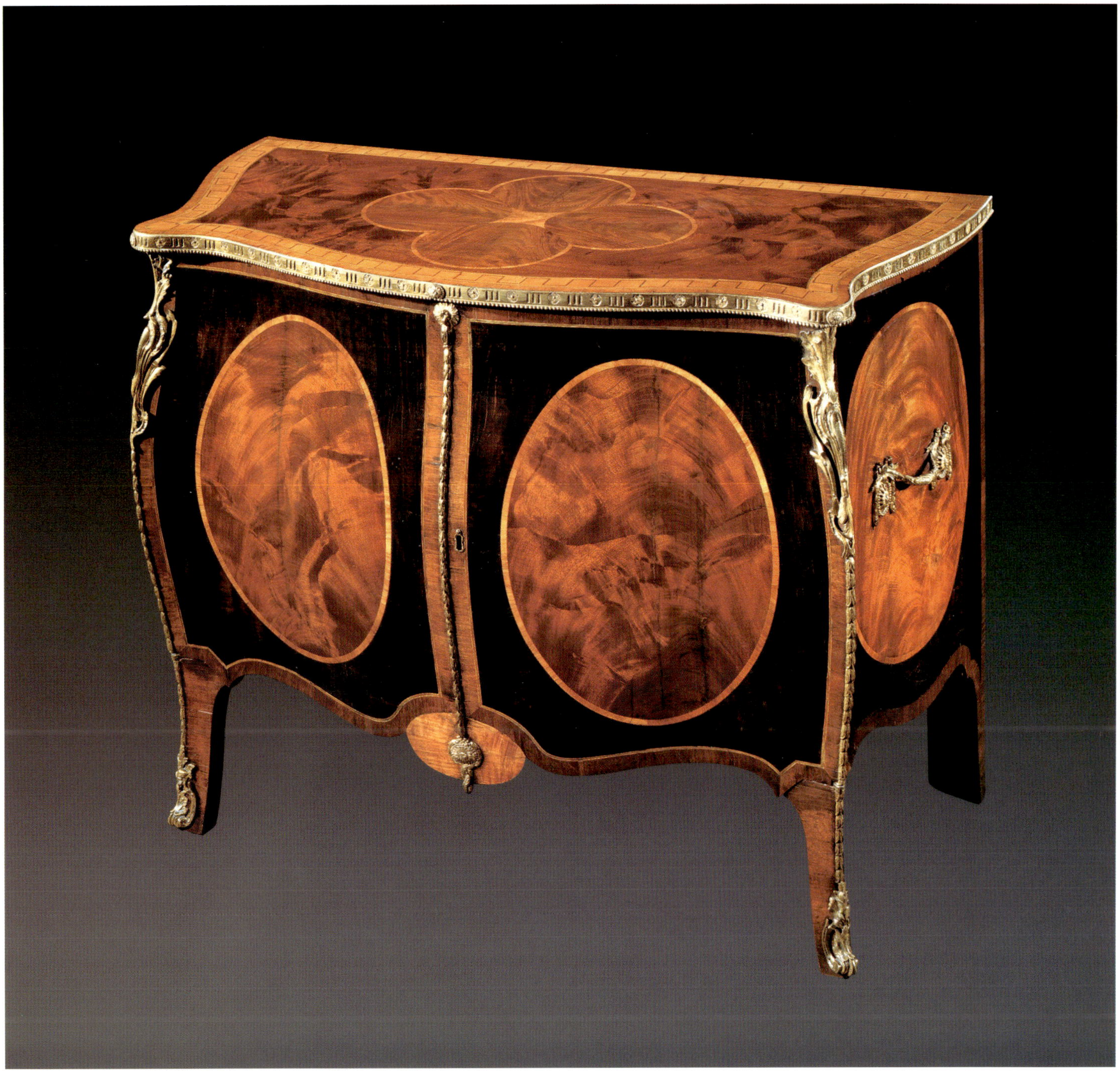

CATALOGUE 20
A serpentine mahogany commode
with carved angles and feet, c.1770.
Attributed to Thomas Chippendale.
H: 33¾" (86 cm); W: 53" (134.5 cm);
D: 24¾" (63 cm).

This commode may be attributed to Thomas Chippendale on the grounds of its close similarity to a pair of commodes almost certainly supplied to Daniel Lascelles, brother of Edwin Lascelles of Harewood House, for Goldsborough Hall, about ten miles from Harewood in Yorkshire.

Although no bills or account books are extant relating to the furnishing of Goldsborough Hall, it is recorded that William Reid, Chippendale's foreman, made several visits to the house between 1771 and 1776. An 1801 inventory of the contents of the Hall includes commodes, and Christopher Gilbert, whilst discussing the furniture at Goldsborough, some of which is now at Harewood, writes: 'Although it would be impossible fully to unravel the two collections, it is possible with a fair degree of confidence to provenance ten or so pieces – besides the dining-room furniture – to Goldsborough, the most distinguished being a pair of serpentine mahogany commodes.'[1]

Gilbert draws attention to the handle pattern and S-shaped keyholes that are associated with Chippendale's *oeuvre*. The attribution of the Goldsborough Hall commodes to Chippendale is accepted, and it is very reasonable that the commode discussed here should follow suit.

PROVENANCE
Ham Court, Worcestershire.
Private collection.

1. Gilbert, *The Life and Work of Thomas Chippendale*, pp. 258–9, Plate 226.

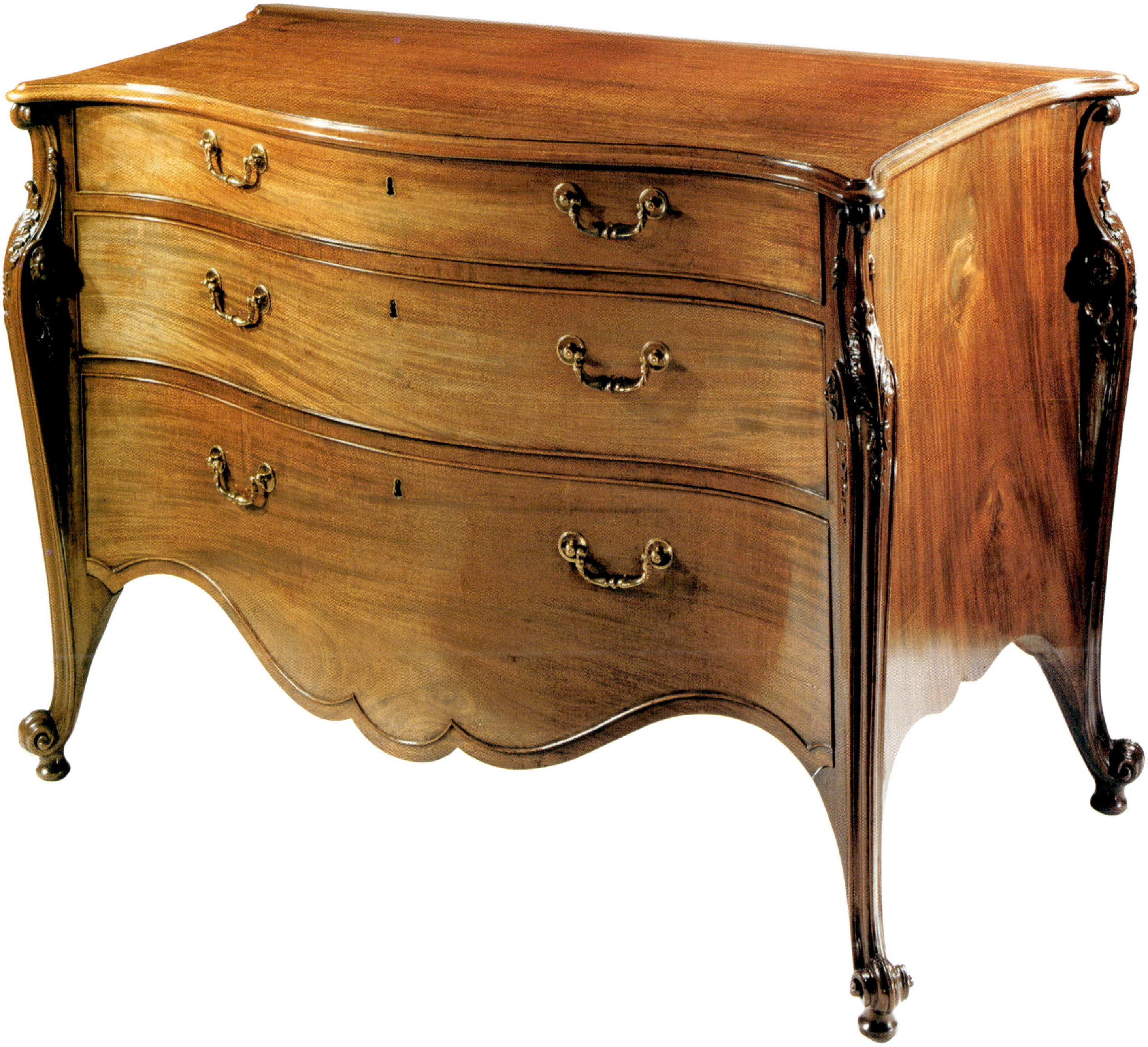

CATALOGUE 21
A sycamore and marquetry side table mounted in ormolu. c.1770. Attributed to Thomas Chippendale.
H: 30½" (77.5 cm); W: 52½" (133 cm); D: 26" (66 cm).

I have had a love affair with this table since I first saw it in 1966 at Idsworth Park, Hampshire, in the collection of Major A. E. Clarke-Jervoise. Hotspur purchased it in 1972 from Christie's. Its attribution to Thomas Chippendale was discussed in an article written by Edward Joy and Brian Kern in 1973.[1]

The authors compared the Clarke-Jervoise table with a documented commode supplied in 1770 by Thomas Chippendale to Sir Rowland Winn for Nostell Priory, Yorkshire, and to a pair of side tables that bore a direct relationship to it. They wrote: 'There were such striking similarities between all three pieces in their form and decorative details, and in particular between the top of the commode and that of one of the side tables, as to leave no reasonable doubt that all these came from the same workshop'[2] – that of Thomas Chippendale in St Martin's Lane where, during the latter half of the 1760s, incipient neoclassicism was emerging from the rococo.

Brian Kern and Edward Joy succinctly sum up the relationship between the Clarke-Jervoise table, a larger and grander version of the pair of side tables, and the three pieces discussed above: 'Its top is so obviously akin to that of the commode and to those of the pair of side tables, in shape, materials, marquetry decoration, outer wide cross-banding in rosewood, inner border of flowers and leaves, and edging of gilt metal guilloches that readers can easily pick out the relevant features.'[3] They continue by discussing the identical gilt metal mounts that are found on the knees, feet and friezes of some of the pieces.

There would appear to be little, if any, doubt that the Clarke-Jervoise table emanated from Chippendale's workshop.

PROVENANCE
Major A. E. Clarke-Jervoise, Idsworth Park, Hampshire.
Christie's London, 23 November 1972, lot 83.
Hotspur Ltd.

1. Joy and Kern, 'A Side Table by Thomas Chippendale', *Antique Collector*, April 1973.
2. Ibid., p. 82.
3. Ibid., p. 88.

231

CATALOGUE 22
A carved gilt wood girandole (one of a pair), c.1770.

A pair of girandoles that epitomise English early neoclassicism and that are extremely elegant, the arms retain their original gilt metal drip pans, which is rare as sadly many of them have been lost over the years.

Girandoles served an important purpose in lighting a room, with the flame of the candles reflected in their mirror-glass backplates. All candles were expensive, whether of tallow (animal fat) or beeswax, the latter being three times as expensive as the former.[1] At the Lord Mayor's banquet at Guildhall in 1761, the room was illuminated by 'near 3,000 wax tapers', reportedly at a cost of £92 4s.[2]

1. *Country House Lighting, 1660–1890*, Leeds, 1992, p. 5.
2. Ibid., p. 8.

233

CATALOGUE 23
A semi-elliptical side table, the gilt wood frame supporting an inlaid harewood veneered top (one of a pair).
c.1770.
H: 35½" (90 cm); W: one, 55¼" (141.5 cm); the other, 55½" (141 cm);
D: 23½" (60 cm).

The legs of these tables, which are carved with a most unusual design of spiral and foliated flutes, are based on those in a drawing for 'two designs for a table'[1] by Matthias Lock. As Lock died around 1765, he could not have been responsible for this neoclassical design.

Between 1788 and 1797, a carver of the same name is recorded at Clerkenwell Green;[2] this was presumably Lock's son, Matthias Lock Junior, and it is he who is responsible for the design under discussion. It was from his descendant, George Lock, that the Victoria and Albert Museum purchased the Lock collection of drawings in 1862–3.

The drapery swag decoration, which is suspended from the fluted frieze, is most elegant; each of the swags is stamped with an identification number on the reverse. The harewood veneered tops are inlaid with semi-circular panels centred by shells from which radiates a sunburst of stiff leaves. These tables are now in the Houston Museum in Texas.

As far as I am aware, there is no record of any furniture being supplied by Matthias Lock of Clerkenwell Green.

1. Ward Jackson, *English Furniture Designs of the Eighteenth Century*, p. 60, Plate 251.
2. Beard and Gilbert, *DEFM*, p. 552.

235

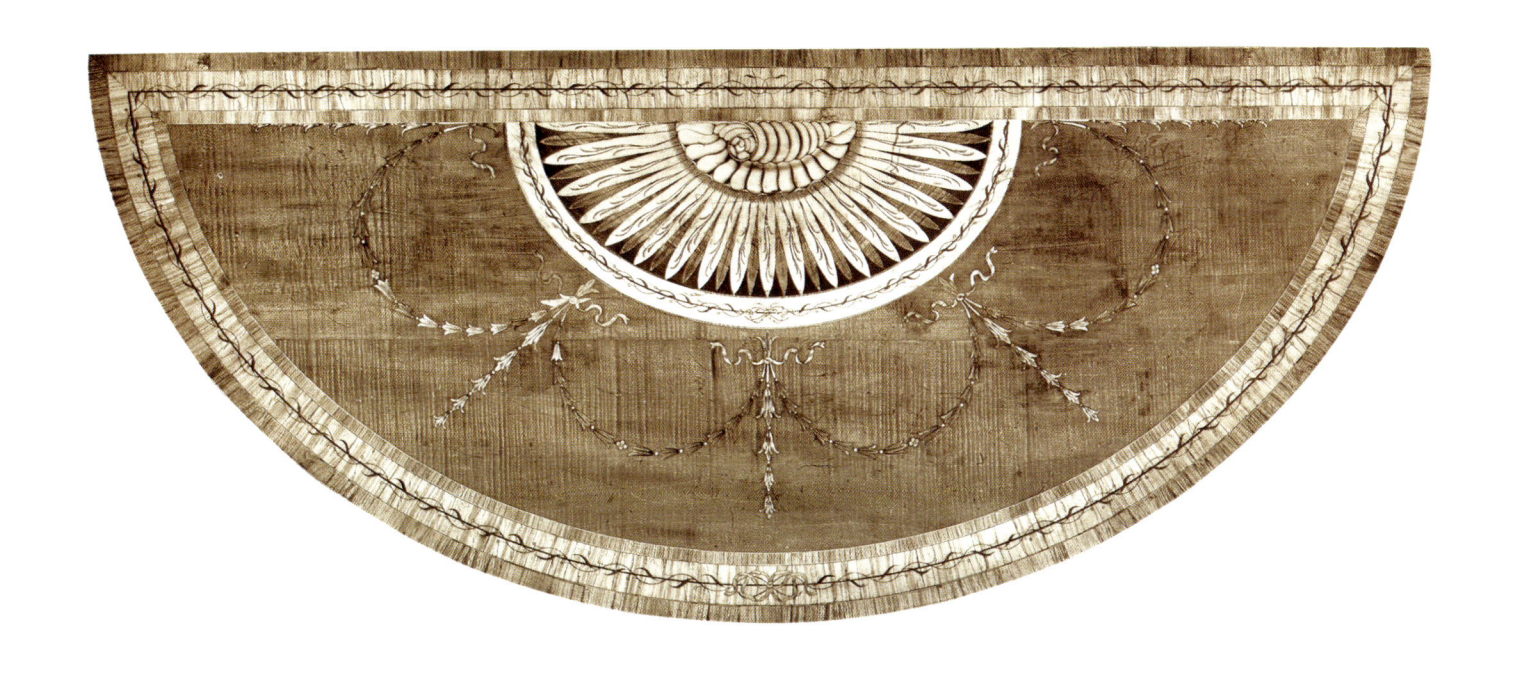

CATALOGUE 24
A lacquered and japanned secretaire, c.1775. Supplied by Thomas Chippendale to Robert and Sarah Child for Osterley Park House in Middlesex.
H: 55½" (136 cm); W: 33½" (85 cm); D: 15¼" (39 cm).

This is another distinguished piece, the history of which I had the greatest pleasure in researching with Robin Kern. This secretaire or 'Lady's Secretary', as it would have been called in the eighteenth century, had been unrecognised when catalogued for an auction in Northumberland in February 1993. Robin asked me to write an article on it, which I did, entitled 'An Addition to Chippendale's Oeuvre', to be published in New York in the June 1996 issue of the magazine *Antiques*. In it I demonstrated that Thomas Chippendale supplied the secretaire in around 1775, to Robert and Sarah Child for Osterley Park House in Middlesex.

The reasons for this attribution and the extraordinary series of coincidences which followed can perhaps be best demonstrated by the following lengthy quotation from an article that I wrote the following year, in the June 1997 issue of *Christie's International* magazine, entitled 'A Tale of Two Secretaires':

This splendid piece of furniture is a very fine example of an English neoclassical upright secretaire in the French taste. Veneered with panels of Chinese lacquer, which would have been painstakingly subtracted from a large Chinese screen, the frieze and border are decorated with English japanning and enriched with carved and oil gilt neoclassical motifs. In November 1773 Thomas Chippendale supplied to Edwin Lascelles of Harewood House in Yorkshire a lacquer secretaire for the State Bed Chamber at a cost of £26. It was described in the invoice as "A Lady's Secretary vaneer'd with your own Japann [lacquer] with additions of Carved Ornaments & Japann'd and part Gilt, the front of the Secretary to rise with Balance Weights". There is at Harewood House today a satinwood and marquetry upright secretaire, which is attributed to Chippendale. Although not included in his extant accounts, it is part of the 1795 inventory taken on the death of Edwin Lascelles. This piece and the lacquer secretaire are identical in form, construction and measurements and they have identically arranged interiors.

I then compared the lacquer secretaire to a dressing commode that was also supplied for Harewood House, again for the State Bed Chamber. This piece, now in the collection of Jon Gerstenfeld,[1] was invoiced by Chippendale as 'A large Commode with folding Doors vaneer'd with your own Japann with additions Japann'd to match with a dressing Drawer and fine locks'. These two pieces of furniture, both invoiced on 12 November 1773, for the same room, the State Bed Chamber, have much in common, but I would describe them as 'first cousins' rather than 'brother and sister'. The secretaire under discussion has various other decorative, stylistic and constructional elements that point to Chippendale's workshop, but space precludes further discussion here.

I had almost completed my article and was confident that the secretaire was the one described in Chippendale's 1773 Harewood account, as was Christopher Gilbert, author of *The Life and Work of Thomas Chippendale*. However, there are at Osterley Park House in Middlesex two very grand lacquer commodes[2] that have previously been attributed to Chippendale, although unsupported by a bill, which have much in common with the secretaire under discussion. I was discussing the merits of these commodes with my colleague, John Hardy, when he had a brilliant recollection. When curator at the Victoria and Albert Museum, with responsibility for Osterley, he recalled having seen an identical lacquer secretaire, illustrated in a view of the Etruscan Room published in 1922 in Arthur T. Bolton's *Architecture of Robert and James Adam*. There it was staring us in the face. The secretaire can be identified as the 'japanned secretaire with pictures and books', which was listed as part of the contents of Mr Child's Dressing-Room when an inventory was taken at Osterley after his death in 1782.

A comparison of the secretaire under discussion with the two Osterley commodes was most rewarding. It was now becoming apparent to Robin Kern, John Hardy and me, when we visited Osterley on that exciting and unforgettable morning, that Chippendale had not only made the secretaire, but that he had also supplied it to Robert and Sarah Child. If this was so, then in all probability he made the two Osterley lacquer commodes too. Happily, the attribution of the secretaire to Chippendale became universally accepted and funds were found from a private benefactor, the National Art Collections Fund and the National Heritage Memorial Fund to purchase the secretaire for the National Trust and return it to Osterley where it belongs. Simon Jervis marked the happy ending to this story by writing an article for *Apollo* in June 1996 entitled 'Acquisition in Focus, a "Lady's Secretary" for Osterley Park'.

However, the story has by no means ended yet. Towards the end of my article in *Antiques* I wrote, 'perhaps the Lady's Secretary that Chippendale supplied to Harewood still awaits discovery'. In 1996 my colleague Edward Lennox-Boyd was researching in the late Robert Symonds's photographic archive at the Winterthur Museum in Delaware when he came across a photograph of a c.1775 black and gilt lacquer upright secretaire. Its similarity to the Osterley secretaire is striking.

This tale has turned up many bizarre coincidences. I had completed this article, as far as this point, by the late afternoon of 10 February 1997, and had obviously hoped that it might be read by the owner of the Harewood secretaire: later that evening I listened to a telephone message from a colleague to hear that the secretaire, which was illustrated in Robert Symonds's photograph, had been delivered to our warehouse. A client had sent it in for advice and my colleagues had recognised it. I could hardly believe it.

It is a splendid piece of furniture, as one would expect: Chippendale at his best. Here was the 'Lady's Secretary vaneer'd with your own Japann with additions of Carved Ornaments & Japann'd and part Gilt, the front of the Secretary to rise with Balance Weights', which Thomas Chippendale supplied to Edwin Lascelles of Harewood House in November 1773 at a cost of £26 for the State Bed Chamber. The hunt was over before it had really begun. James Lomax fully discusses this piece on pages 44 to 47. After being offered at Christie's,[3] it is now back in Yorkshire at Temple Newsam House in Leeds, not far from Harewood House.

PROVENANCE

Robert and Sarah Child, Osterley Park House, Middlesex.
Hotspur Ltd.
National Trust, Osterley Park House, Middlesex.

1. Lennox-Boyd, *Masterpieces of English Furniture: The Gerstenfeld Collection*, pp. 86–9.
2. Coleridge, 'An addition to Chippendale's Oeuvre', *Antiques*, June 1996, illustrated on pp. 866–7.
3. Christie's London, 3 July 1997, lot 80.

CATALOGUE 25
A burr elm veneered writing table mounted in gilt bronze, *c.*1825.
Attributed to Morel and Seddon.
H: 29½" (75 cm); W: 50" (127 cm); D: 27" (69 cm).

This distinguished burr elm veneered writing table can be compared with a pair of sofa tables, part gilded and veneered with amboyna, which were supplied by Morel and Seddon to George IV for Rooms 188 and 197[1] at Windsor Castle in *c.*1828.[2]

They were invoiced at £1,728 for the pair, the table destined for Room 188 being described thus:

To a sofa table of fine amboyna wood highly polished with handsome buhl border of pearl and metals, richly inlaid with tortoise-shell with ormolu mouldings on the edge and richly carved cove rail on standards with carved and ormolu scroll lotus, and rosette ornaments, terminating with enriched plinths and stuffed foot rail covered with the Office gros de Naples, the whole of the carving double gilt in the best manner in mat and burnished gold and standing on improved castors.

The tops of the tables invoiced by Morel and Seddon each have 'a handsome buhl border of pearl and metals, richly inlaid with tortoise-shell', whilst the Hotspur example has a border inlaid with cut brass of a stylised floral repeating design: likewise the 'stuffed foot rail[s]' on the Windsor pair are echoed by the central leather-covered footrest on the example under discussion. These rich golden *bois-clair* tables are also mounted with similar gilt bronze rosettes.

Nicholas Morel, who had worked for the King when he was Prince of Wales at both the Brighton Pavilion and Carlton House, had in 1807 been referred to as 'Upholder Extraordinary' to the Prince of Wales and, with his partner Robert Hughes, as 'Upholders to the Prince of Wales' from 1811 to 1820. For the Windsor Castle commission he formed a partnership with George Seddon, a member of the celebrated and long-established family of cabinet-makers who had large workshops in Aldersgate Street in east London, the use of which was essential to the project.[3] Nicholas Morel and George Seddon won the Windsor Castle commission in 1826.

PROVENANCE
Sotheby's Parke Bernet New York, 23 November 1979, lot 83.
Christie's New York, 19 October 2000, lot 150.

1. Now in the Large or Crimson Drawing-Room.
2. Roberts, *For the King's Pleasure: The Furnishing and Decoration of George IV's Apartments at Windsor Castle*, p. 123, figs 95–7.
3. De Bellaigue and Kirkham, 'George IV and the Furnishing of Windsor Castle', *FHSJ*, 1972, Plates 17a–b.

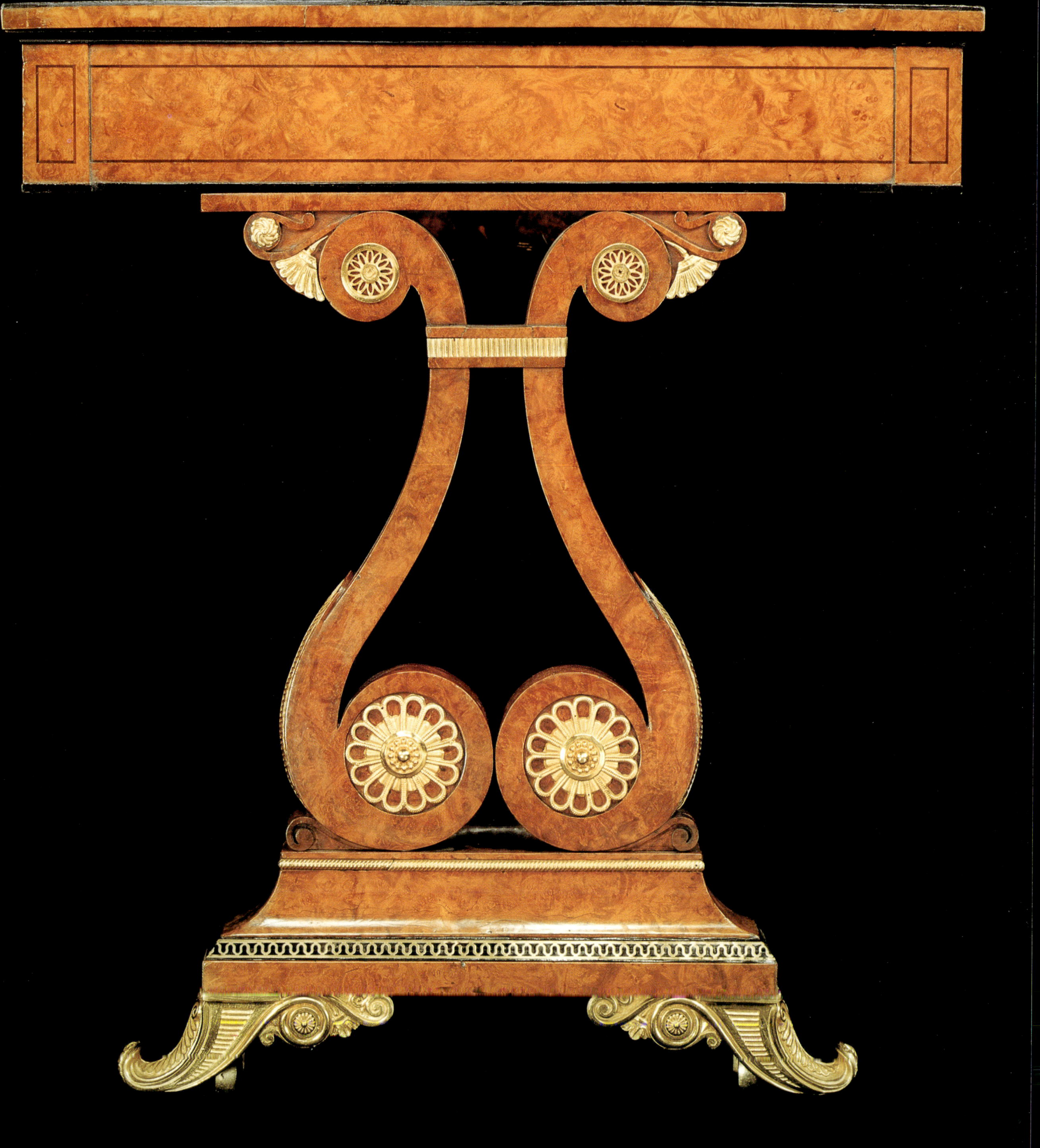

Clocks, barometers and other objects

ROBIN KERN

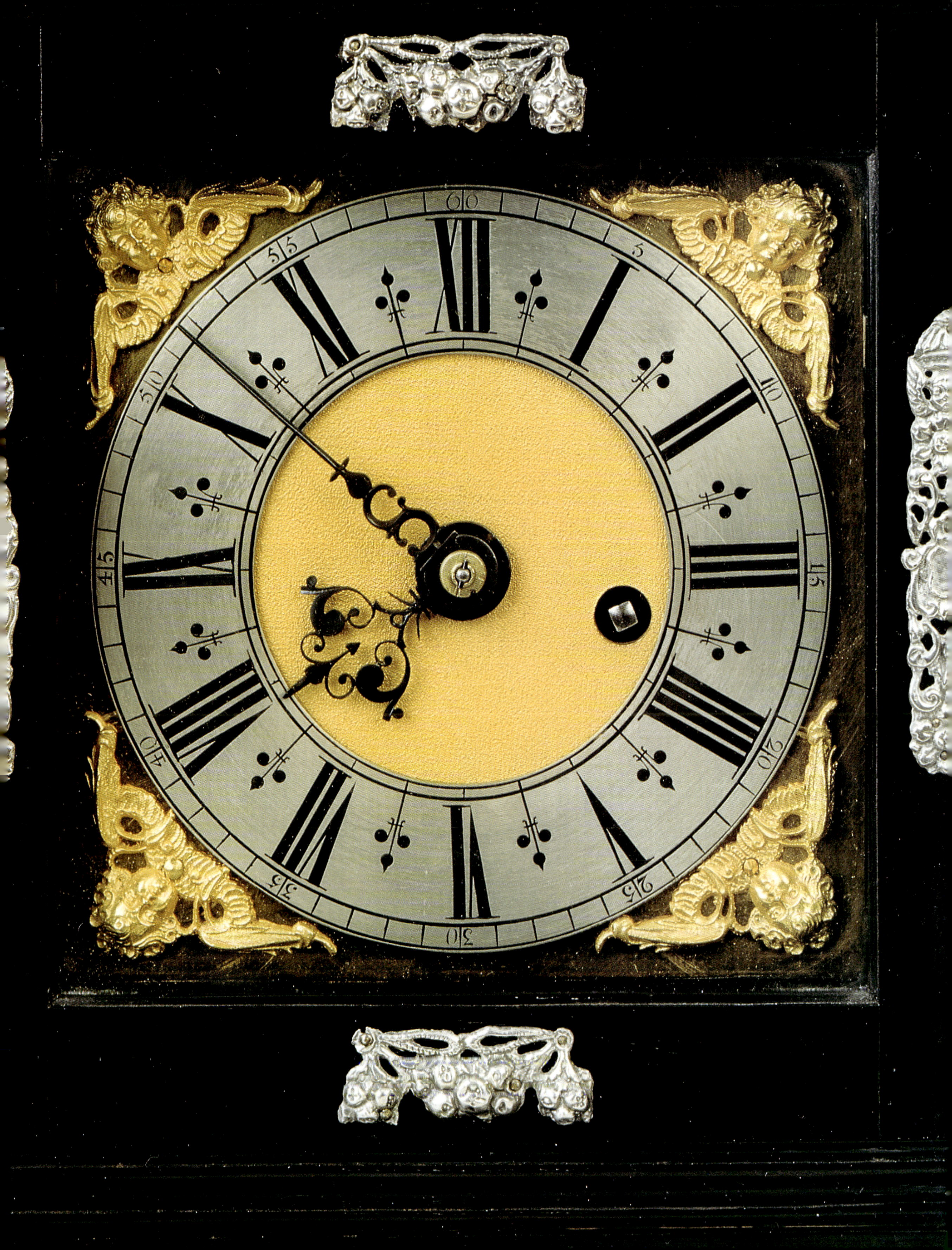

CLOCKS, BAROMETERS AND OTHER OBJECTS

THE EXCITEMENT OF the 'chase' in this wonderful world of antiques is difficult to put into words. Suffice to say that every day brings its surprises and you never know from one day to the next what will turn up, what will be submitted, or who will approach Hotspur about acquiring an object. Days and weeks often pass without news of possible must-have purchases and then the element of buying for the sake of buying creeps in, something that is dangerous and must be kept in check. Patience often brings rewards from the most unusual sources. Coincidence, too, plays an important part in the life of an antiques dealer; and one must not underestimate the contribution made by the friendship of many dealers with whom we have reciprocal deals of one form or another. It is a fact of life that the number of dealers in eighteenth-century English furniture is shrinking, both in London and in the regions – the same thing is happening in America. One of the advantages of being long established is that we are offered back pieces sold in the past and this source is invaluable – it is a most important part of Hotspur's strategy for acquisition.

It has been difficult to select these few pieces, under what might be termed, inelegantly, a 'miscellany', from the many wonderful objects that have passed through our hands over eighty years, but the group I have chosen reflects Hotspur's interests, both specialised and varied; while at the same time each is worthy of note for its quality, for its rarity, for its charm and beauty.

These pieces will be discussed chronologically, beginning with a late seventeenth-century silver-mounted quarter repeating timepiece by the eminent clockmaker Samuel Watson of London, who was Royal Clockmaker to King Charles II (Fig. 1).

Samuel Watson was called 'Mathematician in Ordinary to His Majesty', and at Windsor Castle there is an elaborate astrological calendar clock that he made for Charles II; he also supplied an astrological calendar clock to Isaac Newton. This delightful clock is of diminutive size, being just over fourteen inches high; the case is veneered in ebony with the enchanting contrast of fine silver mounts. It is fascinating in many ways, not least that the silver-embellished basket top incorporates the history

PREVIOUS PAGE, ABOVE & OPPOSITE
1. A silver-mounted quarter repeating timepiece, c.1690.
H: 14½" (37 cm).

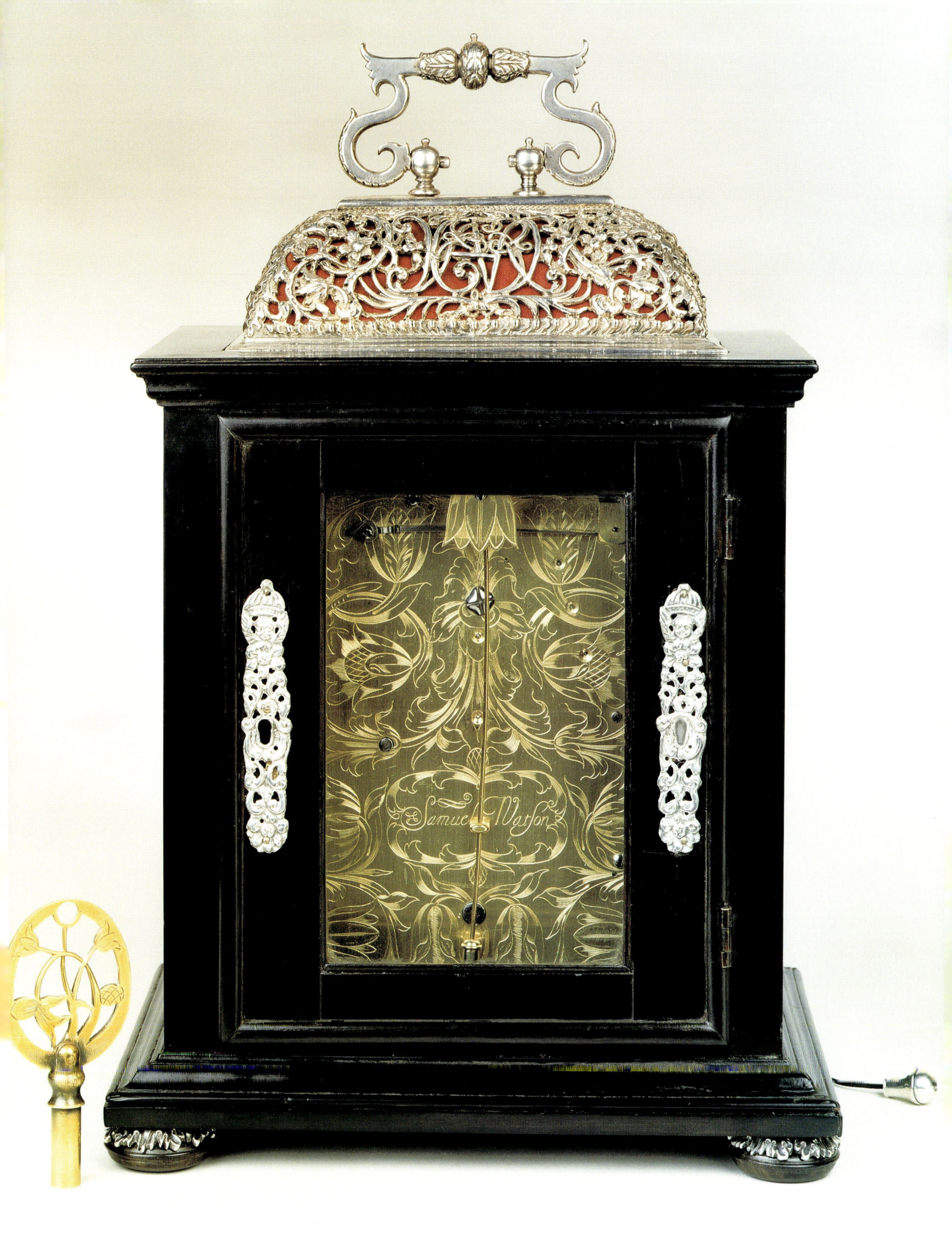
Samuel Watson

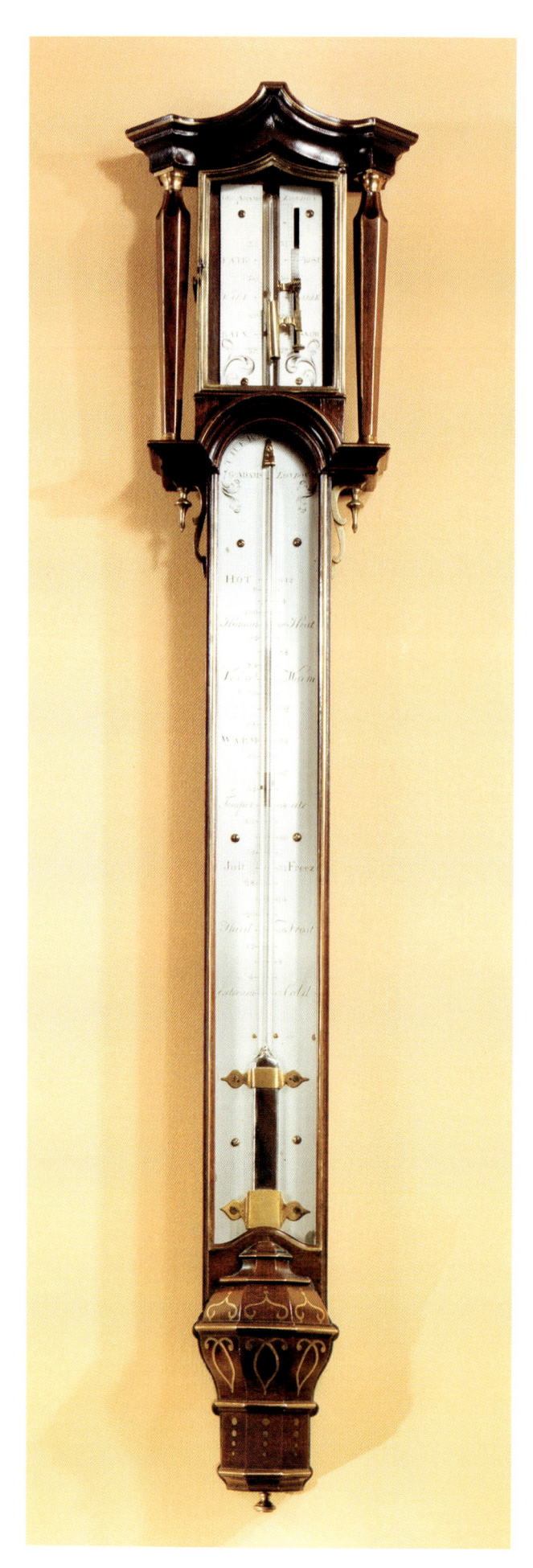

2. A George Adams barometer, c.1760.
H: 37½" (95.2 cm).

CLOCKS, BAROMETERS AND OTHER OBJECTS

of this little clock in the form of the Birch family coat of arms at the front – the crest is on the left- and right-hand sides – while at the back is the monogram or cipher of the Birch family's initials, 'W.C.E.H.I.R.B.B.' All the silver mounts are pierced and backed with crimson silk. The eight-day, seven-pillar movement has a verge escapement with pull quarter repeat on two bells and the tulip engraved back-plate bears the maker's signature.

The very interesting mid-eighteenth-century barometer (Fig. 2), is by George Adams, one of the most eminent instrument-makers of the period, who worked for the Prince of Wales and later for George III. This barometer is of great interest not only for its sophisticated and fine inlaid brass decoration to the mahogany case, but also for its very rare precision-recording 'magnifying glass' mounted on the vernier scale, a feature that I have not seen before.

The shaped pagoda cresting is mounted on two tapering columns inlaid with brass stringing, and written on the arched silvered thermometer plate flanked by gilt metal brackets, is 'Thermometer' and it is signed 'G. Adams, London'. The cistern cover at the base is richly embellished with inlaid brass decoration and closely mirrors the group of inlaid brass furniture that formed the exhibition at the Victoria and Albert Museum in 1994: *John Channon and Brass-Inlaid Furniture, 1730–1760*.[1] The Museum owns a similar barometer.

In my 'Reminiscences' I give an account of my trip to America with Jerome Phillips in 1961, and relate how during our stay we travelled non-stop, visiting clients, museums and other dealers. Alastair Stair, of Stair & Co., who had magnificent premises at that time on East 57th Street, was kindness itself, and in the years to come I visited him twice a year and purchased many handsome pieces. The pole screen (Fig. 3) was a thrilling find, spied in the basement of the Stair & Co. building in the mid-1960s. It comes from the famous Mulliner Collection,[2] and the design for it is based upon two drawings in the first, 1754 edition of Chippendale's *Director*.[3]

The banner frame for the screen is a Fulham tapestry panel depicting a pheasant with foliage decoration that is contained in a superbly and richly

3. A pole screen, c.1754.
H: 64" (163 cm).

1. Goodison, *English Barometers 1680–1860*, Plates 62, 63; Gilbert and Murdoch, *John Channon and Brass-Inlaid Furniture, 1730–1760*, fig. 183.
2. Illustrated in Mulliner, *The Decorative Arts in England, 1660–1780*, fig. 188.
3. Thomas Chippendale, *The Gentlemen and Cabinet-Makers' Director*, first edition, 1754, Plate CXXIV.

4. A long-case clock, c.1755.
H: 70" (178 cm).

OPPOSITE: ABOVE & BELOW
5. The Earl of Craven's urns, c.1755.
H. overall: 72½" (184 cm).

carved pierced mahogany frame in the rococo taste. The fine rococo carving is echoed in the tripod base, again boldly carved and pierced with scroll-work and acanthus decoration; the grand finale being a superbly carved vase of flowers surmounted as a finial, sitting proudly on top of the pole. Pole screens are not the most exciting or indeed saleable objects, but this was a one-off and was included in an exhibition at the Burlington Fine Arts Club in 1920.

In the early years of my career, Hotspur purchased the eighteenth-century long-case clock (Fig. 4), which has remained with the same family ever since. It has a richly carved mahogany case containing a clock by John Pyke, who became clockmaker to George III when he was Prince of Wales. In addition, this fine example has elements of such exquisite carving as to be confidently attributed, stylistically, to the workshop of the Royal cabinet-maker, William Vile. It also holds a double interest for horologists because the pendulum is contained in a waisted pedestal with classical mouldings and retains its original marbleised decoration. The combination of the richly carved dark Cuban mahogany with this marbled stand is extraordinarily beautiful.

Every dealer must have a favourite *pièce de résistance*, such as my next choice (Fig. 5): the magnificent Earl of Craven's urns and pedestals from the Dining-Room at Combe Abbey. I find it difficult to express my admiration for the outstanding quality of these superb pieces, words are simply not enough; they are richly veneered in the finest mahogany of such quality that it takes your breath away. The patination is like bronze; the bodies of the urns are sumptuously carved with drapery swags and goatskin flanked by outrageously carved, horned and bearded goat masks. Each stands on a pedestal, beautifully veneered in the finest figured mahogany with stop-fluted panelled doors below. One cupboard door encloses a metal lined interior for plate warming, the other has a single lead-lined drawer above a tambour cupboard and a deep drawer. I remember how proud we were of these urns and pedestals and my attention was drawn time and time again by my father, who would say: 'These are eye-trainers for the condition of the finest eighteenth-century English furniture.'

The urns were sold in 1968 for the very high

CLOCKS, BAROMETERS AND OTHER OBJECTS

sum in those days of £6,700 and came back onto the market in 1995, when they fetched £450,000 at auction. We have borrowed them back twice to show at important exhibitions.[4]

We come now to another barometer (Fig. 6), one that belongs to the neoclassical period of around 1770, one that must be considered a 'must' for every serious collector of fine English furniture: a barometer by Whitehurst of Derby.

This splendid instrument is a wonderful example of design and proportion. The circular engraved steel dial is inscribed 'Whitehurst Derby' with Arabic numerals and denominations for 'Fair', 'Rain' and 'Changeable', enclosed in a carved mahogany frame with beading, foliate and acanthus decorations. The bow-fronted tapering column above is flanked by finely carved and pierced scrolling acanthus; the column is surmounted by a fine neoclassical urn finial. This is a piece of such elegance that it can easily be understood how a barometer such as this is at the top of the collector's list.

One of the great pleasures of being a dealer is the satisfaction derived from successful restoration. This was the case with the pair of *torchères* of about 1773, illustrated in figure 7. The design for them is recorded at Sir John Soane's Museum. They are by Robert Adam, dated 24 August 1773, and are inscribed 'Designed for Sir Watkin Williams-Wynne of 20 St. James's Square'. When we acquired them they had heavy nineteenth-century over-gilding obscuring the very fine detail underneath. It was quite obvious that restoration was going to take a great deal of time and patience and an exceptionally patient and skilled craftsman and gilder who was prepared to take on this task had to be found. Eventually, such a man was found in Norfolk and the slow, laborious work began. The *torchères* are carved in lime, pine and mahogany; and to ensure that we saved as much original gilding as possible, the over-gilding was dry stripped.

Numerous trips to Norfolk followed, and each time I was stunned at the quality of the fine applied lime-carved detailing. What original gilding we found was treasured and months went by before we saw the final result: it was truly magnificent. One of the great examples of Robert Adam's work finally manifested and we started to ask ourselves who would enjoy

6. A wheel barometer by Whitehurst of Derby, c.1770.
H: 43" (109 cm).

4. *The British Antique Dealers' Association Golden Jubilee Exhibition Catalogue*, Victoria and Albert Museum, 1968, no. 164, Plate 104; and C.I.O.N.A., *International Art Treasures Exhibition Catalogue*, Bath, 1973, no. 103, Plate 95.

CLOCKS, BAROMETERS AND OTHER OBJECTS

these truly perfect objects. We approached Kenwood House in Hampstead, and there they eventually found their home in the hall on either side of the chimneypiece.

At Hotspur we all thoroughly enjoyed the progress of this restoration, which preserved for posterity two remarkable pieces of neoclassical furniture that are now enjoyed by everyone who visits Kenwood House. There is a companion pair of *torchères* at Alnwick Castle.

At the Grosvenor House Fair our firm used to have a strategically placed stand opposite the position for the Royal Loans. As an admirer of finely carved mahogany furniture, one of my favourite pieces is the jewel cabinet supplied by the Royal cabinet maker, William Vile to Queen Charlotte, wife of George III. I was thrilled when this *tour de force* was chosen to be the Royal Loan in 1998. For those who share my enthusiasm for this magnificent cabinet, you will recall the quite exquisite inlaid ivory decoration that embellishes this 'jewel'.

An outstanding pair of cabinets, goes one step further towards the neoclassical period (Fig. 8). The cabinets are quite small in size and are similarly profusely inlaid with ivory and exotic woods with jewel-like precision. My hunch regards the possible maker of these cabinets is John Cobb, partner of William Vile, as the similarity of the inlaid ivory decoration is extraordinary. The superb mahogany carving of Queen Charlotte's jewel cabinet has been replaced with inlays of exotic woods for these little cabinets. Interestingly, the cabinets are enhanced by finely chased ormolu mounts, which are very much in the manner of Matthew Boulton, the fine English maker of ormolu discussed by Nicholas Goodison on pages 94 to 121. Each cabinet has a door enclosing a fitted interior of cedar-lined drawers, and they stand on shaped ormolu baluster-fluted feet with inverted ormolu brackets, faced with acanthus.

We continue in the neoclassical vein with a pair of gilt wood tripod *torchères* (Fig. 9) of quite extraordinary quality and rare design, and that have the original painted *jardinière* tops instead of the usual marble tops to support candelabra. These remarkable *torchères* represent two of the four that were supplied to George, Prince of Wales (later George IV), for his

7. A pair of *torchères*, c.1773. H: 64" (163 cm).

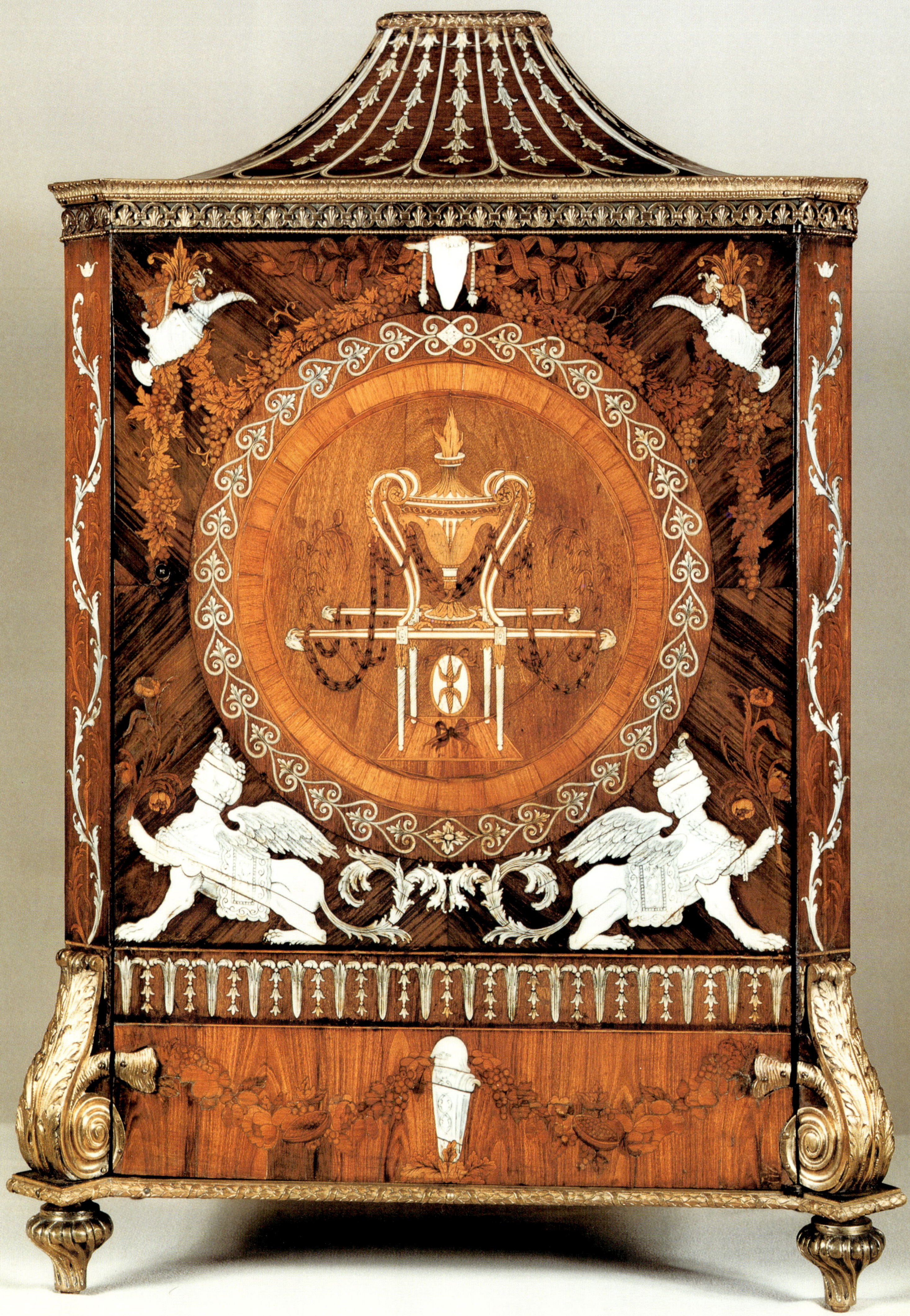

251

PREVIOUS PAGES
8. One of a pair of cabinets attributed to John Cobb, c.1775.
H: 27¾" (70.5 cm); W: 19½" (49.5 cm); D: 13½" (34.2 cm).

ABOVE
9. The original jardinière tops to (OPPOSITE):
A pair of gilt wood tripod *torchères*, c.1782.
H: 48½" (122.5 cm).

CLOCKS, BAROMETERS AND OTHER OBJECTS

rooms at the Queen's House (now Buckingham Palace) in St James's Park. They were supplied by William Gates, a cabinet-maker in St Martin's Lane, who held the Royal Warrant as tradesman to the Great Wardrobe; they were delivered in the quarter ending 5 January 1782.

The lead flower containers, with concave inset jardinière tops, retain their original painted decoration and carved *putti* holding laurel branches. These rest upon a fluted urn that is flanked by three female heads with supports, decorated with garlands of flowers sweeping down to a central stretcher of oval *paterae* with feathers, sunbursts and Apollo masks. The central urn terminates in hoof feet, which in turn rest upon a three-sided fluted plinth, again with a central urn motif, all raised on shaped feet. They seem to display every possible decorative detail belonging to the neoclassical period, but most of all I consider the decorated lead flower containers to be of the greatest interest and, indeed, rarity.

For many years one of Hotspur's great interests has been the work of Matthew Boulton, mainly in ormolu but from time to time another example of Boulton's genre would pass through our hands, such as his cut-steel work – of diamond-like precision – which holds a great fascination for us. Our introduction to this area of Matthew Boulton's *oeuvre* took the form of a dress sword, the hilt decorated with the finest faceted cut-steel studs, like diamonds, of the best possible quality. But on further investigation, it proved to be doubly interesting as we learned that Boulton employed a man named Johann Andreas Kern (our family name), a master cutler who specialised in gold damascening – the art of applying beautiful gold inlay onto the blades of swords. The coincidence was amazing!

The art of cut-steel work was also carried out in Russia, at the Imperial Arms Manufactory at Tula, south of Moscow. Each year on 21 May a fair was held by the master craftsmen at Sofia, a little town near Tsarskoye Selo, for the members of the court and nobility. Two of the best Tula craftsmen were sent to England to see Matthew Boulton's work and so impressed the English cut-steel workers that the Tula craftsmen were offered jobs.

252

253

CLOCKS, BAROMETERS AND OTHER OBJECTS

The Russians copied everything, and the tea caddy of figure 10 illustrates the point perfectly. What appears to be an English tea caddy of about 1780, is in fact one from Tula; copied from the English design by Russian master craftsmen. This example of a polygon form has plates of polished steel over a wood carcass that is secured by polished faceted nails with bands of ivory around the top and bottom. Mounted on the front, back and top of the casket are six faceted polished lozenges, while the steel handle is mounted with revolving faceted steel balls. This really is a jewel. Inside the lid, painted on ivory, are three oval 'oak leaf' frames; arrangements of heartsease pansies adorn the two outer frames. The central frame contains a portrait of a lady with an ermine cape who is wearing beautiful jewels, who has been identified as Anna Feodorovna, the wife of Grand Duke Constantin Pavlovich, brother of Tsar Alexander I. It is known that Maria Feodorovna, the wife of Paul I, was an amateur painter and designer and it would seem that she was responsible for this work. Maria Feodorovna was especially close to Anna Feodorovna, being not only her daughter-in-law, but also sharing German origin.

The next barometer (Fig. 11) is a splendid example of one of John Russell's 'Royal' barometers. Russell was one of the best known clock and watch-makers of his day, who settled in Falkirk in about 1770 and was best known for his handsome wheel barometers. The mahogany case of this example is embellished with gilt brass rope work; above and below the dial are panels of *verre églomisé*, beautifully executed in gold on a black background, with a finial at the top that represents the Prince of Wales's feathers in gilded brass. This particular example has inscribed on the dial 'Watch Maker to His Royal Highness, the Prince of Wales' and can, therefore, be dated before 1811, when the Prince of Wales became the Prince Regent.

An antiques dealer's life can be exciting to say the least, because he never knows what the next day will bring, and the constant search for something of extraordinary rarity is forever on his mind. For me, one of Hotspur's most satisfying acquisitions occurred in 2003 at the Grosvenor House Fair, when we acquired a very fine pair of early nineteenth-

10. A Russian-made English tea caddy, c.1780.
H: 5" (12.5 cm).

CHANG EABLE
29
30
Rain
Fair
J Russell, Falkirk Invenit et Fecit
WATCH MAKER to his R: H the PRINCE of WALES
MUCH RAIN
SET FAIR
STORMY 28 31 VERY DRY

century ormolu ice pails (Fig. 12). Three open-winged eagles stand on pedestals supporting the bowls that are enhanced by finely chased heads of Bacchus, and which retain their original metal liners. Exceptionally heavy and of outstanding quality, these ice pails bear the coat of arms of Viscount Anson of Shugborough. The colour of the gilding is deep and rich, and the standard of workmanship is of the highest order. With much pride we showed them to Nicholas Goodison, who took detailed notes of their design. The following morning he telephoned me to say: 'I have some good news for you about the ice pails.' He had found out that Benjamin Vulliamy, clockmaker to George III, had supplied them, and that they were part of a set of six ice pails made in 1811 for Lord Anson of Shugborough. They cost £438 5s. 2d: a staggering £73 each, which must equate today to about £40,000 each. Not only had he unearthed this information, but he also supplied us with the breakdown costs of each part of the ice pails. Subsequently, prompted by Nicholas, Christopher Payne did further research in the Public Record Office at Kew, and traced the original bill from Vulliamy. This was a most rewarding experience and gave us all great satisfaction.

RK

ABOVE & PREVIOUS PAGE
11. Wheel barometer by John Russell of Falkirk, c.1810.
H: 48" (122 cm).

12. A pair of ormolu ice pails, c.1811.
H: 12″ (31 cm).

CLOCKS, BAROMETERS AND OTHER OBJECTS

CATALOGUE 1
A pair of Chinese painted terracotta figures of a man and a woman with nodding heads, c.1810.
H: 27¼" (69.2 cm).

Their coats painted with flowers on a blue ground are edged with gold, the man holds an octagonal container in his left hand. These figures from Canton belong to a group of 'nodding-head' figures, generally of a mandarin and his wife, made from about the 1780s to the first decade of the nineteenth century. Figures like these were shipped to England, Europe and America and represented Chinese, not Western, people. The name, 'nodding-head', is derived from the head, which is hollow and separate from the body and attached to a long pendulum-like weight, so that when the heads are touched, they nod back and forth.

These figures were made in two sizes, the smaller ones being about ten to twelve inches high, the larger ones being over two feet. A large pair was purchased for the Prince Regent for Brighton Pavilion and can still be seen there today.

LITERATURE
Drawings for The Brighton Pavilion by Augustus Pugin and John Nash.

CATALOGUE 2
A pair of pedestals, c.1775.
H: 55″ (140 cm); W: 13″ (33 cm);
D: 8″ (20 cm).

This pair of late eighteenth-century pedestals is inlaid in the neoclassical taste on the front and sides, with urns and swags on the top panels, above a tapered and waisted trunk that is inlaid with bowed ribbons entwined with graduated huskings, all on a harewood ground, cross-banded in tulipwood.

LITERATURE
Illustrated in Hachenbroch, *English Furniture, the Irwin Untermyer Collection*, Plate 173, fig. 209a.

PROVENANCE
Irwin Untermyer Collection.
Metropolitan Museum.

CATALOGUE 3
A mahogany long-case clock, c.1735.
Case attributed to William Hallett
and the movement to Henry Harrison.
H: 97" (246 cm).

The unusual arched dial of this clock is mounted with spandrels representing the four seasons at the corners of the silver chapter ring, which has a subsidiary ring above it indicating the twenty-nine-and-a-half-day period of lunation; within this is an aperture to view the phases of the moon. This subsidiary ring is flanked by gilt metal figures of Mercury and Pan. The blued steel hands are finely pointed, and the apertures of the winding holes are ringed. There is a further aperture at the base of the dial to view the days of the month. The clock has a three-train striking movement, with the quarters striking on six bells and the hours on a separate bell; the clock is complete with its original brass encased weights and brass bob pendulum.

The outstanding architecturally inspired case has a finely carved swan-neck pediment hood, centred by a carved mahogany figure of Chronos (God of Time). The hood is supported on two fine corbels above interlinked chain motifs that flank the dial; all of which sits on a carved and moulded platform that rests upon a waisted pedestal base. The case is fitted with a hinged door for access to the three weights and pendulum, terminating in a breakfront plinth base carved with acanthus decoration and architectural mouldings.

LITERATURE
Symonds, *English Furniture from Charles II to George II*, p. 288, figs 232, 237.

PROVENANCE
Private collection, USA.

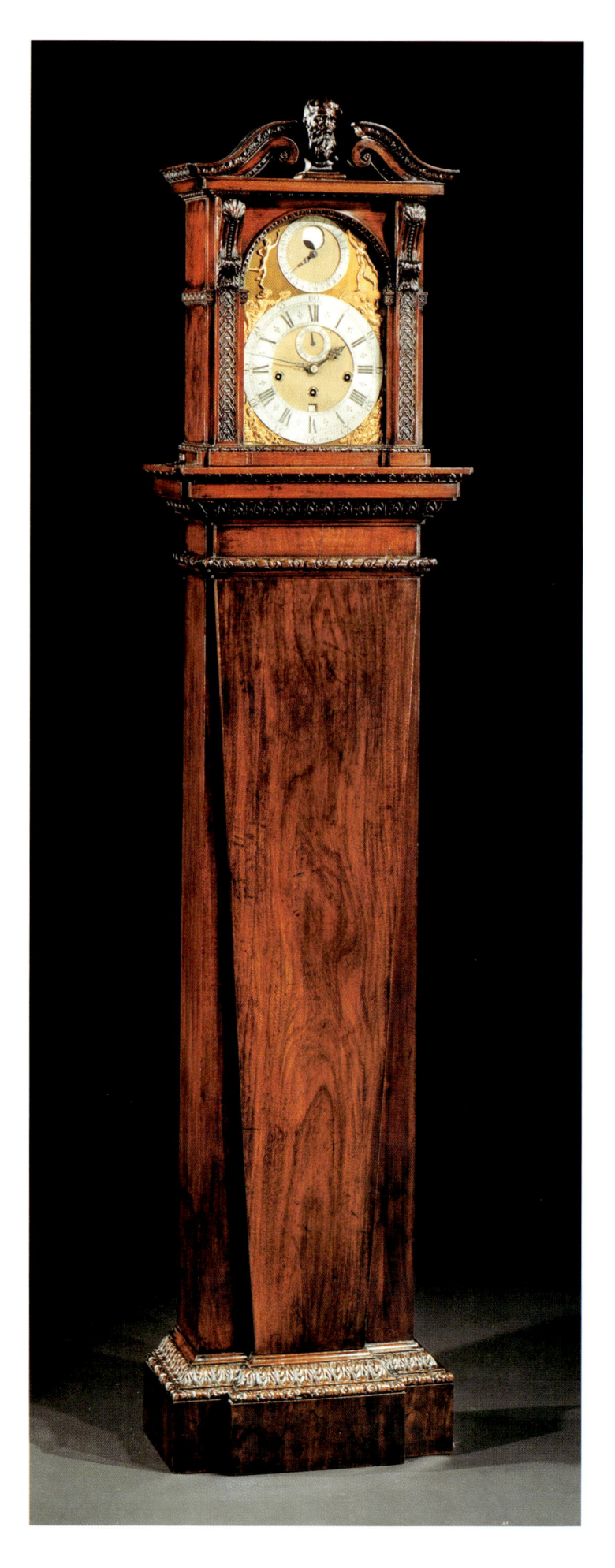

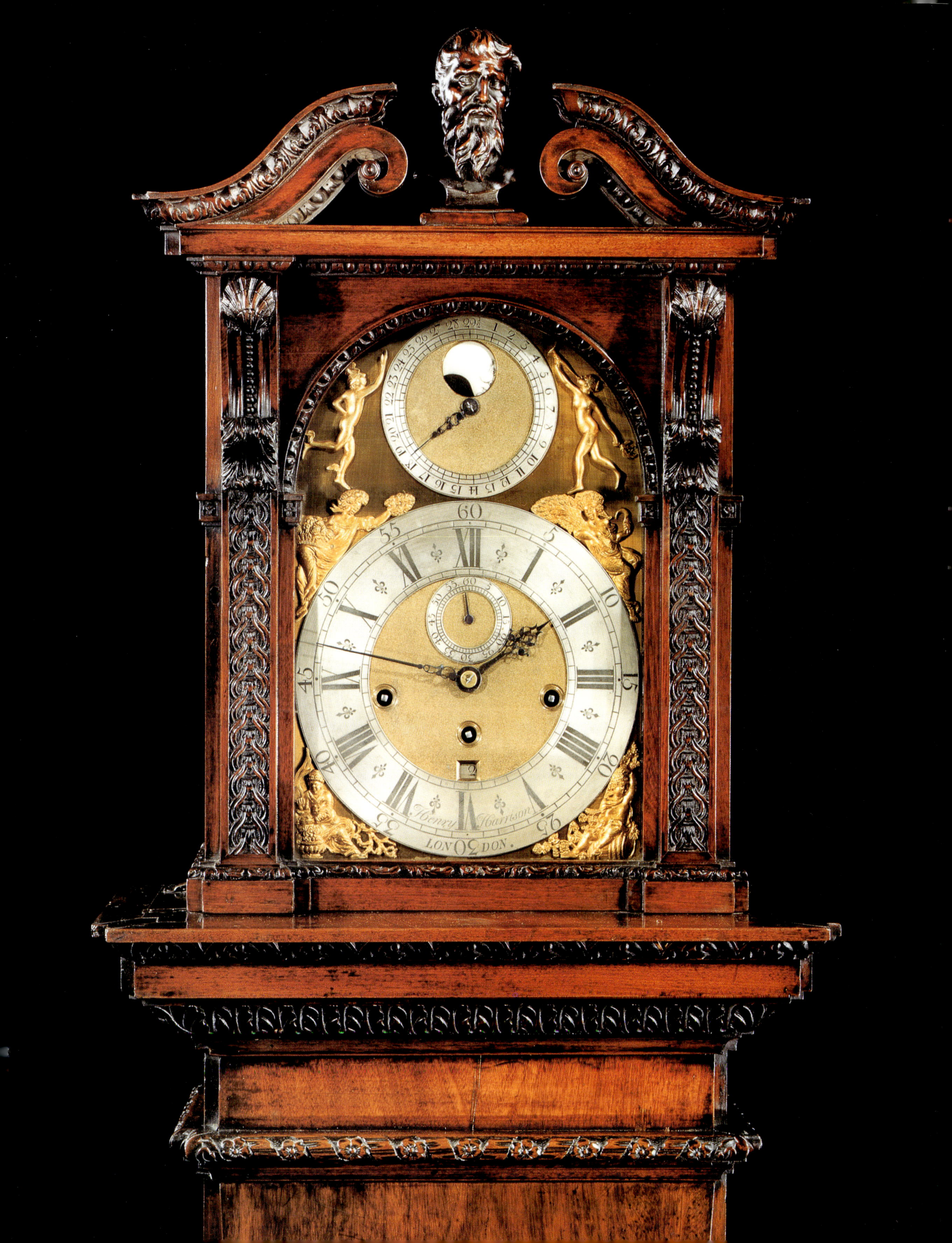
Henry Harrison
LON DON.

CATALOGUE 4
A mantel clock, c.1805.
The movement by 'Bachelard à Paris'.
H: 22″ (56 cm); W: 23¾″ (60.5 cm);
D: 6″ (15 cm).

This mantel clock is of an important size, made in white marble with outstanding quality ormolu mounts and fine two-tone gilding. The white enamel dial is signed by the maker and it has its original hands. The fifteen-day 'sweep seconds' movement with outside countwheel striking is fitted with a gilded bezel that has ormolu cornucopia centred by an eagle with a cherub above; flanked by two seated white marble figures of 'Learning' with a fluted ormolu-mounted column between them, supported on a breakfront stepped white marble plinth that is richly ornamented with ormolu swags, centred by a recessed urn and raised on circular ormolu feet.

LITERATURE
Tardy, *La Pendule Français*, pp. 357, 379.

PROVENANCE
Hotspur Ltd.

CATALOGUE 5
A carved gilt wood cartel clock, c.1755.
H: 34" (86.4 cm); W: 14" (35.6 cm).

The engraved silvered dial signed 'Pat. Cock Nott' is contained within an exuberantly carved and pierced gilt wood case in the rococo manner with 'C'-scrolls. This is surmounted by a carved ho-ho bird under a pagoda. Below the dial is an elaborately carved pendant satyr mask, supported by and terminating in scrollwork.

PROVENANCE
Private collection, United Kingdom.

CATALOGUE 6
A bracket clock, c.1760.
Made by Markwick Markham.
H: 19" (48 cm); W: 12¼" (31 cm);
D: 9" (23 cm).

The case of this bracket clock is veneered in tortoiseshell and embellished with superbly chased ormolu mounts with finely pierced and engraved gilt metal panels at the sides. The clock has a musical movement playing a choice of tunes every third hour, and automaton of ships passing on the Bosphorus above the dial.

The clock has a three-train movement with verge escapement and a beautifully engraved backplate bearing the maker's signature. The movement is fitted with pull side-repeats for both the hour and the music. The silvered dial has Turkish numerals and a date aperture; a bevelled panel signed 'Markwick Markham, London' is surrounded by original painted spandrels. Fine ormolu corbels embellish each canted corner. Four finials and a central carrying handle furnish the top. The whole is supported on boldly shaped and chased ormolu feet.

Markwick Markham, located behind the Royal Exchange in London, was well known for his prolific business with the Turkish market. His name is recorded on many clocks bearing Turkish numerals.

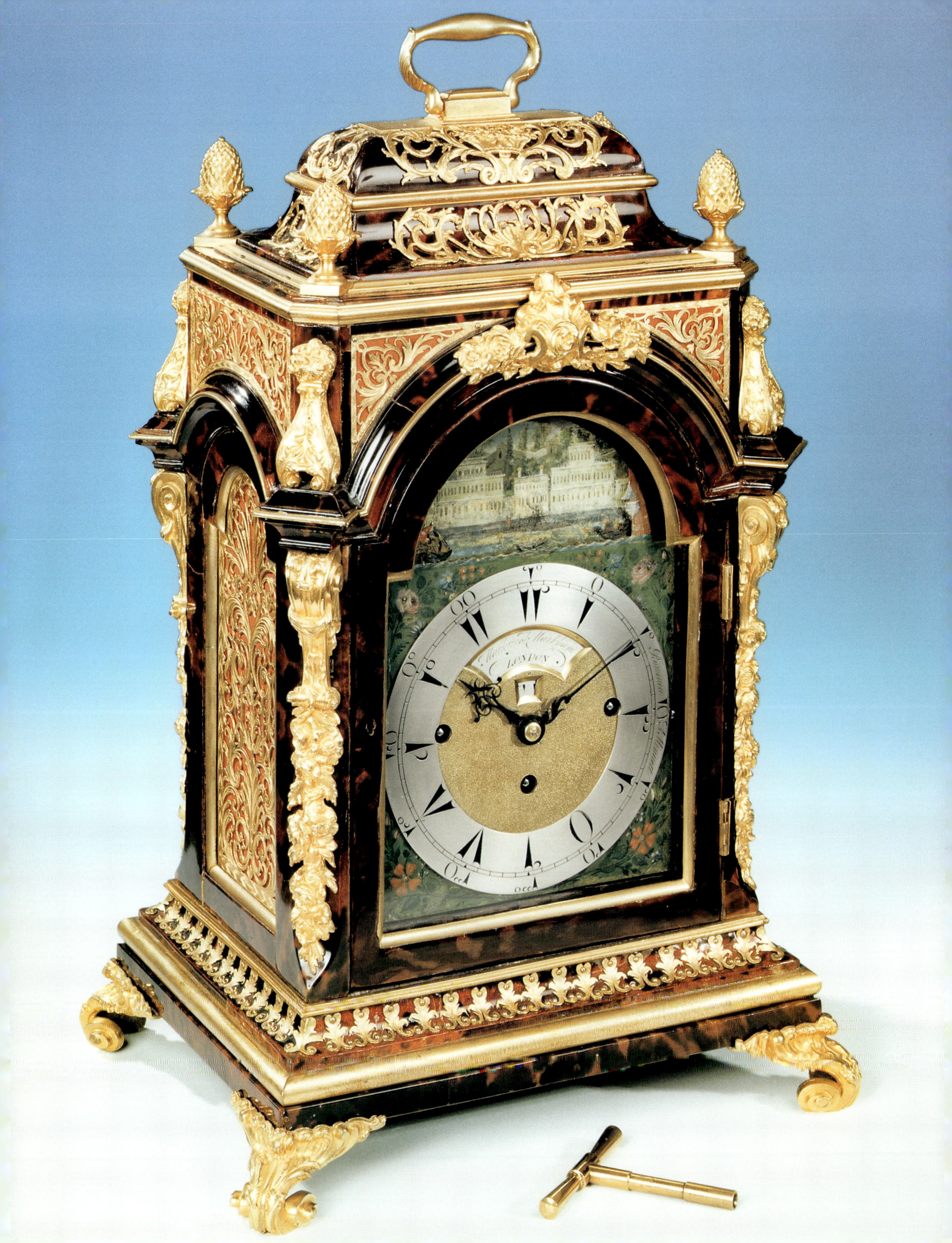
LONDON

CATALOGUE 7
A mahogany barometer with
carved gilt wood enrichments. c.1735.
H: 43" (109 cm).

The arched top of this barometer with three gilt metal finials is supported on delicately turned boxwood columns with gilt wood capitals and bases that flank the two silvered plates upon which is inscribed: 'William Russell. Late W. Jones Esq'. A fluted pilaster conceals the mercury-filled tube that is surmounted by a finely carved and gilt Corinthian capital with a carved gilt wood satyr mask at the base. The satyr's tongue protrudes sideways.

LITERATURE
Goodison, *English Barometers 1680–1860*, p. 168.

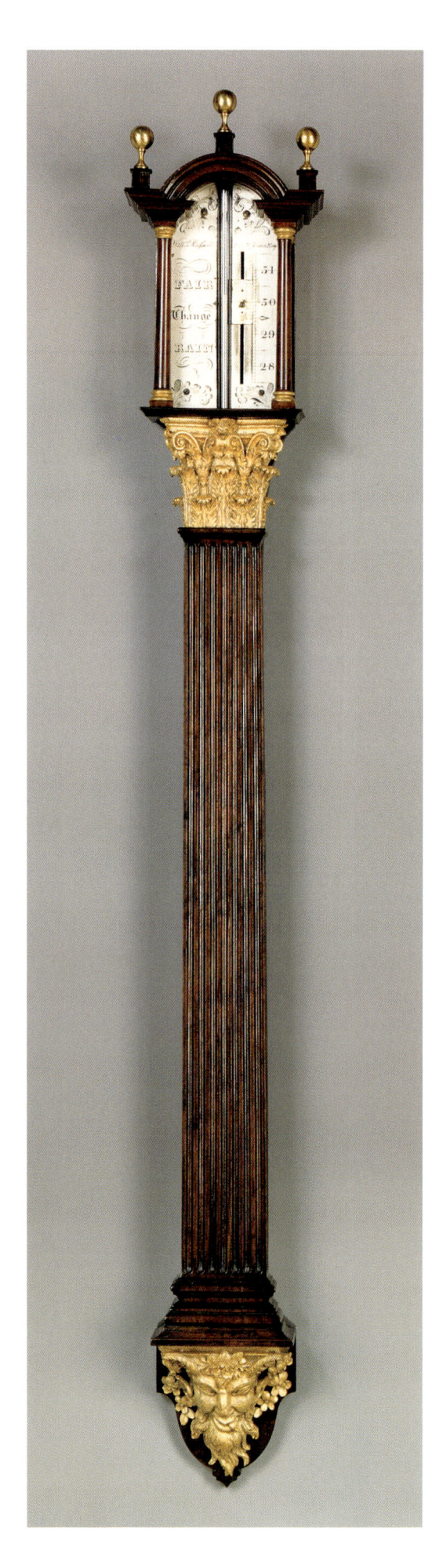

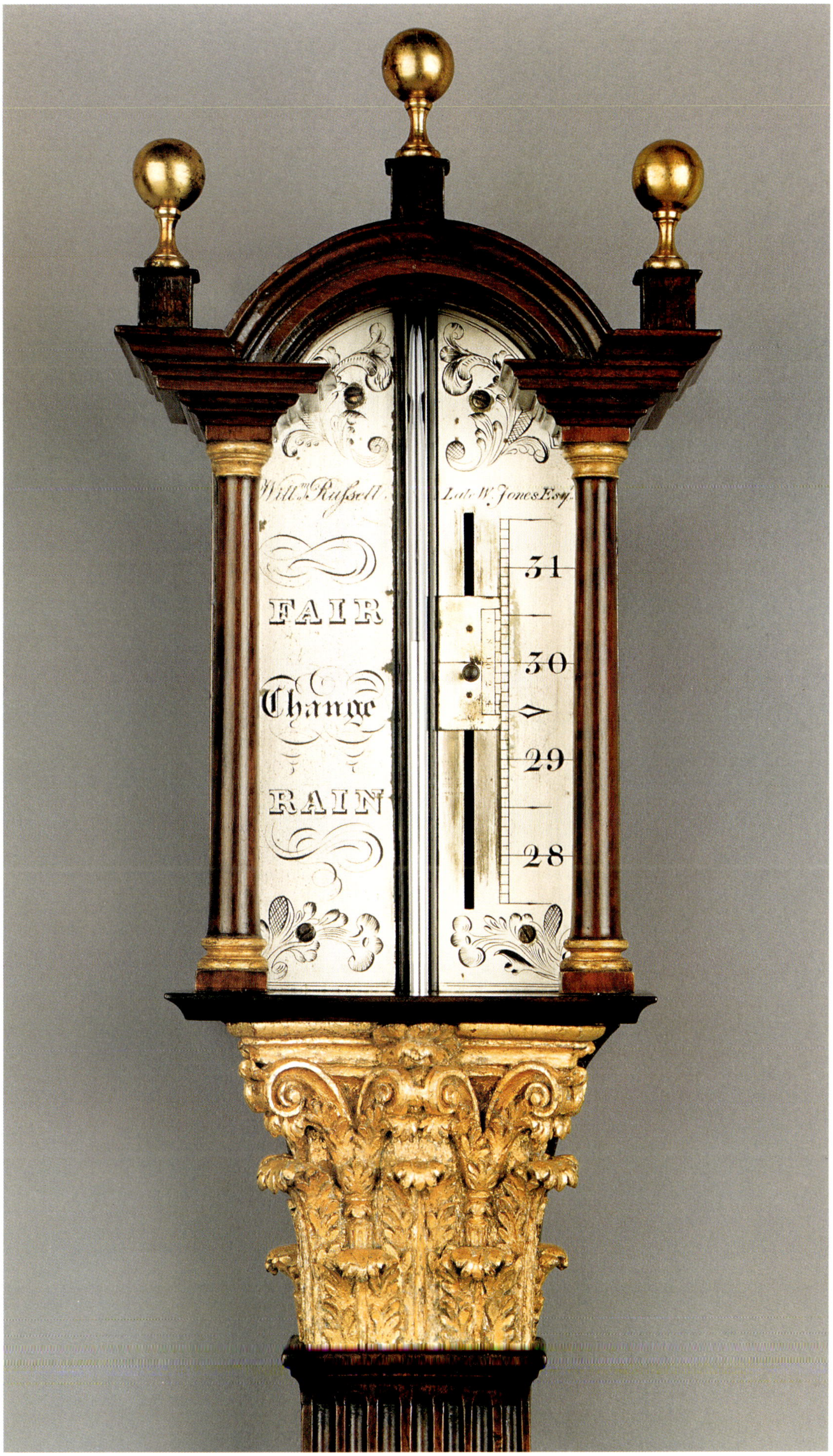
Willm Russell
Late W. Jones Esq.
FAIR
Change
RAIN
31
30
29
28

CATALOGUE 8
A gilt wood chandelier (one of a pair).
c.1755.
H: 39″ (99 cm); W: 43″ (109 cm).

The sheer virtuosity of the fine rococo carving in this remarkable pair of chandeliers beggars belief. Made at the height of the rococo period, these chandeliers are small in scale but vibrant in design and format; each is fitted with six 'S'-scroll arms with gilt wood pans and nozzles that flow from the central baluster's shafts, richly carved with reeds entwined with flowers and bulrushes. These chandeliers are a delight to behold, for both their rarity and their beauty.

PROVENANCE
Almost certainly commissioned by William Stanhope, second Earl of Harrington (d. 1799) for Elvaston Castle, Derbyshire, and thence by descent until sold by the Rt. Hon. Earl of Harrington in 1963.
Private collection, USA.

CATALOGUE 9
A mahogany case containing a
polychromatic shell picture, c.1760.
H: 27½" (70 cm); W: 16½" (42 cm);
D: 5½" (14 cm).

This extremely rare small rectangular case richly carved in the rococo taste, has a carved and pierced 'C'-scroll foliate cresting to the front and sides. The case contains an exquisite picture of flowers in an urn with scroll handles and butterflies constructed from shells. The background is made of ground shells and the case is fitted with a glass front. It is quite astonishing that something so fragile and delicate has survived 200 years or more.

LITERATURE
Example in the Victoria and Albert Museum; illustrated in Edwards and Macquoid, *Dictionary of English Furniture*, revised edition, Vol. 1, page 129, fig. 1.

PROVENANCE
Private collection, USA.

CATALOGUE 10
An organ clock, c.1770. Made by George Hewett of Marlborough.
H: 102" (259 cm).

This extraordinary clock of massive proportions is contained in a richly carved mahogany case with finely figured veneers that can be attributed stylistically to Thomas Chippendale. The eight-day movement has a dead-beat escapement and music with inter-changeable dials. The clock dial shows the moving sun and moon phases, a perpetual calendar, days of the week, months, strike/silent and music/silent, four stops for tunes and a number of pipes used together with five automaton figures with a sweep second hand, all of which is beautifully painted in the manner of Zoffany and finished with chased spandrels.

Included with this clock are three leather-bound manuscripts of tunes from which the organ music has been chosen, signed by the maker George Frederick Hewett.

CATALOGUE 11
A carved gilt wood wall appliqué.
c.1765.
H: 94" (239 cm).

This wall appliqué, in the manner of Thomas Johnson, is richly carved with ribbon-tied crossed boughs, trailing flowers and pomegranates; trailing ribbons flow to an oval of branches and grapes centred with a cross *flambeau*, terminating in a ribbon-tied bow and with graduated husking as a finial.

PROVENANCE
Second Lord Newlands (d. 1929), Grosvenor Square; and Mauldslie Castle, Rosebank, Lanarkshire.
Lady Newlands (*née* Mary Louisa Wellesley Cecil), daughter of the third Marquess of Exeter.
Removed to Burghley House, Stamford, in about 1936.

CATALOGUE 12
A pair of bronze sphinx candlesticks,
c.1810. Attributed to William Bullock.
H: 20" (51 cm); W: 15¼" (39 cm).

This pair of rare, finely modelled and chased bronze sphinx candlesticks follow the design of William Bullock's first advertisement in *Gore's General Advertiser* of 25 July 1805,[1] and were seen in the advertisement for his 'Liverpool Egyptian Hall'. William Bullock, the elder brother of the celebrated furniture-maker George Bullock, established himself in Liverpool in around 1804 as a museum promoter with his 'Liverpool Egyptian Hall'. In 1810 he moved to London to create his famous museum in the Egyptian Hall, Piccadilly.

The sphinxes, with unusual hair buns, have chased pack-saddles on their backs, each of which support tall baluster-shaped candlesticks engraved with hieroglyphics and with three open-winged chimera standing on concave-sided triangular platforms. Engraved on the side of one is: 'Oedipus Expounded Her Riddle' and 'She Then Destroyed Herself'. On the other the riddle is inscribed in reverse so that it can be read when reflected in a mirror. A whorled fluted band with three owls, wings open, supporting the serrated lips of the lamps, embellish the tops of the candlesticks. The sphinxes sit on rectangular Mona marble bases.

Mona marble is a beautiful green stone found in Anglesey: the quarry was part owned by George Bullock. This marble was used extensively on items of furniture, sculpture and works of art from the workshops of William and George Bullock.

The Riddle of the Sphinx
The Sphinx, a monster compounded of the upper part of a winged maiden and the lower part of a lion with a serpent's tail, lodged on a hill near to the city of Thebes and asked every passer-by the riddle: 'Who is it that in the morning walks on four legs, at midday on two, and in the evening on three?' All who failed to give the correct answer were slain by the Sphinx. Oedipus gave the correct answer, 'Man' (who goes on four legs as an infant and uses a stick, a third leg, in old age), at which the Sphinx killed herself. Oedipus having rid Thebes of this monster was rewarded with the hand of Jocasta, his mother, having already murdered his father, King Laius, in a quarrel at the crossroads, not knowing who he was. Thebes was soon subject to a terrible plague – the result of Oedipus's sins – and it was only after consultation of the oracle at Delphi by Creon, Oedipus's brother-in-law, that Oedipus's position was explained. The gods' fury had to be avenged. Jocasta hanged herself and Oedipus put his eyes out with the shoulder pins from her dress.

1. *Gore's General Advertiser*, 25 July 1805, p. 4, col. 4.

273

CLOCKS, BAROMETERS AND OTHER OBJECTS

CATALOGUE 13
A carved gilt wood picture frame (one of a pair), c.1765.
Attributed to William Linnell.
H: 58" (147 cm); W: 54" (137 cm).

A pair of picture frames with very fine quality carved detail that formed part of the original chinoiserie decoration in the Tapestry Room at Ditchley House in Oxfordshire. These elaborately carved rococo frames, with highly pronounced pagoda cresting, contain two journeyman landscape paintings. The frames, which were used as overdoors and which hung beside the overmantel carvings discussed by Anthony Coleridge (p. 206), are attributable to William Linnell.

274

CATALOGUE 14
An oval mahogany wine cooler with elaborate gilt metal mounts, c.1765. Attributed to Samuel Norman.
H: 25" (63.5 cm); W: 27½" (70 cm); D. inclusive: 20½" (52 cm).

This remarkable wine cooler, richly embellished with exceptional gilded brass mounts, belongs to a very small group of similar examples that are comparable to a pair at Aske Hall, supplied to Sir Lawrence Dundas by Samuel Norman in 1763. The extant examples vary in the design of the gilded brass ornamentation, some having end-lifting handles incorporating satyr masks, some with mounts to the knees of the cabriole legs, as in this example, and others that are plain. Though undoubtedly a practical piece of furniture, this wine cooler exhibits unusually sophisticated ornamentation.

CATALOGUE 15
An ormolu mounted Derby biscuit astronomical clock, 1785. By Benjamin Vulliamy.
H: 19" (48 cm); W: 31" (79 cm); D: 11" (28 cm).

An outstanding clock, one of a very few known of this massive proportion, it exhibits a typical broken-fluted white marble column. It has a white enamel dial with a beaded bezel and Roman numerals mounted on a square gilt metal plinth engraved 'design'd by Benjamin Vulliamy London 1785', and standing on a *demi-lune* stepped white marble plinth, flanked by a large Derby biscuit figure of a winged Genius pointing to the clock's dial. Beside this figure is a superbly chased inverted Corinthian capital supporting two small books and a marble scroll engraved 'design'd and executed by B. Vulliamy clock and watchmaker to His Majesty'. On the right there is a Derby biscuit seated figure of Urania holding an armillary sphere with a tripod standing beside her, headed with satyr masks and terminating in hoof feet with swag decoration. A small Derby biscuit *putto* stands in front of the fluted column holding a sextant in his left hand. The marble is inscribed twice with the monogram 'ID'.

CATALOGUE 16
A mahogany tripod table, c.1755.
H: 27¾" (70.5 cm); Diam. of the top 28" (71 cm).

An icon of all tripod tables from the Percival Griffiths Collection, formed with the help of R. W. Symonds, this is a remarkable and outstanding object.

The table retains its original tilt-top with an elaborately carved piecrust edge that is embellished with acanthus decoration and gadrooning. It is executed in fine Cuban mahogany and supported on a tripod base with a fluted stem, carved vase, and legs carved with acanthus, terminating in claw and ball feet. R. W. Symonds[1] notes a 'Mahogany tripod table with piecrust top of unusual design decorated with acanthus foliage. The fine quality of the mahogany forming the top should be noted.'

PROVENANCE
Percival Griffiths Collection.
J. Sykes Collection.

1. Symonds, *English Furniture from Charles II to George II*, figs 184, 185.

CATALOGUE 17
A carved gilt wood and gesso chandelier, c.1725.
H: 37" (94 cm); W: 42½" (108 cm).

To the collector of fine eighteenth-century English furniture, gilt wood chandeliers represent the greatest rarity and are highly prized. This sumptuous example, belonging to the early part of the eighteenth century, is richly carved and gilt with fine gesso decoration. It has eight 'S'-shaped arms that extend from a baluster-shaped body beautifully carved with lambrequins and acanthus. Most unusually, the arms are enriched with applied pewter masks of the goddess Diana – a rare feature that I have seen only once before on a mirror of a similar period.

PROVENANCE
Holme Lacy, Herefordshire.
Hochschild Collection.

EXHIBITED
Fanfare for Europe Exhibition,
Christie's 1973, p. 143 in the catalogue.

ILLUSTRATED
Edwards, *The Dictionary of English Furniture*, revised edition, Vol. 1, p. 333, fig. 16.

CATALOGUE 18
A brass chandelier, c.1770.
H: 68" (173 cm); W: 58" (147.5 cm).

The exceptional size of this brass chandelier dominated our first floor in Lowndes Street causing some anxiety about the strength of the ceiling hook. It is in three tiers with thirty elegant scrolling arms, pans and nozzles that emanate from the balustered stem which is enriched with gadrooning. The chandelier is surmounted by a dove with a sprig of myrtle in its beak.

PROVENANCE
Estate of the Earl of Lonsdale: Lowther Castle, Westmorland.

CLOCKS, BAROMETERS AND OTHER OBJECTS

CATALOGUE 19
A pair of carved gilt wood *torchères*, c.1775. Design attributed to Robert Adam; the possible maker, John Linnell.
H: 67¾" (172 cm).

These eighteenth-century *torchères* are of outstanding quality. They have tapering and fluted stems and carved festoons of swags to circular tops decorated with rams' heads. The candle nozzles have been replaced. The tricorn bases are richly decorated in the neo-classical taste with circular *paterae* and carved swags, all carved with leaves on a fluted plinth with carved feet below.

It is interesting to note a companion and identical pair of candlesticks, although smaller in size, in Sir Watkin Williams-Wynne's (fourth Bart. 1749–89) collection, almost certainly commissioned for his celebrated London house at 20 St James's Square. Built under the direction of Robert Adam, it was one of the most sumptuous buildings of its kind ever to be erected in London.

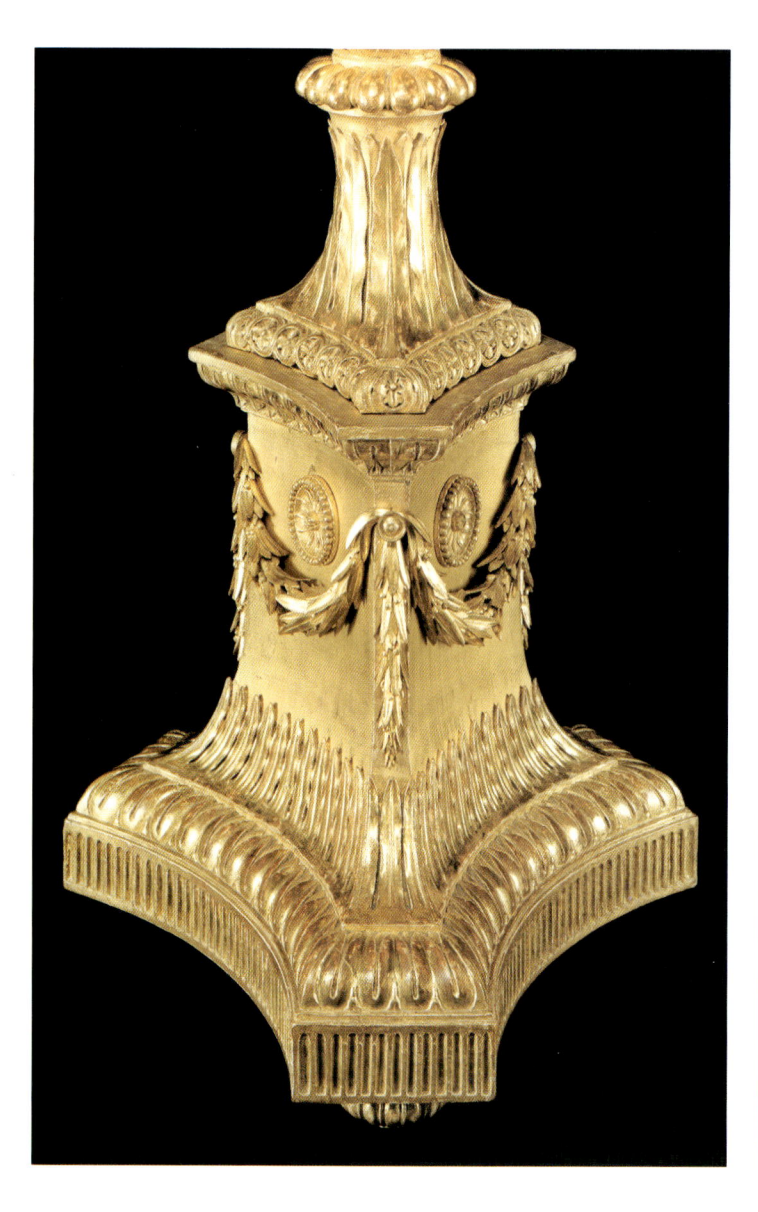

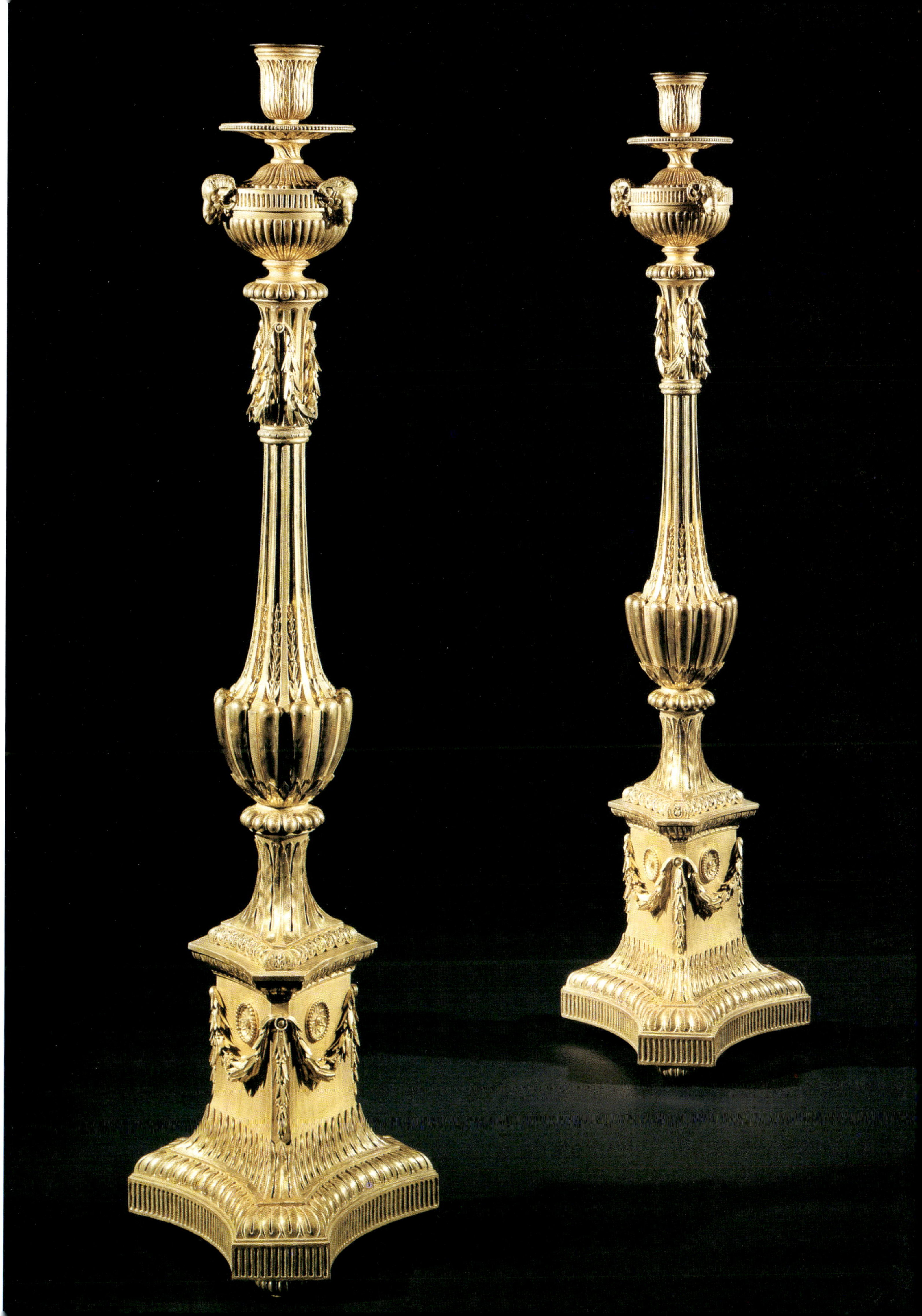

Bibliography

The following abbreviations are used throughout:

The Dictionary of English Furniture (*DEF*)
The Dictionary of English Furniture Makers (*DEFM*)
The Furniture History Society Journal (*FHSJ*)

Sale catalogues are quoted in full in the notes and are not listed in the bibliography.

Beard, G. *Upholsterers and Interior Furnishing in England 1530–1840*, New Haven 1997.
Beard, G. and Gilbert, C. (eds) *Dictionary of English Furniture Makers, 1660–1840*, Leeds 1986.
de Bellaigue, G. and Kirkham, P. 'George IV and the Furnishing of Windsor Castle', *FHSJ*, vol. VIII, 1972.
Bowett, A. *English Furniture 1660–1714 From Charles II*, Woodbridge 2002.
Brown, P. (ed.) *The Noel Terry Collection of Furniture and Clocks*, Leeds 1987.

Caldwell, I. 'John Gumley, James Moore and King George I', *Antique Collector*, April 1987.
Caldwell, I. 'John Gumley, James Moore and the Bateman Chest', *Antique Collector*, February 1988.
C.I.O.N.A. *International Art Treasures Exhibition Catalogue*, Victoria and Albert Museum, London 1962.
C.I.O.N.A. *International Art Treasures Exhibition Catalogue*, Assembly Rooms, Bath 1973.
Coleridge, A. 'A Reappraisal of William Hallett', (*FHSJ*) 5, vol. 1, 1965.
Coleridge, A. *Chippendale Furniture: The Work of Thomas Chippendale and his Contemporaries in the Rococo Style*, London 1968.
Coleridge, A. 'Gilt and Attribution', *Antique and New Art*, vol. 8, No. 19, May 1992.
Coleridge, A. 'An Addition to Chippendale's Oeuvre', *Antiques*, June 1996.
Coleridge, A. 'The Hope-Wier Cabinet', *Antiques*, June 1997.
Cornforth, J. 'Ditchley Park, Oxfordshire II', *Country Life*, November 1988.
Cornforth, J. 'William Linnell at Ditchley', *Country Life*, December 1988.
Country House Lighting, 1660–1890 (Temple Newsam Country House Studies, No. 4, Leeds), 1992.

Dell, T. *Furniture in the Frick Collection*, Princeton 1992.
Dunning, R. *Some Somerset Country Houses*, London 1991.

Edwards, R. 'Attributions to William Vile', *Country Life*, October 1954.
Edwards R. and Macquoid, P. *The Dictionary of English Furniture*, 3 vols, London 1924; Edwards R. *The Dictionary of English Furniture*, revised edition, 3 vols, London 1954.
Edwards, R. and Jourdain, M. *Georgian Cabinet-Makers*, revised edition, London 1955.

Friedman, J. *Spencer House: Chronicle of a Great London Mansion*, London 1993.

Gilbert, C. 'Some Weeks's Cabinets Reconsidered', *Connoisseur*, May 1971.

Gilbert, C. *Furniture at Temple Newsam House and Lotherton Hall*, Bradford and London 1978.

Gilbert, C. *The Life and Work of Thomas Chippendale*, 2 vols, London 1978.

Gilbert, C. and Murdoch, T. *John Channon and Brass-Inlaid Furniture 1730–1760*, New Haven 1993.

Goodison, N. *English Barometers 1680–1860*, second edition, London 1977.

Goodison, N. *Matthew Boulton: ormolu*, London 2002.

Gwynn, *Huguenot Heritage*, Sussex 2001.

Hackenbroch, Y. *English Furniture: The Irwin Untermyer Collection*, Cambridge-Massachusetts 1958.

Hayward, H. *Thomas Johnson and English Rococo*, London 1965.

Hayward, H. and Kirkham, P. *William and John Linnell: Eighteenth-Century London Furniture Makers*, 2 vols, London 1980.

Hayward, J. F. 'Furniture Designed and Carved by Matthias Lock for Hinton House, Somerset', *Connoisseur*, December 1960.

Heal, Sir Ambrose, *London Furniture Makers (1660–1940)*, London 1953.

Joy, E. T. 'A Cabinet from Weeks's Museum', *Connoisseur*, June 1965.

Joy, E. and Kern, B. 'A Side Table by Thomas Chippendale', *Antique Collector*, April 1973.

Lees-Milne, J. *Caves of Ice, Diaries: 1946 & '47*, London 1983.

Lennox-Boyd, E. *Masterpieces of English Furniture: The Gerstenfeld Collection*, London 1998.

Luff, R. W. P. 'Marble Top Tables in England', *Antique Collector*, April 1964.

Marot, D. *Nouveaux Livres de Licts de Differentes Penssees*, Amsterdam 1703.

Mortimer, M. *The English Glass Chandelier*, Woodbridge 2000.

Morton, L. and Stroube, M. *Partridge: French Clocks*, London 2003.

Mulliner, H. *The Decorative Arts in England: 1660–1780*, London 1923.

Murdoch, T. 'The King's Cabinet-Maker: The Giltwood Furniture of James Moore the Elder', *Burlington Magazine*, CXLV, June 2003.

Roberts, H. *For the King's Pleasure: The Furnishing and Decoration of George IV's Apartments at Windsor Castle*, London 2001.

Shrub, D. *The Vile Problem*, Victoria and Albert Museum Bulletin, vol. 1, London, October 1965.

Stratton, A. *The English Interior*, London 1920.

Symonds, R. W. *English Furniture from Charles II to George II*, London 1929.

Symonds, R. W. 'The Serpentine Line in English Furniture', *Antique Collector*, November/December 1944.

Symonds, R. W. 'The English Tea Table', *Antiques Review*, March–May 1951.

Symonds, R. W. 'Portrait of a Collector', *Country Life*, June 1952.

Symonds, R. W. 'Old Mahogany Furniture', *Country Life*, June 1953.

Symonds, R. W. *Furniture Making in Seventeenth- and Eighteenth-Century England*, London 1955.

Symonds, R. W. 'The Chair with a Shell Back', *Antique Collector*, October 1956.

Symonds, R. W. 'Changing Taste in Furniture Collecting', *Connoisseur*, June 1958.

Symonds, R. W. 'Provincial Cabinet-Making in the Eighteenth Century', *Antiques Review*, June–August 1981.

Tardy, *French Clocks The World Over: From Louis XVI Style to Louis XVIII-Charles X* (2 vols), second edition, Paris 1981.

Turpin, A. 'Thomas Pistor, Father and Son, and Levens Hall', (*FHSJ*) vol. XXXVI, 2000.

Ward Jackson, P. *English Furniture Designs of the Eighteenth Century*, London 1958.

Williams, C. (ed.) *Sophie in London*, 1933.

Wood, L. *Catalogue of Commodes in the Lady Lever Art Gallery*, London 1994.

Index

Page numbers in *italic* refer to the illustrations

A

Adair, John, 145
Adam, James, 145
Adam, John, 208
Adam, Robert, 145, 146
    cabinets, 208
    frames, 216
    Grand Tour, 138, 208
    mirrors, 31
    at Moor Park, 142, 143
    sofas, 143, 190
    torchères, 248–9, *280–1*
Adams, George, *244*, 245
Adelaide, 25
Agnew's, 15
Aldby Hall, Yorkshire 40
Allendale, Lord, 31
Alnwick Castle, Northumberland, 249
Althorp, Northamptonshire, 143
amateur collectors, 70–3
Amigoni, 142
Amyand, Claudius, 116
Amyand, Sir George, 116
Amyand, John, 116
Ancaster, Peregrine, 3rd Duke of, 134
Anna Feodorovna, Grand Duchess, 254
Anne, Queen of England, 126, 194
Anson, Viscount, 256
Arbury Hall, Nuneaton, 174
armchairs, *76*, 77, 88, *89*, 145, *155*
Aske Hall, Yorkshire 275
Athenaeum, Bury St Edmunds, 176
Atholl, Duke of, 143, 214
Auckland Museum, 33
auctions, 71, 190
Aykbowm, John D., 160

B

Bachelard à Paris, *262*
Badminton House, Gloucestershire, 206
Barlow, Francis, 206
Barnard, Simone, 15, 189
barometers, 18, 84, *84*, *244*, 245, 248, *248*, 254, 255–6, *266–7*
basins, cut-glass, *167*
Bayou Bend collection, 72
Beard, Geoffrey, 33, 200
Beaton, Cecil, 190
Beaufort, 4th Duke of, 206
Belchier, John, 194
bell, Hotspur's, 12–13, *13*
Bellot cabinet, *41–3*, 44
Bellot family, 44
Belton House, Lincolnshire 15
bergère chairs, *157*
Betts, Thomas, 162, 166
Birch family, 245
Birmingham, 25
Bismarck, Contessa Mona, 77
Blackwell, Geoffrey, 51
Blades, John, 162, *179–81*
Blair Castle, Perthshire, 214
Blairman, John, 23
Blenheim Palace, Oxfordshire, 128, 194
Bonham family, 24
Boodle's Club, St James's, London, 179
bookcases, bureau, *220–1*
Boson, John, 196, 200
Boston, 25
bottle stands, 60, *62*
Boughton House, Northamptonshire, 194
Boulton, Matthew, 11, 19, 25, 37, *37*, 94–120, *102–21*, 161, 249, 252, 254
boxes, stump-work, 80–1, *81*
Bradburn, John, *233*
Brahan Castle, Ross-shire, 33
Bramshill, Hampshire, 31
Bretton Hall, Yorkshire 31
Bristol, 25
British Antique Dealer's Association, 13
Brockenhurst Park, Hampshire, 145
Brocket Hall, Hertfordshire 40
Brown, Capability, 28
Brown, Peter, 11
Bryan, John, 24
Buckingham Palace, London, 40, 252
Bullock, George, 272
Bullock, William, 272, *273*
bureau-bookcases, *220–1*
'Burgoyne's' vase, 37, *107*
Burlington, Richard Boyle, 3rd Earl of, 138, 163, 196
Burlington Fine Arts Club, 247

C

cabinets, 249, *250–1*
    cabinets on stands, *41–3*, 44, *193*
    Hope-Weir Cabinet, 208, *209*
    'Lady's Secretary', 17, 44–7, *45*
    Weeks's cabinet, *35*, 36–7, 40
caddy stands, 56, *57*
Caldwell, Ian, 194
candelabra, *172–3*
candle stands, *52*, 54, 56
candle vases, 37, *102–5*, *107–10*
candlesticks, 'sphinx', *273*
Canterbury, Lady, 138
Carlhian and Beaumartz, 19
carvings, *206–7*
Cathcart, Lord, 99, 118
Catherine II, Empress of Russia, 114
Cator, Charles, 24
Cecil Higgins Museum, Bedford, 160
chairs, *123*, *133*, *135*
    armchairs, *76*, 77, 88, *89*, 145, *155*
    bergère chairs, *157*
    'French' chairs, 138, *138*–41, 142, 143, 145, *147*
    Gainsborough chairs, 11
    hall chairs, *153*
    'ribband back', 136, *136–7*
    side chairs, 33, *34*, 128–30, *129*
    wing chairs, 81–4, *83*, *125*, 126–8, *127*, 130, *131*, *151*
Chambers, Sir William, 97, 98, 99, 114, 116, 118
chandeliers, 160–1, *163–5*, *169*, *175–83*, *268*, *278–9*
Charles II, King of England, 191, 242
Charleston, R.J., 162
Charlotte, Queen, 56, 212, 249
Charrington, Guy, 51
Chatsworth, Derbyshire, 172, 194
Chawner, William, *35*
Cheere, John, 206
Chicago, 25
Chicheley Hall, Buckinghamshire, 202
Child, Francis, 146
Child, Robert, 46, *108*, 236
Child, Sarah, 236
Childwick Bury, Hertfordshire, 64
Chinese mirror paintings, *219*
Chinese soapstone, *210*
Chippendale, Thomas, 29, 145, 210, 214
    chairs, 40, 136–43, *136–41*, 190
    clock cases, 270

commodes, 228, *229*, 236
  The Gentlemen and Cabinet-Makers' Director, 136, *136*, 138, *138*, *140–1*, 142, 198, 202, 214, 216, 220, *220*, 245
  Harewood Library writing table, 33, 37
  'Lady's Secretary', *17*, 44–7, *45*, 236
  secretaires, 236–7, *237*
  side tables, 40, 230, *230–1*
  sofas, 190
Christie's, 12, 60–1, 186, 189
City Art Museum, St Louis, 163
Clarke-Jervoise, Major A.E., 230
Claude Lorraine, 28
clocks: astronomical clock, *276*
  bracket clocks, 37, 264, *265*
  cartel clocks, *263*
  geographical clock, 99–101, 114, *115*
  'King's' clock case, 98–9, 116, *117*, 118
  long-case clocks, *246*, 247, *260–1*
  mantel clocks, *262*
  'Minerva' clock case, 97, 99, 118, *119*
  'Narcissus' clock case, 37, *37*, 97, 120, *121*
  organ clocks, *270*
  quarter repeating timepieces, *241–3*, 242–5
  sidereal clocks, 99–100
  'Temple' clock, *38*, 40
close stools, *39*, 40
Cobb, John, 216, *217*, 226, 249, *250–1*
Cobham Hall, Kent, 14–15
Cole, George, 214
Coleridge, Anthony, 64
Colonial Williamsburg, 51, 72
Combe Abbey, Warwickshire, 247
commodes, *53*, 54–6, 64, *201*, *225–9*
Cornewall, Catherine, 116
Cornewall, Sir George, 116
Corsham Court, Wiltshire, 214, 226
Cotton, Jack, 51
Country Life, 28, 54
Courtauld Institute, 99
Coventry, 6th Earl of, 216
Cox brothers, 176
Craigiehall, West Lothian, 208
Craven, Earl of, 28
Croome Court, Worcestershire, 31, 216
Cullen, James, 208
cut-steel work, 252–4
cutlery urns, 97–8, *112*

D

Darly, Mathias, 134
Darnley, Lord, 29
Delomosne, 161, 162
desks, kneehole, 88, *90–1*
Devonshire, Dukes of, 138, 172
Dillington House, Ilminster, Somerset, 136–8
Dillon, 11th Viscount, 206
Ditchley Park House, Oxfordshire, 31, *206*, *274*
Doddington Hall, Lincolnshire, 163
Drake, William, 146
du Pont, Henry Francis, 72
Dudley House, London, 212
dumb-waiters, *203*
Dumfries, Earl of, 208
Dundas, Sir Lawrence, *141*, 142, 190, 285
Dunkeld House, Perthshire, 214

Duveen, Lord, 21

E

Eardley and Norton, 99
Earl of Craven's urns, 247–8, *247*
Ebury, Lord, 142
Edwards, Ralph, 12, 14, 30, 187, 188, 200
Egerton, Frances, 13, 14
Elizabeth, The Queen Mother, *18*
Emmanuel College, Cambridge, 163
Emmett, William, 31
English Heritage, 15, 189
Esterley, David, 31
ewers: cut-glass, *167*
  ormolu, 97, *111*

F

Faber and Faber, 188
Falcon Glass House, 176
Ferguson, James, 114
figures, terracotta, *258*
Fink, Larry and Lorie, 24
Flaxman, John, 99, 114
Flitcroft, Henry, 206
Ford family, 11
Fortt, Raymond, 14
Fothergill, John, 96, *108*, *110–12*
frames, 28, 30–1, *274*
France, William, 138–42, *233*
France and Bradburn, 136
Frederick, Prince of Wales, 196
French & Co., 11
'French' chairs, 138, *138–41*, 142, 143, 145, *147*
Frick, Henry Clay, 138
Furniture History Society, 47, 188

G

Gainsborough chairs, 11
Galway, Viscount, 64
Garbe, Mr, 101
garnitures, 11
Garrard, 56
Garvan, Francis, 200
Gates, William, 252
Gay, John, 118
Geffrye Museum, London, 25
Gentile da Faenza, Antonio, 99, 114
The Gentleman's Magazine, 200
George I, King of England, 128
George III, King of England, 98, 114, 116, 245, 247
George IV, King of England, 238, 252, 254, 258
Gerreit, Jensen, 126, 192
Gerstenfeld, Jon, 24, 64, 236
Gibbons, Grinling, 28, 30–1
Gibson, Christopher, 196
Gibson, Patrick, 13
Gilbert, Christopher, 25, 33–6, 44–7, 216, 220, 228, 236
Gillows of Lancaster, 44
Ginsburg, Cora, 81
girandoles, 66, *67*, *233*

glass objects and chandeliers, 158–61, *162–83*
Gobelins tapestries, 138, 142
Golden Jubilee Exhibition (1974), 161
'goldfish-bowl' stands, 56, *57*
Goldsborough Hall, Yorkshire, 228
Golle, Pierre, 192
Golodetz, Lionel, 12–13
Gomm, Richard, 222
Gomm, William, 222
Goode, Thomas, 161
Goodison, Benjamin, *32*, 33, 200
Gordon, John, 143, 145
Grahme, James, 192
Grand Tour, 138, 208
Grendey, Giles, *39*, 40–4, *148*
Griffiths, Percival, 54, 64, 277
Grimsthorpe Castle, Lincolnshire, 134
Grosvenor House Antiques Fair, 14, 21, 25, 56, 101, 160, 249, 256
Guilford, 2nd Earl of, 136
Guisachan House, Inverness, 226
Gunton Park, Norfolk, 166

H

Hague, Sir Harold and Lady, 51
Halfpenny, William and John, 134
Halifax, Earl of, 28, 29, 31, 33
Hallett, William, 29, 200, *201*, 216, *260–1*
Ham House, Surrey, 15, 194
Hambro, Olaf, 224
Hamilton, Mary, 202
Hancock, 161, 162, *180–1*
Hanning, John, 138
Harcourt, Simon, 1st Earl, 143
Harcourt, Simon, 1st Viscount, 128
Harcourt House, London, 128
Hardwick Hall, Derbyshire, 124
Hardy, John, 236
Harewood House, Yorkshire, 40, 46–7, 228, 236–7
Harris, Moss, 60
Harrison, Henry, *260–1*
Hart, Geoffrey, 51
Hayward, Helena, 214
Hazlitt's House, Frith Street, London, 19–21, *20*
Heal, Ambrose, 200
Hearst, William Randolph, 21
Heathcote, Sir Gilbert, 134–6
Heidelberg, 19
Hendy, Philip, 28, 29–30
Heritage Lottery Fund, 47
Hewett, George, *270*
Hill, Henry, 54–6
Hill, Nathaniel, 114
Hinton House, Somerset, 198
Hoffman, Madeleine, 212
Hogarth, William, 206
Hogg, Ima, 72
Holburne of Menstrie Museum, Bath, 166
Holderness, Robert D'Arcy, Earl of, 212
Hollings Collection, 31
Hope-Weir, Charles, 208
Hope-Weir Cabinet, 208, *209*
Hopetoun House, West Lothian, 15, 198
Houghton Hall, Norfolk, 128, 130
Houston Museum, Texas, 25, 234
Hugford, Don Enrico, 208

Hughes, Robert, 238
Huguenots, 124-6
Huntington Gallery, California, 25

I

ice pails, 256, *257*
Idsworth Park, Hampshire, 230
Ince and Mayhew, 154, 210, 214, 224, *225*
Infantado, Duke of, 44
Ingram family, 29, 31

J

jardinières, 249-52
Jensen, Gerreit, 126, 192
Jeremy 13
Jervis, Simon, 236
Joel, Jim, 64
Johnson, Jerome, 162, 164
Johnson, Dr Samuel, 88
Johnson, Thomas, 214, *215*, *271*
Jourdain, Margaret, 187, 188
Jowett, Alfred, 51
Joy, Edward, 230

K

Kedleston Hall, Derbyshire, 15, 146
Keil, John, 84
Kennedy, John, 168
Kensington Palace, London, 194
Kenwood House, Hampstead, 25, 142, 249
Kern, Betty, 25
Kern, Brian, 11, *17*, 19, 24, 25, 161, 186-9
Kern, F.E.L., 11, 18, 19, *19*, 28
Kern, Johann Andreas, 252
Kern, Rob, 11, 12-13, 14, 18-23, *19*, 25, 124, 160, 186-7
Kern, Robin, *17*, 19, 23, 25, 50-1, 60, 66, 73-4, 160-1, 186-90
kettle stands, 56-60, *59*, *61*
Kier, James, 96, *108*
Kingzett, Dick, 15
knife urns, *112*
Knight, Frank and Rutley, 186
Knight, Leonard, 13
Knole, Kent, 124
Krehbiel, Fred and Kay, 24

L

la Cour, William de, 134
La Roche, Sophie von, 40
'Lady's Secretary', *17*, 44-7, *45*, 236
Lafount, Moses, 162, 176
Langley, Batty, 44
Langley Park, Norfolk, 210
Lapierre, Francis, 126
Lascelles, Daniel, 228
Lascelles, Edwin, 46, 236, 237
Lawson, James, 142
Lee, John, 138
Lee, Ronald, 18, 33, 60

Lee family, 206
Leeds, 25
Leeds Art Collections Fund, 47
Lees-Milne, James, 136
Leidersdorf, Arthur, 212
Leigh, Augusta, 212
Leigh, 5th Baron, 222
Leigh, 3rd Lord, 134
Lennox-Boyd, Edward, 236-7
Leoni, Giacomo, 142
Lepaute, Jean-Baptiste, 37
Lesturgeon, William and Aaron, 56, *56*
Levens Hall, Cumbria, 192
Lewis, Alec, 13
Lichfield, George Henry Lee, 3rd Earl of, 206
Lichfield, George Lee, 2nd Earl of, 206
Linnell, John, 31, 145-6, *156*, 206, *206-7*, *280-1*
Linnell, William, 206, *206-7*, 214, *274*
Lock, George, 234
Lock, Matthias, 31, 198, *199*, 214, 234
Lock, Matthias junior, 234
London Journal, 126
Lumb, Frank, 13-14
Lumb, Reginald, 13-14, 23-4
Lunar Society, 100

M

McAlpine family, 24
Macaulay, William Babington, 188
Macdonnell, Ronnie, 160
Macquoid, Percy, 187
Maine, Jonathan, 31
Malahide Castle, Co. Dublin, 40
Mallett, 13, 14, 46, 99
Mann, Sir Horace, 208
Manwaring, Robert, 134
Marble Hill House, Twickenham 25
Maria Feodorovna, Tsarina, 254
Markham, Markwick, *265*
Marlborough, Sarah, Duchess of, 128, 194
Marot, Daniel, 126
marquetry, 192
Mary II, Queen of England, 192
Mathie, William, 208
Matthews, William, 116
Mayhew and Ince, *see* Ince and Mayhew
Mayorcas, 81
Meers, Jim, 77
Mekeren, Jan van, 192
Melbourne, 25
Messer, Sam, 11, 12, 24, 48-66
Methuen, Paul, 214, 226
Metropolitan Museum of Art, New York, 11, 24-5, 145, 172, 212, 222
Micklem, General and Mrs, 51
Mills, Mr and Mrs Charles, 224
mirror paintings, *219*
mirrors, 79-80, *80*, 84, *86-7*, 88-92, *93*, 160, *169*, *191*
Moccas Court, Hereford, 98, 99, 116
Moller, Budgy, 12
Moller, Eric, 11, 51, 64, 84
Moller, Ralph, 11, 51
Monday, Kern and Herbert, 19
Montacute House, Somerset, 136
Monument Trust, 47

Moor Park, Hertfordshire, 142
Moore, James, 128-30, *129*, 194, *195*
Morant, John, 145, *146*
Morel, Nicholas, 238
Morel and Seddon, 238, *238-9*
Mulliner Collection, 245
Murray, Alexander, 145
Museum of London, 166
Musgrave, Ernest, 28, 30, 31-3

N

National Art Collections Fund, 47, 236
National Heritage Memorial Fund, 236
National Trust, 236
needlework, 75, 77, 81-4, 130-4, *150-1*
Neilson, Jacques, 142
neoclassicism, 142, 143, 145-6
New York, 11
Newton, Isaac, 242
Noel Terry collection, Fairfax House, York, 24, 202, 204, 212
Norman, Samuel, 138-42, *275*
Normanton Park, Rutland, 134-6
Norton, Eardley, 116
Nostell Priory, Yorkshire, 230
Nuneham Park, Oxford, 143, 145

O

ormolu, 11, 25, 94-120
   candelabra, *172-3*
   chandeliers, *175*
   clock cases, 37, *37*, *38*, 40, 97, *98-101*, *114-21*, *276*
   cutlery urns, 97-8, *112-13*
   ewers, 97, *111*
   ice pails, 256, *257*
   tables, *230-1*
   vases, 98, *102-10*
Osterley Park, Middlesex, 15, 46, *108*, 146, 236-7
Ovid, 134
Oxley Collection, 31

P

paintings, mirror, *219*
Palladianism, 138, 143
paper filigree-work, *78*, 79
Parker, 160
Parker, Samuel, 172
Parker, William, 162, 170, *172-3*
Parker and Perry, 162, *175*, *178*, 179
Parkes, Dan, 99
Partridge, 46, 60, 64
Partridge, John, 60, 64
Pascall, James, 29, 33
pattern books, 136
Payne, Christopher, 15, 25, 161, 189, 256
pedestals, *259*
Pellatt, Apsley, 176
Pelletier, Jean, 194
Pelletier, John, 126
Pelletier, Thomas, 126
Pennethorne, Sir James, 136

perfume burners, *106*
Peter, Alexander, 208
Philadelphia, 25, 161, 164
Philips, John, 114
Philips, Mrs, 101
Phillips, Amyas, 11, 13
Phillips, Jerome, 11, 23, 245
Philips family, 114
picture frames, *274*
pier-glasses, *197*, *215*, *217*
pietre dure, 208, *209*
Pineau, Nicolas, 134
Pistor, Thomas, 192, *193*
Plender, Lord, 51
Poke, Frederick, 51
pole screens, 245–7, *245*
Pope, Alexander, 40
Poulett, Earl, 198
Prestige, Sir John, 51
Pyke, John, 247

R

Radcliffe, Sir Everard, 142
Redburn, Simon, 79
Reid, William, 228
'ribband back', 136, *136–7*
Richards, James, 33
Richardson, Francis, 145
Richardson, George, 145
Ridpath, E. Guy, 51
Roberts, Richard, 126–8, *127*
Roberts, Thomas, 126, 134
rococo style, 138, 142
Rogers, W.G., 28n.
Rotch, Claude, 12, 54
Roubiliac, Louis François, 40
Rowe, Robert, 33, 37
Rubens, Peter Paul, 28
Rubin, Henry, 13
Rudding Park, Yorkshire, 142
Rupert, Prince, 28n.
Russell, John, 254, *255–6*

S

Saint, Gideon, 222
St Giles's House, Dorset, 196
St James's Palace, London, 212
St Martin's Lane Academy, 206
Santwijk, Philippus van, 192
Scarsdale, Lord, 146
sconces, *75*, *77*
screens, pole, 245–7, *245*
Second World War, 21–3, 24, 28
secretaires, *35*, *36–7*, *213*, 236–7, *237*
Seddon, George, 238
Sefton, Earl of, *111*
Selwyn, George, 200
Serlby Hall, Nottinghamshire 64
settees, *39*, 40–4, *84*, *85*, *148*
Shaftesbury, Anthony Ashley-Cooper, 4th Earl of, 196
Shardeloes, Buckinghamshire, 146
shell pictures, *269*
Sheraton, Thomas, 36, 202
Shugborough Hall, Staffordshire, 145, 256
Simson, George, 37
Sir John Soane's Museum, London, 248
soapstone, Chinese, *210*
sofas, 143, 190
Sofia, 252
Soho House, Birmingham, 100
Sotheby's, 14–15, 186
Spangler, J.J., 40
Speke family, 136
Spencer, John, 1st Earl, 143, *145*
Spencer House, London, 143, 145
Spye Park, Chippenham, Wiltshire, 130
Stair, Alastair, 245
Stair & Co., 11, 245
stands, 56–60
  bottle stands, 60, *62*
  caddy stands, 56, *57*
  candle stands, *52*, *54*, 56
  'goldfish-bowl' stands, 56, *57*
  kettle stands, 56–60, *59*, *61*
  tripod stands, *58*
Stoneleigh Abbey, Warwickshire, 134, 222
stools, *55*, 56, 130, *132*, *149*, *152*
Stourhead, Wiltshire, 44
Streatham Lodge, Richmond, 21–3, *22*
Stuart, James 'Athenian', 97, 98, *102*, 138, 143–5
stump-work boxes, 80–1, *81*
Summers, Martin, 224
Suthers, Terry, 46
swags, 28
sweetmeat stands, *171*
swords, 252
Sykes, J.S., 51
Symonds, Robert, 12, 51, 54, 64–6, 84, 187, 200, 220, 236–7, 277
Syston Court, Gloucestershire, 28, 32

T

tables: artist's tables, *205*
  centre tables, 60, *63*, *195*, 222–3
  console tables, *199*
  side tables, 31–3, *32*, *83*, *84*, 230–1, *235*
  tripod tables, *210–11*, 277
  writing tables, 238–9
Taitt, John and Richard, 143, 145
tallboys, 64, *65*
tea caddies, *78*, 79, 254, *254*
Temple Newsam House, Leeds, 25, 26–47, 120, 216, 237
terracotta figures, *258*
Terry, Noel, 11–12, 24; *see also* Noel Terry collection, Fairfax House, York
textiles, *75*, *77*, 81–4, 124, 130–4, *150–1*
Theed, William, 40
Thomas, Alexander, 176
Thornhill, Sir James, 142
Tibats, H., 222
Titian, 28
torchères, 248–52, *249*, *252–3*, *280–1*
trade cards, *20*, *21*
Tree, Mr and Mrs Ronald, 196
tripod stands, *58*
Troy, François de, 40
Tula, Imperial Arms Manufactory, 252–4
Turner, Cecil, 13
Turner and Adams, 170
Turpin, Adriana, 192
Tuscany, Grand Duke of, 208
Tweedsmouth, 2nd Baron, 226

U

United States Department of the Interior, 25
Untermyer, Judge Irwin, 11, 12
upholstery, 124, 130–4
urns, Earl of Craven, 247–8, *247*

V

Vanbrugh, Sir John, 128
Vardy, John, 143
vases, ormolu, 96, 98, *102–10*
Victoria and Albert Museum, London, 12, 14, 25, 54, 166, 194, 198, 202, 206, 212, 222, 234, 245
Victoria Art Gallery, Melbourne, 182
Vile, William, 56, 200, 212, 216, *217*, 247, 249
Vile and Cobb, 136, 138–42, 200
Virgil, 97, 118
Vulliamy, Benjamin, 36, *38*, 40, 256, *276*

W

wall appliques, *271*
wall brackets, *177*
Walpole, Sir Robert, 128
watch stands, 97
Waterford Glass Works, 168
Watson, Samuel, 242–5
Watt, James, 97
Wedgwood, Josiah, 96, 97, *111*, *112*, 170
Weeks's cabinets, *35*, 36–7, 40
Weeks's Museum, 36
Wells-Cole, Anthony, 47
Wentworth Woodhouse, Yorkshire, 31
Westminster, Palace of, 138, *140*
Weston (enameller), 114, 116
White, John, *61*
Whitehurst, John, 99, 100, 114, 116, 248, *248*
William III, King of England, 192
Williams-Wynne, Sir Watkin, 248, 280
Willoughby de Eresby family, 134
Windsor Castle, 126, 194, 238, 242
wine coolers, *275*
wing chairs, 81–4, *83*, *125*, 126–8, *127*, 130, *131*, *151*
Winn, Sir Rowland, 230
Winterthur Museum, 179
Woburn Abbey, Bedfordshire, 206
Wolff, Joel, 13
Wolsey, Sam, 13, 23
Wood, Lucy, 226

Y

York Assembly Rooms, 163

Z

Zoffany, John, 270

Photographic acknowledgements

Every effort has been made to contact the original copyright holders and the publishers would be pleased to make good any errors or omissions brought to their attention in future editions. The illustrations may not be reproduced without prior permission from the copyright holders.

Christie's Images on pages: 52, 53 (detail 49), 55, 57, 58, 59, 61, 62, 63, 64, 65, 67, 205, 247.

Raymond Fortt photography on pages: 41 (details 27, 42, 43), 103, 107, 111, 112, 113, 137, 139, 157, 167, 203, 210, 211, 213, 219, 231 (detail 230), 233, 235, 245, 246, 248, 250 (detail 251), 252, 253, 258, 259, 274.

P. J. Gates (Photography) Limited on pages: 13, 17, 22 (below), 23, 69, 75, 76, 78, 80, 81, 82, 83, 84, 85, 86, 87 (detail 70), 89, 90, 91, 93, 104, 108. 109 110, 117, 119, 125, 127, 129, 131, 132, 133, 135 (detail 123), 140, 141, 144, 147, 148, 149, 151 (detail 150), 152, 153, 154, 163, 165, 169, 171 (detail 172), 173, 175, 176, 177, 178, 179, 180, 181, 191, 193, 195, 197, 199 (detail 185), 206, 207, 209, 215, 217, 221, 222 (detail 223), 225, 227, 229, 237, 238, 239, 242 (detail 241), 243, 244, 249, 254, 256 (detail 255), 257, 260, (detail 261), 262, 263, 265, 266 (detail 267), 268, 269, 270, 271, 273, 275, 277, 278, 279, 281 (details 280).

Nicholas Goodison on pages: 37, 102, 105, 106, 115 (detail 95), 121.

Courtesy of Leeds Museums and Galleries (Temple Newsam House) on pages: 32, 34, 35, 38, 39, 45.

Mallett and Son (Antiques) Limited on page 276.

National Gallery of Victoria, Melbourne, Australia on pages: 183 (detail 159).